The Curious Culture of Economic Theory

# The Curious Culture of Economic Theory

Ran Spiegler

The MIT Press
Cambridge, Massachusetts
London, England

The MIT Press would like to thank the anonymous peer reviewers who provided comments on drafts of this book. The generous work of academic experts is essential for establishing the authority and quality of our publications. We acknowledge with gratitude the contributions of these otherwise uncredited readers.

This book was set in Palatino by Westchester Publishing Services. Printed and bound in the United States of America.

The author's preference is to use binary pronouns in this work. The MIT Press recognizes all gender identities and recommends the use of gender-neutral pronouns.

Library of Congress Cataloging-in-Publication Data

Names: Spiegler, Ran, author.
Title: The curious culture of economic theory / Ran Spiegler.
Description: Cambridge, Massachusetts : The MIT Press, [2024] | Includes bibliographical references and index.
Identifiers: LCCN 2023028463 (print) | LCCN 2023028464 (ebook) | ISBN 9780262548229 (paperback) | ISBN 9780262379021 (epub) | ISBN 9780262379038 (pdf)
Subjects: LCSH: Economics. | Economics—Sociological aspects.
Classification: LCC HB171 .S7155 2024 (print) | LCC HB171 (ebook) | DDC 330.01—dc23/eng/20230713
LC record available at https://lccn.loc.gov/2023028463
LC ebook record available at https://lccn.loc.gov/2023028464

# Contents

# Preface

This book is a collection of essays about the professional culture of economic theory. When is a theoretical result "taken seriously" for economic applications, and how do theorists try to influence this judgment? What determines whether a new theoretical subfield adopts a "foundational" or an "applied" style? Why have theory papers become so long, and how do journals and readers handle this trend? How do theorists respond to economists' taste for "rational" explanations of human behavior? Each question addresses the norms that economic theorists apply as they produce, evaluate, and disseminate research. The essays in this book explore these questions and others. Through them, I hope to illuminate our culture—at least as I have experienced it since the turn of the century.

In a strange way, the book is a product of the COVID-19 pandemic. Lockdowns, school closures, and travel restrictions disrupted my cherished work habits as an economic theorist (no more sketching models in cafes or proving theorems in airport lounges), and suddenly gave a comparative advantage to a different kind of project that is not *in* economic theory but *about* it: a project that would allow me to mull over an idea for as long as I wanted and implement it in brief, unpredictable spurts of activity.

At the same time, the pandemic intensified the kind of introspection that writing about one's own culture demands. When the crisis went global in March 2020, several members of my international research community decided they were not going to sit this one out. Theorists who hadn't shown a strong bent for policy-oriented research suddenly began composing pieces about how to do viral tests more efficiently, or how to make epidemiological models better at accounting for behavioral responses to mitigation policies. Some of these pieces were garden-variety applied theory inspired by the situation, but others had a direct policy pitch. Some of us claimed to have temporarily abandoned economic theory altogether, realizing there were more important and urgent things.

This reaction was short-lived. But from my subjective perspective, it seemed to reflect a deep-seated anxiety about the role of theorists within the economics profession and in society at large. Theorists regularly live with this anxiety: witness our constant attempts to write papers that would appeal to the "general reader" (translation: labor economists; they are not "general," and they have better things to do than read our papers). The COVID-19 crisis brought this anxiety to the surface.

This combination of factors impelled me to try something I had wanted to do for a long time: write about economic theory in a style that I thought I had seen in other disciplines but not in my own. It would involve a bit of intellectual history, but it wouldn't be a "proper" history-of-economic-thought treatise. It would have its share of polemic, but it wouldn't campaign for any particular position. Its selection of topics and commentaries would be subjective, but the discussions would be grounded in objective, pedagogically oriented exposition of concrete pieces of economic theory. It would occasionally get technical, but it wouldn't be written exclusively for connoisseurs. Conversely, while it would present concrete examples of economic theory in a deliberately accessible manner, it wouldn't be a popular-science book. And it would make some use of my own work experience, but it certainly wouldn't be a "scientific autobiography."

Instead, it would be a collection of "cultural criticisms" by a working theorist: not a philosopher or historian who perceives this culture from afar; nor an aristocrat of the profession who has lost touch with the everyday business of economic theory. Too often, our community leaves the task of "talking about the profession" to its mightiest big shots. But isn't it more interesting to hear the perspective of active theorists outside the profession's house of lords? True, in recent years, social media is filled with academic commentary by a growing and diverse crowd of economists. Yet, there is still a big difference between the brief, jumpy Twitter thread, however sharp and articulate, and the measured, longer-breathed, and carefully organized essay form—the genre to which the chapters in this book belong.

There is an additional factor behind this book. In the years 2015–2021, I served as a coeditor and then chief editor of the journal *Theoretical Economics*. This experience has given me several opportunities to muse over our professional culture and occasionally try to nudge it ever so slightly.

Who is the intended audience of this unusual "cultural criticism of economic theory"? Obviously, I will be happy if members of my research community of economic theorists read it and find it thought-provoking. Hopefully, they'll be intrigued by the "cultural criticism" spin on classics from the last quarter-century and find it worthwhile to assign as a complementary reading in (core or advanced) graduate-level economic-theory courses. However, I am also targeting economists from other subfields, who often look at theorists with varying mixtures of bemusement, puzzlement, and disapproval. I know that I would be very curious to read an introspective analysis of the professional culture of, say, applied microeconomics. By the same token, I hope that academic economists of various stripes will take an interest in the present text. Philosophers and historians of science may use the book's content as valuable raw material for their more professional and systematic discourse on the methodology and sociology of contemporary economics. Finally, I have tried to pitch the occasional technical discussions at a level that readers with minimal graduate-level exposure to economic theory will be able to grasp. Those readers, who frequently encounter rants about economic theory in popular and social media, might be curious to learn a bit about what this curious culture looks like from the inside.

I am grateful to Yair Antler, Oren Danieli, Kfir Eliaz, Nathan Hancart, Elhanan Helpman, Michele Piccione, Ariel Rubinstein, Heidi Thysen, and Dan Zeltzer for their comments on an earlier draft of the book, and for their general support for this project. I also benefited from comments on specific chapters by Duarte Gonçalves, Stephen Morris, and Philipp Strack. Tuval Danenberg helped preparing the index and bibliography and offered excellent additional comments on the substance. Finally, I wish to thank Emily Taber, the MIT Press editor, for valuable exchanges that helped me improve the book. All remaining lame self-referential jokes are mine.

Ran Spiegler
Tel Aviv, September 2022

# 1    Apps and Stories (an Introduction)

## The Oppressors Have Become the Oppressed

In the epilogue of their blockbuster book *Mostly Harmless Econometrics* (2009), Josh Angrist and Steve Pischke write, "If applied econometrics were easy, theorists would do it."[1] As academic jokes go, this one is reasonably funny. But coming at the end of a book that didn't display the slightest interest in economic theory (and why would it?), the joke feels gratuitous. It prompts the reader to look for some hidden resentment behind the joke.

Such resentment against economic theory and economic theorists is something the authors could have picked up during their formative years as graduate students. The late 1980s were peak years in terms of the status of economic theory within the broader economics profession. The field had gone through the so-called game theory revolution and was busy rewriting graduate-level economics textbooks. Graduate programs put a large premium on abstract formal modeling and accompanying mathematical techniques. This created dismay among students, who had other reasons for pursuing an academic career in economics.

David Colander and Arjo Klamer captured this mood in a *Journal of Economic Perspectives* article titled "The Making of an Economist," which they later expanded into a book.[2] During interviews with students in top graduate programs, they observed that their interlocutors didn't like the outsized role of economic theory and mathematical technique in their curriculum:

As to the things they liked least, the majority of comments focused on the heavy load of mathematics and theory and a lack of relevance of the material they were learning.

Still, the students understood the culture they were immersed in:

They are convinced that formal modeling is important to success, but are not convinced that the formal models provide deep insight into or reflect a solid understanding of the economic institutions being modeled. Believing this, they want to be trained in what the profession values. Thus we find that students who believe they are not being taught the most complicated theory feel deprived and unhappy because they worry about the ability to compete.

The sense that "real economists" are being oppressed by a subculture that fetishizes formal modeling and mathematical pizzazz keeps resurfacing from time to time. Here is Thomas Piketty's memorable quote:[3]

The discipline of economics has yet to get over its childish passion for mathematics and for purely theoretical and often highly ideological speculation, at the expense of historical research and collaboration with the other social sciences.

Occasionally, the expression of this sentiment carries political overtones. Paul Krugman's famous 2009 *New York Times* article "How Did Economists Get It So Wrong?" associated it with political conservatism and a strong belief in the postulates of rational choice and competitive markets:[4]

The economics profession went astray because economists, as a group, mistook beauty, clad in impressive-looking mathematics, for truth. . . . As memories of the Depression faded, economists fell back in love with the old, idealized vision of an economy in which rational individuals interact in perfect markets, this time gussied up with fancy equations. . . . The central cause of the profession's failure was the desire for an all-encompassing, intellectually elegant approach that also gave economists a chance to show off their mathematical prowess.

Krugman's beef was with macroeconomic rather than microeconomic theory (which is what most academic economists associate with the term "economic theory"), but the resentment is similar: a culture in love with "fancy equations" derails the discipline from its right path. It is significant that Krugman lumps "theory loving" with belief in rationality and markets (and implicitly, with right-wing politics). He's not the only one performing this trick (Kay 2012), and I'm not the only one who noticed (see Michael Woodford's [2011] response to Kay's article).

These gripes about the unwarranted dominance of theory in economics have become less frequent over the years. Once the game theory revolution was complete and the textbooks were rewritten, economic theory reached a stage of consolidation and gradually reassumed its traditionally marginal position in the professional landscape. At the same time, the status of empirical work in economics has risen dramatically. Increased computing power, proliferating data sets, and greater confidence in their methods have made empirical economists happier about the state of affairs. They have developed a sense that the discipline is moving in the right direction and becoming more scientific. When David Colander wrote a sequel to *The Making of an Economist* in 2007, he was pleased to report that twenty years after the original Colander-Klamer interviews, the students at top graduate programs were at ease with the more modest role of theory in their education.[5]

Indeed, the balance of power between theorists and "real economists" has shifted. A popular narrative has emerged: once upon a time, data was scarce, and so we had to base economic analysis on theoretical arguments, but now there is plenty of data and we know how to deal with it, and so the theorists can return to the back seat, where they belong; the inmates no longer need to run the asylum.

A parallel trend, which may or may not be related, is the increasing career premium for publishing papers in what my longtime collaborator Kfir Eliaz calls the "high five" journals.[6] This trend has become so strong that people now refer to it as the "curse" or "tyranny" of the "top five."[7] Since members of this mighty fist orient themselves as "general readership" journals, authors are expected to address the "general reader," who is—needless to say—not a theorist. This further shifts the balance of power. Theorists can no longer settle for satisfying each other; they are busy pleasing members of other fields.

This attitude is a one-way street: labor economists probably don't have theorists in mind when submitting their work to the top-five journals, whereas theorists are expected to put themselves in the labor economists' shoes. The eminent theorist Debraj Ray, until recently a coeditor at the *American Economic Review*, once told me that his editorial decisions on theory papers are guided by what he called the "Mark Gertler test"—namely, whether he can successfully pitch the paper to his NYU colleague, the leading macroeconomist Mark Gertler. I replied that I wonder whether Gertler would apply a "Debraj Ray test" if he handled a macroeconomics paper as an *AER* editor.

## The Applied Dimension

Theorists' anxiety about their place in the broader economics community is nothing new. I remember that, in 2000, Kfir Eliaz and I went to

Bilbao for the first World Congress of the Game Theory Society. I had recently finished my PhD; Kfir was about to finish his. We surveyed the colleagues who swarmed the large conference halls and played the silly game "economist or modeler": the task was to classify every senior theorist we saw into one of the two categories, "real economist" or "mere modeler" (the two of us clearly belonged to the latter).

Yet, the pressure on theorists to define themselves vis-à-vis applied economists and seek their affirmation has only grown stronger over the last two decades. For a recent demonstration, we need look no further than the 2020 economics Nobel Prize that went to Paul Milgrom and Robert Wilson. As any theorist would agree, these are two highly deserving laureates who made several landmark contributions to economic theory. And yet, a huge portion of the background information provided by the prize committee was devoted to the laureates' *practical* work on auction design at the service of governments or private companies.[8] The message was not lost on commentators. Tyler Cowen (2020) wrote in his blog,[9]

The bottom line? If you are a theorist, Stockholm is telling you to build up some practical applications. . . . The selections themselves are clearly deserving and have been "in play" for many years in the Nobel discussions. But again, we see the committee drawing clear and distinct lines.

The pressure to be practically useful is arguably the most powerful force that acts on contemporary economic theorists. In the course of this book, we will have many opportunities to see the pull of this "applied dimension" at work.

### The Aesthetic Dimension

Another dimension represents a view of economic theory that emphasizes "artistic" or "aesthetic" values—particularly the tickle that we get when encountering a good *story*, dressed in the language of a formal economic model. Here is what Robert Lucas had to say in 1988, in a beautiful commencement address to University of Chicago students, which was later published under the title "What Economists Do" (and it is significant for our story that Lucas was a chief villain in the narrative that Krugman's 2009 journalistic piece concocted):[10]

Economists have an image of practicality and worldliness not shared by physicists and poets. Some economists have earned this image. Others—myself and many of my colleagues here at Chicago—have not. I'm not sure whether you will take this as a confession or a boast, but we are basically story-tellers, creators of make-believe economic systems. . . . In any case, that is what economists do. We are storytellers, operating much of the time in worlds of make-believe. We do not find that the realm of imagination and ideas is an alternative to, or a retreat from, practical reality. On the contrary, it is the only way we have found to think seriously about reality.

I don't know if Lucas felt this way later in his life, but I know that Ariel Rubinstein does. In various lectures and essays, such as his Econometric Society presidential address or popular-science-ish book, appropriately titled *Economic Fables*,[11] Rubinstein presented the unadulterated view of economic models as stories. According to him, our response to a successful economic model is like the response to a good fable. It is not a scientific response but an "artistic" one. It is a recognition that the model offers an abstract representation of reality that we find edifying in a way that we cannot or will not subject to a properly scientific test.

## Ticking Boxes

The culture of economic theory can be viewed as an intricate maneuver between the applied and the aesthetic, the "scientific" and the "artistic." A theorist's professional identity has a lot to do with how she locates herself in the space defined by the applied and aesthetic dimensions.

Of course, the theorists' value system is not two-dimensional; they use additional criteria to guide their own work and evaluate the work of their peers. One criterion is technical brilliance. Above-average aptitude for math is a key part of many theorists' self-worth: Krugman got that one right! Theorists' sense of mathematical superiority offers partial compensation for their sense of inferiority on the "usefulness" dimension. As the latter became more acute, theorists felt a need to double down on the former. Over the last two decades, economic theory has become outwardly more technically demanding.

Another criterion is conceptual innovation, the mission of broadening the scope of what formal models can say about economic behavior. In the revolutionary 1970s and 1980s, when economic theory exerted its "oppressive" power over the rest of the economics profession, expanding the language of economics was a shared core mission among theorists. Even in today's postrevolutionary phase, our culture still rewards theorists for pushing economics' conceptual envelope (although demand for this kind of work appears to be weaker now).

These four coordinates—the applied, the aesthetic, the technical, and the conceptual—have always shaped the professional culture of economic theory. Changes in our culture amount to changes in the relative weights that we assign to them, but also in our expectations as to *how many* of these dimensions a single piece of economic theory should occupy. My impression is that, over the years, this number has gone up, especially when it comes to "high five" publications. Yet, ticking multiple boxes with a single paper—offering a conceptual innovation *and* demonstrating it with a convincing "economic application," or writing a thought-provoking story that *also* shines with flashy mathematical technique—is a devilishly difficult feat. It may be a fool's errand, but many theorists still try, fueled by the increasing pressure to score top-five publications. This tendency is another key factor that defines the contemporary culture of economic theory.

**Structure . . .**

This book is a series of explorations into how theorists deal with the pressures that shape our professional culture, especially the tension between "applied" and "aesthetic" values.

Chapters 2, 3, and 4 are devoted to the interplay between "pure" and "applied" approaches to economic theory. Chapter 2 explores the fine line that separates the applied from the paradoxical, using the theory of "global games" as a test case. Chapter 3 continues this theme, highlighting various rhetorical and stylistic devices that economic theorists use to escape paradox and lend an "applied" veneer to their models. Chapter 4 shifts attention from individual papers to entire subfields. Using behavioral economics as a test case, it explores how subfields "choose" to orient themselves in the pure-applied spectrum.

Chapters 5, 6, and 7 are a series of reflections on various aspects of the current culture of economic theory: the "rationalizing" mode of explanation that is so popular in economics, the growing dimensions of theory papers and the resulting practice of relegating material to "supplementary appendices," and the norms that govern our evaluation of incremental modeling innovations.

In chapters 8 and 9 I get more personal and use my own work to illustrate two themes: the emerging culture of "market design" at the expense of the older competitive-equilibrium culture, and the "artistic" nature of economic models as stories. I conclude in chapter 10 with brief thoughts about the future of economic theory.

## ... and Style

The style of this book's essays seems to be new in economics. Economists have used the essay form before, but usually to talk about methodology or to support a position in a debate between schools of thought. The essays in this book, by contrast, are not about core methodologies or philosophies of economic theory. Instead, they address the style of its delivery, the rhetorical gambits its practitioners employ, and the ancillary modeling choices they make, as well as the norms that shape audiences' response to these rhetorical and stylistic moves. This is why I classify the essays as "cultural criticisms." I should qualify this label by saying that I have no expertise in the academic disciplines that are usually associated with this term and make no attempt to establish links to those disciplines. I am an expert economic theorist but an amateur cultural critic.

The manner in which I execute my cultural criticisms is not methodical, but allusive and impressionistic; the claims and judgments I make along the way are informed, but also subjective. Yet, the book is not all fluff: my discussions of style and rhetoric are grounded in concrete models from the literature, such as the e-mail game, Bayesian persuasion, or rational inattention. While the selection of these examples is subjective and reflects my own experience, their description is as precise and self-contained as possible while striving for minimal notation and math. This mixture of precise (yet accessible) exposition of formal models and impressionistic verbal discussion is, as far as I can tell, a novelty in economics. It hopefully makes the book a valuable companion to "proper" texts in microeconomic-theory courses. At any rate, approaching the text as if it is meant to be fully objective and tightly argued can lead to misunderstandings.

In an attempt to preempt some of the misunderstandings that my style can generate, I wish to alert the reader to two features of this style. First, when an essay in this book highlights a rhetorical effect in some modern economic-theory classic, the reader might infer that I am suggesting the authors *deliberately* engineered the effect. That would be what literary critics call an *intentional fallacy*—namely, a tendency to over-attribute literary effects to authorial intent.[12] Therefore, I ask the reader to resist this instinctive response: I am merely proposing an interpretation of the paper's reception by our profession, whether its authors intended it or not.

A second possible reaction to my "cultural" take on economic theory is that it reflects some kind of disrespect for its scholarly value. That would be a false impression that has less to do with my attitude to economic theory and more to do with the "cultural criticism" mode itself. For example, I make liberal use of scare quotes; that will not be sarcasm but a useful distancing device that enables me to dissociate terms from their conventional interpretations.

The suggestion that successful pieces of economic theory make their impact partly through rhetorical devices and calibration of audiences' stylistic expectations does not diminish from their status. In this sense, I am in agreement with McCloskey (1985), possibly the most well-known foray into the role of rhetoric in economics. I am less sure that this agreement extends to our basic attitudes to economic theory. When I first read *The Rhetoric of Economics*, it felt like yet another grudging response to theorists' 1980s oppressive reign (and a very well-written one). This is definitely not going to be the case here. Unlike McCloskey, I am a theorist. Accordingly, my "cultural criticism" of economic theory is an affectionate one. The bewildering professional norms that govern what "works" and "doesn't work" in the world of economic theory can be a source of frustration, but they also fascinate me. Economic theory's elusive mixture of "scientific" and "artistic" elements is probably what attracted me to it in the first place. I don't think I would have been drawn to the field if it had been too far on either side of the art-science spectrum. Maybe the mixture will change in the future, in which case it is likely to attract a different type of scholars. Maybe it is already changing.

# 2 The Paradox around the Corner

## Coordinated Attack

Imagine a scene from ancient times. Two armies—call them A and B—face a common enemy. The enemy is camping in a valley and therefore vulnerable to an attack from the surrounding hills. There is a snag, however. Three snags, actually. First, the attack must be coordinated: neither army is big enough to overcome the enemy on its own. Second, even a coordinated attack can be successful only if enemy forces are depleted to begin with. An unsuccessful attack—whether because it is uncoordinated or because the enemy is strong—is deadly and humiliating; no army general would want to launch an attack unless he is sufficiently certain it will be successful. Which brings us to the third and final snag: *only army A* has a vantage point that enables it to observe the size of enemy forces.

To a modern reader, this doesn't sound like much of a predicament. When army A's general learns from his watchmen that the enemy is feeble, all he has to do is pick up a secure phone and call his counterpart at army B, and they can coordinate the attack. But remember, these are ancient times. No phones. The two parties must rely on a different communication protocol. Army A sends a messenger on a camel. The messenger must climb down the hill, ride through the valley, and climb up to army B's location.

It's a somewhat dangerous ride. There is a small chance that the messenger will be spotted and executed by a gang of robbers. If the messenger makes it to army B's camp, conveys the good news, and fixes the time of the attack, he turns back and rides all the way back to army A's camp, facing the same risk of getting caught. If he reaches it, he informs army A that he has conveyed the good news to army B. But the protocol is not over: the messenger saddles up and makes yet another trip to army B's camp, in order to let army B know that army A knows that he broke the good news to army B.

And so, our camel-riding messenger keeps traveling back and forth between the two camps. Each time he crosses the valley, there is a small chance he will be captured by the robbers, and the communication will be broken. However, if this chance is very small, the communication protocol is the best simulation of modern, simultaneous communication that the ancient technology can offer. With very high probability, the messenger will make a large number of trips, thus assuring army A that army B knows that army A knows that army B knows . . . that army A knows that conditions are ripe for a successful attack, where the length of this chain of iterated knowledge is arbitrarily high. Eventually, the messenger will be caught and therefore the communication chain will be finite. Our army generals will never attain what game theorists call "common knowledge"—namely, an *infinite* chain of iterated knowledge. But they can get awfully close. (As with any made-up story like this, the reader is expected to ignore certain unrealistic features, such as that, by the time the messenger completes more than a couple of rides, it will be too late for an attack.)

And here's the question. Suppose the messenger never came back from his first voyage to army B's camp. Will the general of army A order an attack? How would the answer change if the messenger came back from the first voyage but not from the second? And what if the messenger managed to complete forty-nine trips before his eventual demise?

**The E-mail Game**

Fast-forward to our present day. The scenario I have described is known in the computer science literature as the "coordinated attack problem."[1] It is a parable that was meant to illustrate the difficulty of attaining a coherent state of knowledge in a distributed computing system.

But the computer scientists did not address our *behavioral* question: How will the army general make the strategic decision whether to attack, given this imperfect communication protocol? Addressing this question requires us to describe the situation in a way that will capture both its informational intricacies and their implications for the generals' behavior. In other words, we may want to write it down as a *game*.

In 1989, Ariel Rubinstein published a paper that did precisely that.[2] The first thing his paper did was to remove the anecdotal aspect of the game and replace it with an abstract, storyless $2 \times 2$ game, which does, however, fit the coordinated attack story. The next thing he did was to modernize the communication method. In the 1980s, electronic mail was a shiny new technology for academics, and messages that failed to arrive at their destination were not unheard of.

Rubinstein described the following communication protocol, in which e-mails replaced the human camel-riding messenger. A priori, the enemy is weak with probability $p$, which is below ½ but arbitrarily close. When army A's general learns that the enemy is weak—and *only* then—his computer sends an *automatic* message to army B's computer. When this message arrives at its destination, army B's computer sends an automatic confirmation message to army A's computer, which in return sends an automatic confirmation message to army B's computer. This orgy of confirmation e-mails continues until one of the messages fails to reach its destination. Each message has an independent failure probability of $q$. Therefore, conditional on the enemy being weak, the probability that the communication stops after a total of $K$ messages is $q(1-q)^{K-1}$. At the end of this process, the computer screen of each army general displays the total number of messages that his computer *sent*. This number encodes the general's state of knowledge.

For example, when army A's general sees the number 2 on his screen, this means that his computer sent the original message and another confirmation message but did not receive confirmation for the latter. Thus, army A's general knows that the enemy is weak; he knows that army B knows that it is weak; but he does not know whether army B's general knows that he (army A's general) knows that army B knows that the enemy is weak. This is because he does not know whether the failure to receive confirmation of his second message was due to failure of his last outgoing e-mail or failure of the subsequent incoming confirmation e-mail from army B's computer.

A larger number on a player's screen thus represents a higher level of iterated knowledge. As with the ancient messenger story, the e-mail communication protocol stops after finitely many rounds with probability one. Therefore, the two generals will never reach the infinite chain of iterated knowledge that defines common knowledge. However, if $q$ is small, they are likely to reach a high level of iterated knowledge.

Having described the game's information structure, let us write down its payoffs, which reflect the coordinated attack story. Suppose that, when an army does not attack, it gets a payoff of 0 for sure. In other words, not attacking is a safe action. In contrast, attacking is a risky action: it yields a gain of 1 if the attack is successful and a loss of 1 if

|            | Attack | Don't attack |
|------------|--------|--------------|
| Attack     | x, x   | −1, 0        |
| Don't attack | 0, −1 | 0, 0        |

**Figure 2.1**
Payoffs in the e-mail game.

the attack is unsuccessful. Recall that the attack is successful if and only if the enemy is weak and the other army attacks as well. This payoff structure can be encapsulated by the 2×2 payoff matrix in figure 2.1 (the value of $x$ is 1 when the enemy is weak and −1 when it is strong).

The numbers have been cooked so that if an army general is clueless about whether an attack is going to be successful (by clueless I mean that the chances are fifty-fifty), he will be indifferent between attacking and abstaining because the expected payoff from attacking will be

$$0.5 \cdot 1 + 0.5 \cdot (-1) = 0$$

## Nash Equilibrium

In the e-mail game, a strategy for a player is a function that assigns one of the two actions for each number on his computer screen. Rubinstein conventionally applied the solution concept of Nash equilibrium to this game. In Nash equilibrium, each player's strategy always prescribes an action that maximizes the player's expected payoff given his information, taking the other player's strategy as given.

In the common-knowledge benchmark—that is, the case of $q = 0$, in which the e-mail communication never breaks down and players' chain of iterated knowledge is infinite—each of the 2×2 payoff matrices that fit $x = 1$ and $x = -1$ can be analyzed in isolation. When the enemy is strong, there is a unique Nash equilibrium, in which neither army attacks. Indeed, attacking is manifestly a strictly dominated action: it yields a fixed payoff of −1, whereas not attacking yields a fixed payoff of 0. When the enemy is weak, there are two "pure" Nash equilibria: in one equilibrium, neither army attacks; in the other, both attack. The latter is a good equilibrium, as it gives both players a payoff of 1, whereas the bad equilibrium gives them both a payoff of 0.

But what about the e-mail game—that is, the case of $q > 0$? Here comes a surprise. Rubinstein showed that no matter how small $q$ is, the e-mail game has a *unique* Nash equilibrium, in which neither player attacks—regardless of the number on his computer screen.

The proof is by mathematical induction on the cumulative number $m$ of messages that are sent before the communication breaks down. When $m$ is an even number, we will examine the behavior of army A; when $m$ is odd, we will examine the behavior of army B.

Let's start with $m = 0$. This corresponds to army A learning that the enemy is strong (and therefore his computer doesn't send any message). We saw that, in this case, attacking is strictly dominated, hence army A will not attack.

How about $m = 1$? This corresponds to army A sending a message that goes astray: army B is not receiving any message. But the general of army B doesn't know whether this is because the enemy is strong or because the enemy is weak, but the first e-mail from army A failed. In other words, army B cannot distinguish between $m = 1$ and $m = 0$. Using Bayes' rule, the conditional probability that $m = 1$ is

$$\frac{pq}{pq + 1 - p}$$

(I remind the reader that $p$ is the prior probability of a weak enemy, and $q$ is the probability that a message goes astray.) Since $p < \frac{1}{2}$, this conditional probability is less than ½. If $m = 0$—that is, the enemy is strong—attacking is unsuccessful by assumption. Therefore, the probability that army B's attack will be successful given that army B receives no message is below the breakeven point of ½. The upshot is that regardless of what army B believes about A's behavior, it will not attack when $m = 1$.

Now comes the masterstroke. Suppose we proved the claim for all integers up to some $m > 0$. That is, we proved that both armies choose not to attack when the cumulative number of sent messages is at most $m$. Now suppose that the cumulative number of sent messages is $m + 1$, and consider the player who didn't receive the last message. This player doesn't know whether the total number of sent messages was $m$ or $m + 1$. In other words, he knows that the last message his computer sent either failed or reached its destination and the confirmation message failed. By the inductive argument, the opponent doesn't attack in the former scenario. What is the probability of that scenario? That is, given that an army didn't receive confirmation for its last outgoing message, what is the probability that the message failed?

A cute Bayesian calculation will give us the answer. The probability the outgoing message failed is $q$. The probability that the outgoing message arrived and the ingoing confirmation message failed is $(1-q) \cdot q$. The total probability that the player didn't receive confirmation for the last message he sent is the sum of these two probabilities. Bayes' rule tells us that conditional on this event, the probability that the outgoing message failed is

$$\frac{q}{q+(1-q)q}$$

This number is greater than ½. Therefore, regardless of what the player thinks about how the opponent will behave in case he did receive the player's last message, the probability of a successful attack is less than ½. Therefore, the player will prefer not to attack. We have thus proved the claim for $m+1$, which—by the logic of mathematical induction—means that we have proved it, full stop.

Note that in this proof, for large values of $m$, there is no uncertainty as to whether the situation is ripe for a successful attack: both players know that the enemy is weak. The proof makes it clear that the result is all about the *strategic* uncertainty due to each player's uncertainty about his opponent's *high-order* knowledge. It is a minor uncertainty in the sense that the player does not know whether that level is $K$ or $K-1$, where $K$ can be arbitrarily large. The constant, independent failure rate per message implies that $K-1$ is more likely than $K$; and the inductive argument implies that in the more likely case of $K-1$, the opponent doesn't attack.

The inductive reasoning is more than a mathematical proof technique. It has a deeper behavioral meaning: the outcome is driven by iterated elimination of strictly dominated strategies. Each round of the proof corresponds to a stage in this iterative procedure. The argument that army A won't attack when $m=0$ corresponds to deleting all strategies in which he attacks when the enemy is strong. The argument that army B won't attack when $m=1$ corresponds to deleting all strategies in which the army attacks when it sees zero on its computer screen. The argument that army A won't attack when $m=2$ corresponds to deleting all strategies in which the army attacks when it sees the number 1 on its screen. And so forth. This solution concept is weaker than Nash equilibrium: in a general finite game, the set of outcomes that survive the procedure contains the set of Nash equilibria. In the e-mail game, the two coincide because a unique outcome survives the procedure.

## Paradox

How should we interpret the stark result? Rubinstein makes it clear that he doesn't treat the Nash equilibrium outcome in the e-mail game as a plausible prediction. First, he puts the term *prediction* under scare quotes. Second, he refers to the result explicitly as *paradoxical* and compares it to other well-known vignettes of game theory, like the Chain Store or Centipede Games—both examples of how inductive reasoning leads to a behaviorally implausible prediction.[3] While the term "paradox" is philosophically deep and multifaceted, I use it here the way I believe most game theorists do in this context: simply to characterize a theoretical prediction that powerfully clashes with our intuition about what actual behavior would look like.

Indeed, the e-mail game is written as a thought experiment that we can easily run in our head. Would we attack if we saw a high number on our computer screen? Most of us would. In fact, there is a sense in which the communication protocol makes coordinated attack a focal point. A high number on one's computer screen, when one knows that the opponent also saw a high number, is an implicit invitation to coordinate on the efficient outcome (attacking when both know the enemy is weak). There is a clash between this intuition and the game-theoretic "prediction." Refutation of this prediction in the thought experiment has been confirmed by actual lab experiments.[4]

How do we respond to this paradox? One obvious response is that it is an empirical refutation of standard game-theoretic methods. My experience from teaching this example is subtler: the students' response seems more "artistic" or "aesthetic." It is in fact a marvelous *joke*. Indeed, when I explain the inductive argument, many students begin smiling. I deliberately play it for laughs by conjuring up the image of the camel-riding messenger. That poor messenger, riding back and forth on his camel toward his inevitable demise. No matter how many rounds he manages to complete, he will never assuage the generals' fear that their army will be the only one launching an attack. Funny, in a sadistic sort of way. A bit like watching someone slip on a banana peel.

The source of this humor is that the e-mail game highlights a serious and real concern: that successful coordination in many important situations is hampered by strategic uncertainty due to incomplete high-order knowledge. The relentless logic of iterated elimination of dominated strategies takes this realistic phenomenon to an absurd extreme. This is what makes it funny: the over-the-top execution of a basically sound logic. But the absurd humor doesn't mean the exercise has been empty entertainment. After seeing the example, we understand something—namely, the role of high-order beliefs in coordination problems—better than before.

The "artistic" response to the e-mail game doesn't require us to know its broader context, the evolution of game theory, and its role in economics. A "scientific" response does. The e-mail game was a watershed in the history of game theory. It showed the crucial role of common knowledge for strategic interactions that contain an element of a coordination problem. It was the first example to demonstrate that even an apparently small incomplete-information perturbation of a common-knowledge environment can dramatically change the game-theoretic analysis. Preoccupation with robustness to common-knowledge assumptions was in the air. Around the same time, Robert Wilson issued his famous "Wilson critique," which cautioned against mechanism-design exercises that rely on common-knowledge assumptions.[5]

Even more than that, the e-mail game is the first example in the economics literature that I am aware of that demonstrated the behavioral implications of high-order beliefs in situations of incomplete information. The 1970s were the heyday of "information economics," showing that asymmetric information can have dramatic effects on economic interactions, but the examples that economists thought about in the 1970s and 1980s involved only "first-order" asymmetric information: one player knew something, another player didn't. In the e-mail game, players may both know that the situation is ripe for an attack, but coordination will be thwarted because of a small asymmetry in their high-order information.

All these heady considerations were latent in Rubinstein's 1989 paper. But the immediate experience of reading or teaching the paper is simply that it is funny—the best piece of high humor in modern economic theory that I am aware of.

## Global Games

In 1993, Hans Carlsson and Eric van Damme published a wonderful paper that offered a general treatment of a class of games like the e-mail game.[6] These games have a coordination component that is captured by some parameter. In a complete-information version, as a result of this coordination effect, there are multiple Nash equilibria for some parameter values, but there are strictly dominant actions for other parameter values. We perturb the game by introducing uncertainty regarding this parameter, such that there can never be common knowledge of its true value.

Carlsson and van Damme referred to this class of games as "global games." The "global" aspect of the game is the influence of certain regions of the space of parameter values on players' behavior in very distant regions, due to strategic reasoning.

While Rubinstein analyzed a specific example, Carlsson and van Damme offered a general analysis of global games. Nevertheless, they did make use of a leading example. The payoff function is given by figure 2.2, which is a tiny variant on figure 2.1.[7]

Now perform two additional changes. First, while in the e-mail game $x$ takes two possible values, suppose now that $x$ can take any real value in the interval $[-2, 2]$. Second, players' information regarding the value of $x$ follows a different protocol. Player 1 observes a signal $t_1 = x + e_1$, and player 2 observes a signal $t_2 = x + e_2$, where $e_1$ and $e_2$ are independent random variables that are uniformly distributed on the interval $[-\varepsilon, \varepsilon]$, where $\varepsilon > 0$ should be viewed as a small number. That is, each player doesn't get to see the number $x$ with absolute precision. Instead, he gets to see $x$ with some noise. The smaller $\varepsilon$, the smaller the noise. The limit $\varepsilon \to 0$ corresponds to "almost common knowledge," in much the same way that a large number on players' computer screens captured "almost common knowledge" in the e-mail game. These are two different notions of "almost." Each of them makes sense in terms of its underlying information technology.

Carlsson and van Damme showed that the game has an essentially unique Nash equilibrium, in which each player attacks when he receives a signal above ½ and refrains from attacking when he receives a signal below ½.[8] This is remarkable. Even if $x = 0.49$ and $\varepsilon$ is extremely small, such that players observe $x$ with arbitrarily high precision, they will almost surely coordinate on a suboptimal outcome.

|              | Attack       | Don't attack   |
| ------------ | ------------ | -------------- |
| Attack       | $x, x$       | $x - 1, 0$     |
| Don't attack | $0, x - 1$   | $0, 0$         |

**Figure 2.2**
Payoffs in the Carlsson–van Damme game.

Carlsson and van Damme's result highlights a feature that was only latent in the e-mail game, and that is the role of *risk dominance*. An action is risk dominant if it maximizes the player's expected payoff against a uniform belief over the other player's actions. In the payoff function given by figure 2.2, attacking is risk dominant when $x > \frac{1}{2}$ and not attacking is risk dominant when $x < \frac{1}{2}$. Thus, when players' signals are arbitrarily precise, Nash equilibrium selects the risk-dominant action.

Like robustness to common knowledge, the notion of risk dominance was also "in the air" when Carlsson and van Damme performed their exercise. John Harsanyi and Reinhard Selten had introduced the concept in a recent book.[9] Evolutionary game theorists showed how risk-dominant actions are selected by evolutionary dynamics in which players "learn" to play coordination games.[10]

The proof of Carlsson and van Damme's result, like Rubinstein's, is based on iterative elimination of strictly dominated strategies. In the first step, we consider negative values of a player's signal $t$. For such values of $t$, the expectation of $x$ conditional on $t$ is below zero, such that attacking is strictly dominated. Thus, players will not attack when they see a negative signal. But now consider the case of a small, positive signal. The player believes that, in expectation, $x$ will be equal to $t$, such that coordinated attack would bring a small benefit. However, when $t$ is close to zero, the probability that the other player received a negative signal is close to $\frac{1}{2}$. Therefore, the probability that the other player attacks cannot be significantly greater than $\frac{1}{2}$. Because the expectation of $x$ conditional on $t$ is small, the expected gain from a coordinated attack is small compared with the cost of a solo attack. Therefore, the player will prefer not to attack. Thus, in the second round of the iterative procedure, we eliminate strategies that prescribe attacking to small positive values of $t$. In the third round, we eliminate strategies that prescribe attacking to slightly higher values of $t$. And in the following rounds, we keep gobbling up regions of $t$ up to $\frac{1}{2}$, such that after infinitely many rounds, we eliminate all strategies that prescribe attacking to signals below $\frac{1}{2}$.

The case of signals above $\frac{1}{2}$ is a mirror image. In the first round, we eliminate strategies that prescribe not attacking to signals above 1. In subsequent rounds, we eliminate strategies that prescribe not attacking to lower signals, and after infinitely many rounds, we eliminate all strategies that prescribe not attacking to signals above $\frac{1}{2}$. This leaves us with a strategy of attacking when $t > \frac{1}{2}$ and not attacking when $t < \frac{1}{2}$ as the essentially unique outcome of successive elimination of strictly dominated strategies.

### Paradox? What Paradox?

Although the structure of players' incomplete information is different in the Rubinstein and Carlsson–van Damme games, they both lead to a unique Nash equilibrium that is obtained by iterative elimination of dominated strategies, featuring similar strategic reasoning. One might therefore expect Carlsson and van Damme to treat their result as "paradoxical," just as Rubinstein did. Yet Carlsson and van Damme very emphatically deny that their result is paradoxical. Instead, they claim that it is a *useful* result that resolves the indeterminacy of the coordination game under common knowledge. Recall that when the value of $x$ is commonly known (which corresponds to $\varepsilon = 0$ in their example), there are two "pure" Nash equilibria when $x$ is between 0 and 1: coordinated attack and coordinated failure to attack. The latter is inferior to the coordinated attack outcome, but as far as Nash equilibrium is concerned, it is an equally valid prediction.

Unlike Rubinstein, Carlsson and van Damme talk about prediction without scare quotes. They regard Nash equilibrium as a recipe for predicting outcomes in games—and note that the recipe is only partially satisfactory because of its indeterminacy when $x$ is between 0 and 1. They subject the game to a realistic perturbation, such that players do not observe $x$ with complete precision—who can ever observe anything with complete precision?—et voilà! The same recipe delivers a crisp, unique prediction that seems to make sense: players coordinate on the risk-dominant action.

For Carlsson and van Damme, there is no paradox: the unique equilibrium is merely a consequence of applying the same conventional solution concept to a tiny variant on the original game; and moreover, this variant is more realistic than the original game because it relaxes the far-fetched assumption that players observe the state of nature with absolute precision.

Thus, while Rubinstein's and Carlsson and van Damme's examples are very similar, their surrounding rhetoric couldn't be more different. Rubinstein invites his readers to mock his "prediction" and explicitly frames it as paradoxical, whereas Carlsson and van Damme invite the reader to think of the result as bringing us closer to a realistic and valuable prediction. Consequently, they call on their readers to go out and seek areas of economic activity that exhibit indeterminacies due to coordination effects and impose a similar incomplete-information perturbation in order to get unique predictions.

This call was heeded. Morris and Shin (1998) was an influential model of currency attacks, based on the idea that speculators' incentive to attack a currency depends on their beliefs about economic fundamentals and other speculators' behavior, in a way that resembles the coordinated attack problem. Goldstein and Pauzner (2005) revisited the well-known Diamond-Dybvig model of bank runs. This is a scenario in which an individual depositor's decision whether to withdraw his money from the bank depends on his assessment of the bank's solvency as well as his belief regarding other depositors' behavior. There are many more examples; this is not the place for a serious list. Morris and Shin's (2003) review article would be a good starting point for interested readers. Because these models are written in the applied-theory mode, their assumptions are meant to approximate a concrete economic environment. This means that they do not always fall neatly into the rigid global game framework, and some analytical work is needed to bridge this gap. But the main thrust of these works emanates from the Carlsson–van Damme example.

### Between the Absurd and the Applied

How can two examples that are so similar give rise to such different responses? Both examples introduce small incomplete-information perturbations into the same underlying game. Although the perturbations are different, they lead to the same prediction: the risk-dominant action is taken as the consequence of iterated elimination of strictly dominated strategies. The proof method is basically the same. How could the same result lend itself to a "paradoxical" or an "applied" pitch at the authors' pleasure?

I can think of a few explanations. First, explicit intentions matter. Rubinstein announces his result as a paradox, while Carlsson and van Damme announce theirs as a prediction without scare quotes. The authors essentially tell their readers how to think about their results, and readers usually do as they are told.

Going into details, the "states of nature" in the two examples are different. In Rubinstein's example, the state is binary, whereas in Carlsson and van Damme's it is continuous. Continuous variables tend to convey a "realistic" impression, whereas binary variables are often used for pedagogical or "merely illustrative" purposes. The enemy's strength is not *really* binary; there are many degrees of strength. Therefore, an example that describes it as a continuous variable announces itself as more "descriptive" than an example that describes it as a binary variable.

Furthermore, the players' noise structure has an "applied" connotation in Carlsson and van Damme's example. The typical reader has seen countless examples of applied-economics exercises in which decision-makers observe a real-valued economic variable with additive noise. Usually the noise in such works is normally distributed, rather than uniformly distributed as in Carlsson and van Damme's example. And indeed, when Morris and Shin present their version of the example in their 2003 review, they use normal noise distributions. This lends an air of "applied economics" to the exercise. In contrast, the elaborate e-mail protocol in Rubinstein's example has been constructed for the specific purpose of this example. No "applied-economics" paper has ever used anything like it.

Viewing this from outside the economics culture, a reader might think this is getting things backward. Rubinstein's protocol describes a concrete mechanism for generating asymmetric information, based on an actual technology. And everyone has had experience with messages that fail to reach their destination! In contrast, the additive noise specification is obviously a mathematical abstraction. Rubinstein's protocol is more tangible and, in this sense, more realistic than Carlsson and van Damme's abstract specification. Nevertheless, the conventions of economic theory condition us to treat the former as "artificial" and the latter as "realistic."

These factors may explain why we are primed to view Carlsson and van Damme's game in "applied" terms. But why don't we think of the result itself as absurd, given that it has the same underlying reasoning as Rubinstein's? Morris (2002) grappled with this question. He claimed that players' equilibrium strategy in Carlsson and van Damme's example can be described as a heuristic of responding to a "Laplacian" belief that the opponent is equally likely to play the two actions. In other words, it is natural and simple, and doesn't require sophisticated strategic reasoning. But so is the equilibrium strategy in the e-mail game! What can be simpler than playing the same action regardless of one's information?

In my opinion, there are two reasons for our tendency not to be "outraged" by Carlsson and van Damme's prediction. First, in their example, a player's signal $t$ plays a double role: (1) it gives him information about the value of $x$, which determines the value of a successful attack; (2) it measures the player's layer of mutual belief that efficient coordination is possible. The latter role mirrors the number on the player's computer screen in the e-mail game, but this role is masked by the first role. The e-mail game throws players' degree of mutual knowledge in the reader's face; Carlsson and van Damme's example conceals it behind a payoff-relevant detail.

Second, consider our instinctive assessment of the difference between a few key numbers—the cutoff value $t = \frac{1}{2}$ that determines whether players attack, and the values 0 and 1 of $x$ at which attacking becomes a dominant or dominated action. The difference between $\frac{1}{2}$ and 0 doesn't seem large because it is on the game's payoff scale. Therefore, it doesn't surprise us that players might demand a "cushion" that protects them against the risk of a miscoordinated attack. In fact, the appropriate unit of measurement for gauging the difference is $\varepsilon$, which quantifies the precision of players' signals. When $\varepsilon$ is infinitesimal, a signal $t = 0.4$, say, is "infinitely larger" than $x = 0$ in these terms, and therefore the model effectively predicts that players demand an *infinitely large* safety cushion in order to coordinate with their opponent. This pitch sounds more paradoxical, doesn't it? Thus, while Rubinstein's framing of the information structure invites us to regard a huge number on the computer screen as an invitation to be supremely confident that the opponent realizes that coordinated attack will be successful, Carlsson and van Damme's framing obscures this—the difference between 0.4 and 0 looks small, not like the arbitrarily large multiple of $\varepsilon$ that it is.

We see that small stylistic and rhetorical differences can make all the difference between viewing a stark result as a credible, useful prediction or as a funny paradox. Such is the distance between the applied and the absurd in economic theory.

**Holdups and Ultimatums**

Global games are not an isolated example of this fine line. Here is another example, which is a key building block in the modern theory of the firm. It played a crucial role in the development of the theory of incomplete contracts.[11] Imagine a worker who is about to enter a venture with a firm. Before doing so, she decides whether to make an investment in firm-specific human capital. The cost of this investment is $c$, where $0 < c < 1$. Prior to the investment, the value of the output she can produce for the firm is 1. After the investment, it jumps to 2. Because the gain from the investment outweighs the cost, investing is the economically efficient thing to do.

If the two parties can sign an advance contract saying, "If the agent makes the investment, she commits to produce X for the firm and receive W in return," they can bargain ex-ante over the value of W. Conventional bargaining models with complete information predict immediate agreement on some value W. The efficient outcome will prevail.

But now suppose that such contracts are infeasible. The product X is impossible to define before it has been developed, and a contract that doesn't specify exactly what X is cannot be enforced by the courts. The ability to describe X arises only *after* the worker has made her investment. Only at that stage can the two parties bargain over the division of surplus. A typical telling of this story doesn't specify the bargaining process and instead assumes that the worker's share in the surplus is some $\lambda < 1$.

But what is the divided surplus? By the time the two parties enter the bargaining, whatever investment the worker has made is a *sunk cost*. Therefore, her rational calculation will ignore it. The relevant surplus for the bargaining process is 1 if the worker did not make a prior investment, and 2 if she did. Given that her share in the surplus is $\lambda$, the worker's benefit from making the investment is $\lambda \cdot (2-1) = \lambda$. If $\lambda < c$, the worker will not make the investment, and the efficient outcome will not prevail.

This is the holdup problem: when parties cannot write advance contracts, their incentive to make efficiency-enhancing investments is dampened because they anticipate that the future bargaining process will treat these investments as irrelevant sunk costs.

Where is the lurking paradox in this story? Let's look at the bargaining process. Consider the extreme case of $\lambda = 0$, where the holdup problem is at its worst. This value of $\lambda$ means that the firm has all the bargaining power in its relationship with the worker. In conventional game-theoretic models of bargaining, this extreme bargaining power can derive only from the assumption that the firm makes all the offers. In the simplest case, the firm makes a single take-it-or-leave-it offer to the worker.

But, of course, this bargaining protocol is known as the *Ultimatum Game*. A proposer offers a division of some amount of money. The responder says yes or no. If he rejects the offer, no one gets anything. A huge experimental literature, starting with the seminal paper by Güth, Shmittberger, and Schwarze's (1982), documents people's behavior in this take-it-or-leave-it bargaining game. The experiments are usually run over small stakes, although enterprising experimentalists have been able to run them over reasonably large stakes—for example, by running NSF-funded experiments in poorer countries.[12] The robust finding is that the proposer makes an offer that is substantially far from claiming the entire surplus for himself. The modal offer in low-stakes experiments is a fifty-fifty split of the surplus. In the rare occasions that an offer gets dangerously close to the standard prediction, the responder usually rejects it.

Like a few other classic experiments in the history of behavioral economics, this one didn't really have to be performed. Our intuition about it is so robust that we could carry it entirely in our head as a thought experiment, like the e-mail game. As Colin Camerer quipped, only economists find the Ultimatum Game surprising.[13] Indeed, in the early days following the Ultimatum Game, economists proposed various outlandish explanations for this experimental finding. When the dust settled, I think that there was one clear winner, having to do with perceptions of *fairness*. The selection of the two parties into the proposer-responder roles is arbitrary. As a result, the responder doesn't think that the proposer's first-mover advantage entitles him to a disproportionate share of the surplus, and therefore resents the proposer when he behaves as if he *is* entitled. Might doesn't make right. The responder is willing to give up money to express this resentment. Anticipating this sentiment, the proposer is reluctant to antagonize the responder with an unfair offer.

One strand in the voluminous experimental literature explored what can affect the responder's fairness judgments. For example, suppose the identity of the responder is not random, but selected according to a prior trivia quiz. In this case, the proposer *did something* to get the first-mover advantage, and therefore it is more acceptable if he exploits it. Offers in this variant on the Ultimatum Game are somewhat more favorable to the proposer than in the bare-bones version.[14]

But now let us return to the holdup problem with $\lambda = 0$. Not only is the bargaining process following the worker's investment equivalent to the Ultimatum Game, but the parties' behavior prior to the bargaining phase also intensifies the *responder's* sense of entitlement. We can imagine her fuming (expletives deleted): "I made this sacrifice, learning new skills and acquiring new technologies, losing sleep and risking a divorce, and now you're telling me that I should disregard it because it's a *sunk cost*?! So that you can enjoy all the benefits of my investment?!" In other words, the protocol of the holdup game doesn't mitigate the fairness considerations that the Ultimatum Game has revealed; on the contrary, it makes them more prominent. An astute employer will recognize it and make a generous offer to the worker. From this point of view, the sunk cost actually strengthens the worker's bargaining position because it lends credibility to her threat to burn all bridges if she doesn't get her fair share. It's the exact opposite of the usual sunk-cost story. (Of course, when stakes are large, we shouldn't expect a fifty-fifty split, but an allocation that lies somewhere between this benchmark and the standard, proposer-take-all prediction.)

The paradox that lurks underneath the holdup problem is that its standard economic argument runs against the fairness-based interpretation of the Ultimatum Game. Why are we willing to look the other way and pretend that the Ultimatum Game argument is irrelevant to the holdup problem? Somehow, we have managed to compartmentalize our knowledge. Yes, we know that the Ultimatum Game is one of the most robust and frequently run experiments in the history of experimental economics, and we realize that it will upset the classical argument in the holdup problem, upon which such an important literature has been erected. But we seem to have this tacit agreement not to mix these two pieces of knowledge.

One can argue that economists use experimentally refuted theories all the time. For example, we regularly use expected utility theory despite classic experimental refutations like the Allais paradox.[15] The analogy is not accurate. When we apply expected utility theory, we usually don't rely on the specific configuration of Allais's experiment. In contrast, the holdup problem is a specific argument about the role of sunk costs in bilateral bargaining, which runs against the insights we learned from the Ultimatum Game.

This example illustrates yet another variety of the phenomenon that this chapter has examined. Here it is a matter of our willingness, or lack thereof, to approach an economic application from a slightly different perspective that would link it to a different body of literature within economics (in this case, experimental economics) and absorb the lessons this literature might teach us. If we do look at this other literature, the application suddenly becomes "paradoxical."

## A Tight Space

This is the condition of economic theory: paradox can always be just around the corner. Move a bit away from it, and you have a triviality. Move a bit toward it, and you have a result no one can trust. The space in which you can use the tools of economic theory to say something that is not trivial and has some credibility is tight. Rhetoric, stylistic tricks, and arbitrary conventions can determine whether you land in the area of paradox or away from that cliff.

In his Econometric Society presidential address, Rubinstein (2006) referred to the "dilemma of absurd conclusions"—namely, the fact that any economic model can be twisted and extended to the point where it will deliver paradoxical results. What this chapter has shown us is how apparently minor and superficial details of the model's delivery and its surrounding rhetoric can bounce us back and forth between the absurd and the applied.

The reader may think that, by making such a claim, I am diminishing economic theory. I don't think I am. That the serious and the grotesque can be very close is a fact of life. If living in the post–November 2016 world has taught us anything, it is that sometimes, ridiculous things should be taken very seriously (as if we hadn't known this already). That economic theory can accommodate this irony is a measure of its ability to portray an essential aspect of human interactions.

# 3 The Applied-Theory Style

## Applied Theory versus "Applied Theory"

If economic theory often teeters on the verge of paradox, how do theorists cope with this condition? After all, we usually prefer to keep a safe distance from the brink of paradox. Most of us try to convince our audience that our theoretical exercises offer relevant lessons about real-life economic phenomena—that what we do isn't what the gentle souls at econjobrumors.com refer to as "mathurbation." When the intensity of these attempts to establish real-life relevance exceeds a certain threshold, the exercise invites an appreciation as an "applied" contribution. The example of global games from chapter 2 showed how theorists can create an "applied" impression out of raw material that could just as easily generate a "paradoxical" effect.

The traditional distinctions between pure and applied theory are familiar. One distinction is that an applied-theory piece has concrete real-life empirical phenomena as a starting point; explaining them is the piece's raison d'être. Alternatively, an applied-theory paper may be motivated by a policy problem; the theoretical exercise is expected to deliver a policy prescription. A piece of pure theory lacks these ambitions. The flip side is that an applied-theory piece does not aim at a conceptual or technical innovation: it takes an existing model off the shelf (as well as existing methods for analyzing it) and adapts it to the concrete economic situation at hand. By comparison, a piece of pure theory usually has the ambition to expand our arsenal of models or advance our conceptual and technical understanding of existing models, without insisting on the exact mapping between these models and a concrete economic reality.

This description is rough, partial, and imprecise. I am also not sure it matches how practicing theorists would categorize specific instances.

In particular, I speculate that the original motivation behind many papers that we classify as applied theory is different from the one that eventually graces their introductions. Some of these papers are "literature-driven" outgrowths of existing classes of models; their stated "economic motivation" is not what intrinsically motivated the theoretical exercise, but a post hoc plea for its economic relevance.

Trying to come up with a crisp, accurate distinction between pure and applied theory is not a simple task: the pure-applied axis may well be a continuum rather than a dichotomy. At any rate, as philosophically interesting as this question may be, it is actually *not* my concern in this chapter. For what I am interested in here is not applied theory but "applied theory"—namely, not the theoretical exercise's methodology but the *style* of its delivery. This chapter examines papers that do not obviously belong to the pure or applied categories. They are unmistakably *about* real-life situations, yet they are not propelled by concrete empirical regularities or policy questions. This gives these papers considerable wriggle room in terms of how to connect the abstract model with economic reality. What I refer to as the *applied-theory style* is a collection of modeling choices, rhetorical gambits and stylistic devices that the papers employ in order to thicken this connection.

An "applied-theory" exercise is as much a caricature of economic reality as a "pure theory" one. Yet, rather than making this caricature-like nature manifest, the "applied theory" piece, much like "realist art," sublimates it by means of various stylistic tricks—mediated by conventions held by its readers—to create an impression that the correspondence between the economic model and economic reality is straightforward, thus enhancing the perception that the theoretical exercise has direct economic relevance.

What are these tricks and conventions? How do successful practitioners of the applied-theory style manage to pull them off? These are the questions I address in this chapter.

## Mahler versus Stravinsky

So, is the "applied-theory" style mere fakery? Is it nothing more than putting lipstick on a pig? That is not how I think about the issue. To clarify my position, I would like to use an analogy from "classical" music, by comparing two twentieth-century composers. Gustav Mahler is known for the rhetorical intensity of his compositions, epitomizing the Romantic tradition of using musical devices to stir and mimic emotions. By contrast, Igor Stravinsky is equally well-known for his cool-ness of expression and his avoidance of straightforward links between musical occurrences and human emotions. Listeners will have their own preferences over the "rhetorical temperature" of their classical music. Personally, I'm on Team Stravinsky. But this does not stop me from appreciating Mahler's tactics and sometimes even enjoying them.

I think of the distinction between the "pure" and "applied" styles in similar terms. "Pure theory" represents "cool rhetoric," whereas "applied theory" means amping up the rhetorical devices that the paper employs to establish a tangible correspondence between model and reality. Per-sonally, I'm on Team Pure. But this does not stop me from appreciating the devices that masters of the "applied" style use to enhance the impact of their work on their readers. Perhaps I am even envious of them, because I don't actually know how they do it! Trying to make sense of this style is no sign of disrespect toward it. It is provocative only if we deny that these devices have anything to do with how economic-theory papers are received by their readers.

This chapter explores in some detail three classic examples from the economic-theory literature. In each case, I identify various expositional devices that elevate the paper's "applied" status. Readers may disagree whether the individual examples are intrinsically pieces of pure or applied theory. However, recall that this is of secondary importance. My point is that each of these examples use "applied-theory" stylistic tropes to increase the chances that a broad audience of economists will take their theoretical argument more "seriously."

## The Role of Modeling Choices

Before delving into these exercises in amateur style criticism, we should note that the line between style and substance is not always crystal clear. In particular, the *modeling choices* that a theory paper makes play a role in shaping readers' perception of the paper as "pure" or "applied." Accordingly, my discussion treats modeling choices as an aspect of the "applied-theory" style.

For instance, we already saw in chapter 2 how using a Gaussian parameterization of uncertainty has an "applied" connotation, unlike the discrete, geometric distribution over the length of communication chains in the e-mail game. More generally, a model in which variables take values in a continuum is usually regarded as more "applied" than a model with binary variables. With a continuum of actions, it is possible to define agents' preferences by smooth utility functions and use calculus to find optimal actions. This, again, gives the paper an "applied" look. A parametric model invites us to perform comparative statics—that is, analyzing how the model's "solution" (whether it is given by constrained maximization or an equilibrium concept) changes with the free parameters. A theory paper that emphasizes such comparative-statics exercises has better chances to be perceived as "applied." In general, analysis trumps combinatorics as the mathematical language that carries "applied-theory" papers.

Let's make this operational. Take a representative sample of economists and have them manually classify thousands of economic-theory papers into "applied" and "pure" (paying them the standard MTurk rate for this task). Then train a fancy machine-learning algorithm with this data in order to learn the applied/pure classification. My conjecture is that a paper in which agents' choice set is the set of real numbers and their preferences are given by a quadratic utility function with some free parameter is considerably more likely to be classified as "applied," relative to a paper in which agents face binary choices and their preferences are not parameterized—independently of the substantive applied/pure distinction. (The algorithm will make an exception to this rule: it will often classify "market design" papers, which almost invariably involve discrete math, as "applied.")

If my speculative conjecture is correct, why would that be the case? Are smooth, parametric functions over a continuum more "realistic" than nonparametric functions over a discrete set? I don't have a deeper answer than the one my hypothetical machine-learning algorithm would provide. Historically, economists who used models in the "applied" mode made greater use of parametric functions that enabled straightforward, calculus-based comparative statics. This has led us, human economists, to associate certain types of formal exposition with "applied theory" and others with "pure theory." I don't think there is much more to it.

## Doing It Now or Later

Our first example is a classic from one of the peak periods of behavioral economics: Ted O'Donoghue and Matthew Rabin's "Doing It Now or Later" (1999). Behavioral economics covers many aspects of the psychology of decision-making. But when it suddenly burst onto the stage of mainstream economics in the mid-1990s, it was mostly through the phenomena of limited self-control and taste for immediate gratification. O'Donoghue and Rabin's paper presented a simple example of how these phenomena lead to procrastination.

Here's how I used to teach the example. A decision-maker faces a repeated choice between performing a task and delaying it. When he performs it, the problem is over. When he delays it, he faces the same problem in the next period. If he chooses to delay for $T-1$ periods, he is forced to perform the task at period $T$ (the deadline) and the problem is over.

The decision-maker exhibits "present bias." At any moment in time, he dislikes performing the task "now" and would like to do it later, but not *too* late. This causes his preferences over the absolute timing of performing the task to change over time. At any period $t$, the decision-maker's ranking is $t+1 \succ t \succ s$ for every $s > t+1$.

To analyze the behavior of a decision-maker with changing tastes, the standard operating procedure in economics relies on an idea that originates from Strotz (1955), which treats the decision-maker at any decision node as a distinct agent. Thus, the decision problem is turned essentially into a *game* between multiple "selves." O'Donoghue and Rabin argued that to apply the appropriate solution concept to this game, we need to make an assumption about the decision-maker's ability to anticipate his future preferences. They distinguished between two cases.

1. A "sophisticated" decision-maker is perfectly able to predict his future preferences. At any point in time, he fully predicts the behavior of future selves. Therefore, it makes sense to analyze behavior in the decision problem as if we are applying a conventional solution concept to the game between the multiple selves. Subgame perfect equilibrium captures the idea that each self responds optimally to a correct prediction of the behavior of future selves.

2. A "naïve" decision-maker always believes that his future preferences will be identical to his current preferences. Therefore, his decision at any period is taken as if he solves a multi-period decision problem like a rational decision-maker with stable preferences, which happen to be his current preferences.

Let us characterize the behavior of these two types of decision-makers in the task-completion problem. At any period $t < T$, the naïve decision-maker prefers to perform the task at $t+1$. Therefore, he will choose to delay the task at any period $t < T$. The outcome is that he will put off performing the task until the deadline $T$.

Now consider the sophisticated type. We can apply backward induction to find the unique subgame perfect equilibrium. In the final period $T$, the decision-maker is forced to perform the task. He correctly predicts this at period $T-1$. Since his preference at this period is $T \succ T-1$, he will not perform the task at $T-1$. Continuing the backward induction procedure, consider period $T-2$. The decision-maker correctly predicts that if he delays now, he will perform the task at period $T$. Since his preferences at period $T-2$ satisfy $T-2 \succ T$, he will perform the task at $T-2$. The reader can now guess how this is going to play out. At period $T-3$, he will delay; at period $T-4$, he will not; and so forth. Ultimately, the sophisticated type performs the task at any period $t$ if and only if $T-t$ is an *even* number. On the equilibrium path, the decision-maker will complete the task by the end of the *second* period.

How does this sound to you as a prediction? I can attest that when I presented this result in class, students often smiled—not unlike the way they reacted to the e-mail game we discussed in chapter 2. After the serious and economically relevant introduction about limited self-control and procrastination, a prediction that hinges on the *parity* of the number of periods before the deadline sounds frivolously absurd. Rather than a "serious" prediction, it is reminiscent of those whimsical backward-induction exercises that game theory beginners encounter.

Can one use such an absurd prediction if one wants to evaluate the role of sophistication in task completion by decision-makers having a taste for immediate gratification? If we only look at behavior along the equilibrium path, the conclusion is that naïve decision-makers will delay performing the task until the deadline, whereas sophisticated decision-makers will complete the task early. This comparison is compelling. But can we take it seriously, knowing the strange *off*-equilibrium behavior?

At any rate, this is not how O'Donoghue and Rabin pitched their exercise. First, they adopted the language of utility functions rather than preferences to describe the example. In particular, they used the "hyperbolic discounting" utility function to represent these preferences. We will have more to say about this in chapter 4. At this stage, it suffices to note that under this utility function, the decision-maker's rate of substitution between payoff flows at periods $t$ and $t+1$ depends only on whether he makes this assessment prior to period $t$ or exactly at period $t$. For a wide range of parameter values, the utility function induces the time-dependent preferences that I described above. However, presenting a model in terms of utilities lends it an "applied" color, whereas the description in terms of preference relations is associated in economists' minds with a more abstract and pedagogical approach. O'Donoghue and Rabin's description effectively primed readers to view the exercise through an "applied-theory" lens.

Second, and more importantly, O'Donoghue and Rabin's presentation focused on the finding that, along the equilibrium path, the sophisticated type completes the task by the end of the second period, long before the naïve type does. It played down the weird off-equilibrium behavior. Although this pattern does appear in one of their examples, their exposition didn't make a big deal out of it. This is consistent with the "applied" style. While the off-equilibrium pattern is fundamental to the outcome, it is something that an outside observer of the decision-maker's behavior cannot directly identify; only the timing of task completion is observable. An "applied" perspective emphasizes the latter at the expense of the former.

This example offers further illustration of the expositional strategies that can steer a potentially paradoxical message away from the brink and invite a more "applied" appreciation. In the case of global games, this was mainly a matter of using an information structure that, while abstract, is more familiar to applied economists than Rubinstein's concrete and highly specific e-mail protocol. In the "doing it now or later" case, the trick is to focus on the equilibrium path and deemphasize off-equilibrium behavior. These are discreet moves, but I believe they have a large effect on the reader's perception of the nature of the exercise: a "serious" result that is meant to be predictively credible, rather than an ironic result that teases the reader with its absurd elements.

## The Jury Model

In the mid-1990s, two teams of game theorists with economics and political science backgrounds—David Austen-Smith and Jeffrey Banks, and Tim Feddersen and Wolfgang Pesendorfer—published a series of influential papers that used the theory of games with incomplete information to study strategic voting in large elections as well as in small groups such as committees or juries.[1] Perhaps the most provocative among these studies was Feddersen and Pesendorfer (1998), in which they presented their celebrated "jury model." This paper was published in a major political science journal, not in an economic-theory journal. Perhaps accordingly, the paper establishes an "applied" tone at the very outset:

According to Lord Devlin, "Trial by jury is not an instrument of getting at the truth; it is a process designed to make it as sure as possible that no innocent man is convicted." . . . It is commonly thought that requiring juries to reach a unanimous verdict is exactly the mechanism that protects innocent defendants and that this protection comes at the cost of an increased probability of acquitting a guilty defendant. We construct a model that demonstrates how strategic voting by jurors undermines this basic intuition. The unanimity rule may lead to a high probability of both errors, and the probability of convicting an innocent defendant may actually increase with the size of the jury. We also demonstrate that the unanimity rule is an exceptionally bad rule. A wide variety of voting rules, including simple majority, lead to much lower probabilities of both errors.

With this opening paragraph, the authors are telling us that they are not just going to show us a thought-provoking theoretical effect of strategic voting: they will make an argument that bears on a real-life problem of grave importance. Their gambit is a promise to demonstrate that contrary to conventional wisdom, the unanimity rule is pretty bad at preventing the conviction of innocents, once we take jurors' strategic voting into account.

Here is a simple version of the model, which I enjoy teaching in my game theory courses. A group of $n > 2$ "jurors" independently decide whether to vote in favor of convicting or acquitting a defendant. A priori, the probability that the defendant is guilty is ½. Before submitting her vote, each juror receives a private binary signal of accuracy $q > ½$. This means that when the defendant is guilty, the juror receives a "guilty" signal with probability $q$ and an "innocent" signal with probability $1 - q$. These probabilities are independent of the other jurors' signals. Likewise, when the defendant is innocent, the juror receives a "guilty" signal with independent probability $1 - q$ and an "innocent" signal with independent probability $q$. The larger $q$, the more accurate the juror's signal.

In line with the jury trial story, voting follows the unanimity rule: the defendant walks free unless *all* jurors vote to convict him. To complete the model, we need to define jurors' preferences. Feddersen and Pesendorfer assume the jurors have a *common* interest: all they care about is making the right decision. Specifically, each juror gets a payoff of 1 when the right decision is made (a guilty defendant is convicted, an innocent defendant is acquitted) and 0 when the wrong decision is made.

There is something strange about this model, if we wish to regard it as a faithful description of how juries in real-life criminal trials behave. The jurors in the model don't talk with each other; any communication stays out of the model. In addition, their signals are private and conditionally independent, even though they presumably sat through the testimonies and were exposed to the same information. Here is how Feddersen and Pesendorfer addressed this concern:

We assume the signal is private information. Since jurors observe the same facts at the trial and engage in deliberations prior to taking the final vote, the assumption may seem inappropriate. Yet, there are several reasons the complete disclosure of private information through the deliberation process may not occur. For example, some jurors may have technical knowledge that is relevant for the decision but that cannot be fully communicated in the limited amount of time available. Furthermore, while all jurors agree that they prefer convicting the guilty and acquitting the innocent, each may have a different threshold of reasonable doubt. Even such minimal preference diversity may create incentives for jurors not to reveal their private information in deliberations. For example, a juror predisposed to convict may be reluctant to reveal her innocent signal lest another juror with a higher threshold who received a guilty signal vote to acquit. Since we do not model the effect of jury deliberations, determining that effect from a theoretical standpoint is beyond the scope of this article.

The rhetoric is interesting. The authors use the possibility of heterogeneous preferences (which lead to heterogeneous subjective conviction thresholds) as a potential impediment to truthful sharing of personal expertise, even though their main model rules out such heterogeneity. And while it is true that asymmetric expertise and imperfectly aligned incentives can prevent *full* sharing of information ("knowledge cannot be fully communicated," to use the authors' language), does this justify the extreme assumption that *no* knowledge is communicated?

None of this would matter if Feddersen and Pesendorfer employed low temperature, "pure theory" rhetoric: let's see what standard game-theoretic modeling of strategic voting implies under the unanimity rule. From that perspective, taking the simplest model and imposing the starkest assumptions (a common interest, conditionally independent private signals, no communication) helps us focus on the essence of the theoretical argument. It is only when the paper tries to establish relevance in an "applied" sense that more vigorous hand-waving is needed.

## Pivotal-Voting Reasoning

Let us turn to the analysis of Nash equilibrium in this game. An elementary but important observation is that the model has a "bad" equilibrium in which all jurors vote to acquit, regardless of their private information. The reason is that when a juror believes her opponents follow this strategy, she realizes that she can never unilaterally affect the outcome, and therefore she is indifferent between her two feasible actions. Following the "lazy" strategy of voting to acquit regardless of her information is optimal.

The question is whether there are Nash equilibria in which jurors vote in a way that reflects their private information. In particular, is there an equilibrium with *sincere voting*, in which each juror votes to convict if and only if she has a "guilty" signal? It turns out that the answer is *negative*. The reason is insightful.

Put yourself in the shoes of a juror who received an "innocent" signal. She believes that the other jurors vote sincerely. Moreover, as an expected-utility maximizer, she only cares about contingencies in which her action affects the outcome. Under the unanimity rule, the juror's vote makes a difference if and only if all other jurors vote to convict. Although this "pivotal event" is a hypothetical contingency when the juror contemplates her decision—and a low-probability one at that when $n$ is not small—it is actually the only contingency that matters because it is the only one in which her vote affects the outcome. Therefore, the juror chooses as if she *actually* learned that all other jurors voted to convict. But given the other jurors' strategy, this contingency arises if and only if they all got a "guilty" signal.

Now, the juror says to herself: OK, I got this "innocent" signal, but $n-1$ other jurors got a "guilty" signal. Our signals are equally accurate, and the prior probability that the defendant is guilty is ½. Therefore, it is more likely that my opponents are right and I am wrong than the other way around. The juror's conclusion is that she should vote to convict the defendant, *against* her private information. This means that the guessed strategy profile, in which all jurors vote according to their signal, is *not* a Nash equilibrium: when a juror believes her opponents follow sincere voting, her best reply is to vote to convict regardless of her signal.

This is a remarkable example of what behavioral game theorists call "contingent reasoning." The individual player realizes that the consequences of her action depend on a contingent event, and therefore reasons as if the event actually took place. The best-known instance of contingent reasoning is the "winner's curse" from auction theory. In a standard auction, an individual bidder cares about the value of the object only when she wins. However, this hypothetical event conveys information about the other bidders' private information because their bids are systematically related to their information. Therefore, a rational bidder who knows her opponents' bidding strategies will choose her own bid in a way that takes this information into account, as if she actually won the auction. We will revisit the winner's curse in chapter 5.

Having shown that sincere voting is inconsistent with Nash equilibrium, Feddersen and Pesendorfer proceeded to analyze the symmetric Nash equilibrium that is socially optimal (according to jurors' preferences) under the unanimity rule. They showed that, in this equilibrium, jurors vote to convict when they receive a "guilty" signal and randomize between the two actions when they receive an "innocent" signal. As a result, even the socially optimal equilibrium involves a non-negligible probability of convicting innocent defendants, regardless of how large the jury is. Other majority voting rules outperform the unanimity rule in this regard, because the inference from the pivotal event in which a juror's vote is decisive isn't as strong as in the case of the unanimity rule.

I enjoy teaching this model because of the subtlety of the game-theoretic argument of pivotal voting. But there's a difference between appreciating the cleverness of a game-theoretic argument and finding it realistic. As we saw in chapter 2, Rubinstein (1989) presented the relentless iterative reasoning that characterizes equilibrium behavior in the e-mail game as a paradox. By comparison, Feddersen and Pesendorfer's paper does not present the pivotality argument as paradoxical. Indeed, it underlies the paper's substantive claim that the unanimity rule leads to excessive conviction of the innocent.

So, is the pivotal-voting reasoning realistic or is it paradoxical? Should we believe that real-life voters will focus on the rare hypothetical event in which their vote is pivotal, and draw statistical inference from this event as if it has already happened, taking their knowledge of other voters' strategies into account? To me, this reasoning is too sophisticated to be realistic—especially given the rarity of the hypothetical pivotal event, which makes it difficult to learn about its implications from past experience. I would have been content with presenting the model as a thought-provoking exercise with a semi-paradoxical flavor.

However, given that Feddersen and Pesendorfer presented their model in a more "applied" mode, realism of the contingent reasoning that underlies their equilibrium analysis became a pressing matter for other economists. This encouraged experimental work that tried to test it in laboratory settings. The evidence is mixed.[2] I imagine that the impetus for such experimental inquiry would have been weaker had Feddersen and Pesendorfer delivered their exercise in the "pure theory" style.

Remember how Morris (2002) tried to defuse the paradoxical aspect of Nash equilibrium behavior in global games, by pointing out that it can be interpreted as an intuitive heuristic of optimizing against a "Laplacian" belief. In a similar vein, Andrew McLennan (1998) showed that the optimal symmetric Nash equilibrium in symmetric common-interest voting games like the jury model has a natural heuristic interpretation. Suppose each voter asked, "What is the mixed strategy that would maximize our expected payoff if we all followed it?" This is sometimes referred to as a "Kantian" heuristic, because it applies Immanuel Kant's categorical imperative.[3] Her answer to this question would be to play the exact mixed strategy that Feddersen and Pesendorfer characterized. In particular, it outperforms sincere voting. The reason is that given the voters' preferences—specifically, how they weigh the errors of convicting the innocent and acquitting the guilty—the unanimity rule is suboptimal, and the voters' equilibrium behavior tries to undo its deviation from optimality.

The apparent lesson from McLennan's result is that we don't *have to* interpret voters' equilibrium behavior in terms of the counterintuitive contingent reasoning; the Kantian heuristic of acting in a way that would benefit everyone if everyone followed it produces the same behavior. However, when we conclude that Nash-equilibrium reasoning in a particular game is counterintuitive or unrealistic, should this conclusion be affected by the observation that the behavior that Nash equilibrium predicts is also consistent with some *other* heuristic that has nothing to do with Nash equilibrium (also bearing in mind that McLennan's equivalence argument would break down if we perturbed the model and introduced preference heterogeneity among voters)?[4]

So, how should we regard the jury model? As a demonstration of the subtle effects that the concept of Nash equilibrium (more specifically, the idea of best-replying to a low-probability hypothetical event as if it actually happened) entails in games with incomplete information? Or, alternatively, as a credible prediction of what can go wrong in real-life jury trials because of their reliance on the unanimity rule? Feddersen and Pesendorfer's rhetoric took the latter course. Judging from the profession's response, this rhetoric has worked. To this day, the jury model continues to be "taken seriously" for "applied" purposes.

The lesson is that, sometimes, to be successful with the applied-theory style, one needs to face the unrealistic features of the model and the paradoxical features of its analysis, and simply stare them down. If you take them to be realistic, maybe others will. To paraphrase *Seinfeld*'s George Costanza, it's not a paradox if you believe it.

## Bayesian Persuasion

In 2011, Emir Kamenica and Matthew Gentzkow published what proved to be one of the most influential papers in economic theory in the past decade.[5] It was one of the key works that shifted theorists' view of the information structure of a game from an exogenous feature to an element of ex ante *design*.

The simplest way to describe the Kamenica-Gentzkow model is as a cheap-talk, sender-receiver interaction. It builds on the classic model of strategic communication by Crawford and Sobel (1982). In this two-player game, a "sender" privately observes an exogenous state of nature and chooses a costless message. A "receiver" then observes the message and chooses an action. Players' payoffs are functions of the state and the receiver's action. When the sender's preferences are state-independent while the receiver's preference is state-dependent, we have a *persuasion* situation. This simple model became the basis for one of the richest literatures in modern economic theory.

The Kamenica-Gentzkow variant's starting point is the observation that the sender in the original Crawford-Sobel model has a commitment problem. The receiver's choice of action relies on her interpretation of the sender's message. In Nash equilibrium, this interpretation is based on correct knowledge of the statistical mapping from states to messages. The sender may have an incentive to take advantage of the receiver's interpretation and deviate from her supposed strategy. For example, when the public trusts a central banker's utterances, the central banker may have an incentive to milk her reputation and state that the economy is in good shape even when it isn't. This incentive constrains the amount of information that can credibly be communicated in Nash equilibrium. If the sender could *commit ex ante* to a communication strategy, then by definition this vulnerability would disappear, and perhaps the sender could communicate more information—and possibly increase the chances that the receiver will act in the sender's interest.

## Going to a Party

Here is a simple example that illustrates this idea. The example's formal content is taken from Kamenica and Gentzkow (2011), but its anecdotal aspect borrows from an idea that Kfir Eliaz and I once played with.[6]

You and your partner occasionally go to parties. Before you go out, your partner solicits your opinion about what he is wearing. Your partner's appearance is either good or bad. You can tell but he cannot, as you live in a mirrorless house. The prior probability of the good scenario is $p < \frac{1}{2}$. Your partner is willing to go to the party only if the probability he assigns to the good possibility is at least ½. You want to attend the party regardless of your partner's appearance.

A communication strategy for you is a function that assigns some probability distribution over some set of messages to each of the two states of nature (good appearance, bad appearance). What is the communication strategy that maximizes the chances you will go to the party, under the assumption that your partner is rational, knows your communication strategy, and uses Bayes' rule to form his posterior belief?

A key property of Bayesian updating is that it satisfies the so-called *Martingale property*: the expected posterior belief is equal to the prior belief. It turns out that once we remove the credibility constraint, the Martingale property remains the only constraint that the sender faces. In the party-going example, it means that regardless of your communication strategy, with some positive probability your partner's posterior probability of the good state will be weakly below $p$. For example, if your communication strategy is entirely uninformative (because you send the same random message in both states), your partner's posterior will be equal to the prior $p$ for sure. In this case, he will never go to any party. If, on the other hand, your communication strategy is fully informative (you always truthfully report the state), your partner's posterior will be 1 with probability $p$ and 0 with probability $1 - p$. In this case, he will go to the party with probability $p$.

But you can actually do better than this. Observe that having a posterior probability of the good state $q$ that strictly exceeds ½ is wasteful: any $q \geq \frac{1}{2}$ would be just as good in terms of getting your partner to attend the party. Observe that having $q$ lie strictly between 0 and ½ is also wasteful: any $q$ below ½ would lead your partner to skip the party. The Martingale property essentially gives you a "budget" that constrains the distribution over your partner's posterior beliefs. If you want to maximize the probability that $q \geq \frac{1}{2}$, the best you can do is let the only posteriors be 0 and ½. Let $\Pr(q)$ represent the probability that the posterior belief $q$ is realized. By the Martingale property,

$$\Pr\left(q = \frac{1}{2}\right) \cdot \frac{1}{2} + \Pr(q = 0) \cdot 0 = p$$

Therefore, $\Pr(q = \frac{1}{2}) = 2p$. This is the maximal probability with which you can persuade your partner to go to the party. It is *twice* the frequency you could get with the truthful communication strategy. The lesson is that even within the straitjacket of Bayesian updating, strategic communication has "persuasive power": it can increase the chances that the receiver will act in the sender's interest, relative to truthful communication.

Your ability to commit to a communication strategy does all the work here. Suppose you couldn't commit. Then, if your partner expects you to follow this strategy, you would have an incentive to deviate from the strategy and tell him he looks good even when your random strategy prescribes telling him he doesn't. When you lack commitment power, your partner would never go to the party in Nash equilibrium.

## The Prosecutor Example

Kamenica and Gentzkow didn't use a frivolous example such as my party-going story. Like Feddersen and Pesendorfer, they invoked the more serious setting of a criminal trial. (What is it with these economic theorists? Too many court dramas on their TV diet?) Their analogue of my appearance-obsessed partner is a judge, while the informed sender is a criminal prosecutor who chooses which evidence to seek. A communication strategy is thus reinterpreted as an *information acquisition* strategy, or a "signal function." The commitment assumption is justified by the realistic rule that prosecutors cannot conceal evidence from the court. For example, if the prosecutor orders a DNA test, she is forced to disclose the results, regardless of whether they support her case.

The prime attraction of the criminal-trial story for Kamenica and Gentzkow was thus that it gave them a context in which the commitment assumption is convincing. Certainly more than in the party-going anecdote, where one would have to resort to weak informal arguments such as long-run reputational concerns in order to justify neglecting the sender's credibility problem.

Yet that same story calls into question the realism of the twin assumption that the sender has every information acquisition strategy at her disposal. DNA tests correspond to a small set of signal functions. Is *every* signal function implementable by some test that the prosecutor can order and whose results she must disclose? This seems highly implausible. By comparison, this richness assumption is *not* problematic under the original interpretation of communication strategies, because nothing seems to constrain how the sender randomizes over messages in any given state.

If the authors employed "pure theory" rhetoric, the assumption that the sender has commitment power *and* an unrestricted domain of feasible signal functions would not be problematic. The point of the exercise would be to get a better understanding of the respective roles that the sender's credibility problem and the receiver's Bayesian rationality (specifically, the Martingale rule that characterizes Bayesian updating) play in the familiar Crawford-Sobel model of cheap talk. In the simple persuasion problem given by Kamenica and Gentzkow's leading example, the demarcation is stark: when the sender has no commitment power, she is entirely incapable of persuading the receiver to act in the sender's interest, yet with commitment power she can double the probability of persuading the receiver relative to the truth-telling benchmark.

Taking this route, one could go further and ask what happens when we tamper with the assumption that the receiver forms beliefs via Bayesian updating according to a correct perception of the sender's strategy. For example, in 2021 I published a couple of papers with Kfir Eliaz and Heidi Thysen that explored this question.[7] We showed that in certain models with a non-Bayesian receiver, the sender can persuade the receiver with probability one—independently of whether she has commitment power.

In contrast, Kamenica and Gentzkow's paper argues for a more "applied" relevance of the Bayesian persuasion model. This made the twin assumptions that the sender has commitment power *and* a rich strategy space a harder sell. Nevertheless, the criminal-trial image effectively helped Kamenica and Gentzkow's paper to be "taken seriously."

### Three Introductions and a Conclusion

In fact, this was part of the overall style of the Kamenica-Gentzkow paper. Consider the tone of its opening paragraphs:

Suppose one person, call him Sender, wishes to persuade another, call her Receiver, to change her action. If Receiver is a rational Bayesian, can Sender persuade her to take an action he would prefer over the action she was originally going to take? If Receiver understands that Sender chose what information to convey with the intent of manipulating her action for his own benefit, can Sender still gain from persuasion? If so, what is the optimal way to persuade?

These questions are of substantial economic importance. As Donald McCloskey and Arjo Klamer (1995) emphasize, attempts at persuasion command a sizable share of our resources. Persuasion, as we will define it below, plays an important role in advertising, courts, lobbying, financial disclosure, and political campaigns, among many other economic activities.

The first paragraph employs "pure theory" rhetoric, but the second paragraph is more "applied" in style, with its allusion to significant economic sectors like advertising or lobbying. This second paragraph employs a clever rhetorical device. If the prosecutor example is carefully tailored to make the commitment assumption sound plausible, no such attempt is made for the other examples the authors mention in that second paragraph. What are the commitment mechanisms in advertising or political campaigns? Kamenica and Gentzkow's rhetoric manages to insinuate the relevance of their abstract model for important economic activities, without taking the trouble to demonstrate the realism of their joint assumptions of commitment and signal-space richness for any of these activities. This apparently suffices for establishing "applied" credentials in the paper's introduction; readers probably don't expect a more closely argued linkage at such an early stage.

The authors do sweat more later in the paper, where they devote an entire subsection to defending the commitment assumption with references to financial rating agencies, school grading policies, tobacco advertising and drug trials, replete with footnote links to court rulings and medical journals' editorial guidelines. These are clear "applied-theory" tropes.

Now compare this with the two opening paragraphs in Crawford and Sobel (1982):

Many of the difficulties associated with reaching agreements are informational. Bargainers typically have different information about preferences and even about what is feasible. Sharing information makes available better potential agreements, but it also has strategic effects that make one suspect that revealing all to an opponent is not usually the most advantageous policy. Nevertheless, it seems clear that even a completely self-interested agent will frequently find it advantageous to reveal some information. How much, and how the amount is related to the similarity of agents' interests, are the subjects of this paper.

While our primary motivations stem from the theory of bargaining, we have found it useful to approach these questions in a more abstract setting, which allows us to identify the essential prerequisites for the solution we propose. There are two agents, one of whom has private information relevant to both. The better-informed agent, henceforth called the Sender (S), sends a possibly noisy signal, based on his private information, to the other agent, henceforth called the Receiver (R). R then makes a decision that affects the welfare of both, based on the information contained in the signal. In equilibrium, the decision rules that describe how agents choose their actions in the situations in which they find themselves are best responses to each other.

The difference in rhetoric shows how the culture of economic theory changed from 1982 to 2011. In 1982, the model was utterly novel, a key moment in the "game theory revolution" of microeconomic theory. There was no need to talk about advertising or political campaigns. By 2011, the model itself was familiar. Tweaking it by assuming the sender has commitment power probably wasn't enough to attract readers; raising the "rhetorical temperature" helped in this regard. Recall that Kamenica and Gentzkow published their paper in the "general interest" *American Economic Review*, whereas Crawford and Sobel's paper came out in *Econometrica*, a journal that lacked this orientation back in 1982.

For a more contemporaneous illustration of what "pure theory" rhetoric might look like, we can turn once again to the work of Ariel Rubinstein, who—together with Jacob Glazer—wrote a series of papers that used game theory to illuminate aspects of persuasion.[8] While the Kamenica-Gentzkow model imposes no constraints on the sender beyond the receiver's Bayesian rationality, Glazer and Rubinstein focused on strategic effects of persuasion that arise when there *are* constraints on the messages that the sender can submit or the receiver can process. It is instructive to compare their rhetoric with Kamenica and Gentzkow's. Here's a quote from the concluding section of Glazer and Rubinstein (2006):

This paper has attempted to make a modest contribution to the growing literature linking economic theory to linguistics. Our purpose is not to suggest a general theory for the pragmatics of persuasion but rather to demonstrate a rationale for inferences in persuasion situations.

And here's a quote from the introduction of Glazer and Rubinstein (2001):

Let us emphasize that we do not intend to provide a general theory of debates. Our only aim is to point out that the logic of the optimal design of debate rules is subtle and contains some features which are not intuitive.

The difference is stark: claiming to derive aspects of pragmatics (a subject studied by philosophers and linguists) from a game-theoretic exercise that imposes prior constraints on feasible communication, versus identifying persuasion with Bayesian updating and claiming relevance for advertising and financial reporting.

One wonders whether the literature on Bayesian persuasion and information design would have attracted the impressive caliber of theoretical talent that it did if Kamenica and Gentzkow had chosen the low temperature, "pure theory" rhetoric: if instead of talking about prosecutors and judges they had told a vignette about a couple getting dressed for a party.

## "Nobody Knows Anything"

This is a famous quote by the screenwriter William Goldman (who wrote the script for *All the President's Men*, among other works). He meant that despite their vast experience and market research, Hollywood producers still don't know what makes a movie successful. After the long look we have taken at several modern classics of economic theory that made use of the "applied-theory" style, I have to conclude that Goldman's motto might fit here, too. I don't really know how the authors managed to pull it off.

Although I did point out various expositional devices in these modern classics that lend them an "applied" look, it is still something of a mystery why these devices worked. One could easily imagine audiences enjoying the clever theoretical arguments without accepting the pitch that these arguments should be "taken seriously" for empirical predictions or policy prescriptions. Some mysterious process of professional reception bestowed an "applied" status on these models, and from then on theorists got "permission" to develop these models without worrying about the "applied legitimacy" of their investigation. By this definition, an "applied-theory" piece is an exercise involving a model that has already received the "applied" certification. How did that model get certified in the first place? Well, nobody knows anything.

# 4    The Path of Least Theory

## Indoctrination Camp

In the summer of 1998, I flew from Tel Aviv to Palo Alto for a two-week summer camp in behavioral economics, sponsored by the Russell Sage Foundation. This was the third cohort of a summer school that began in 1994. Richard Thaler was one of the main driving forces behind this remarkable institution. In his scientific autobiography *Misbehaving*,[1] he argued that it was a key component in his successful campaign to make economists more open to alternatives to *homo economicus* originating in psychological research.

The summer camp brought together promising students, from all over, who had shown an interest in behavioral economics. Many of them later became some of the most prominent economists of my generation. The main speakers were leaders of the behavioral economics movement: Colin Camerer, David Laibson, George Loewenstein, Matthew Rabin, and Thaler himself. There were also a few special guest stars such as Daniel Kahneman.

This wasn't an ordinary summer camp. Some students jokingly called it an "indoctrination camp." There was a clear sense of a deliberate, forceful campaign. There were practical tips about how to succeed in academia as a behavioral economist. There were sermons (mainly by Thaler) that took shots at pet peeves. At the end of the camp, we were given T-shirts. The back of the T-shirt featured something like a behavioral-economics brigade firing slingshots at a fortress named "expected utility theory." Like I said, no ordinary summer camp.

As a Tel Aviv University student, I arrived at the summer school from a milieu in which interest in abstract economic theory and curiosity about ideas from psychology went hand in hand. Ariel Rubinstein had just published his book *Modeling Bounded Rationality*, which pitched his version of "psychology and economics" as an avant-garde area in economic theory.[2] Amos Tversky came to give talks and collaborated with Ariel on an experimental game theory paper.[3] Tzachi Gilboa had recently joined the economics department, and was busy incorporating ideas from psychology into his own brand of "behavioral" decision theory, in the form of case-based decision theory.[4]

In this intellectual environment, economic theory and behavioral economics seemed destined for a happy marriage. Moreover, it looked like the future of behavioral economics *depended* on the cultivation of a certain type of "pure" theory. As a student of Ariel's, I was naturally influenced by his outlook. Having sensed that the game theory revolution had exhausted its conceptual innovations, Ariel looked to "psychology and economics" as a new source of ideas that would rejuvenate economic theory. From this perspective, theorists could get ideas from psychologists and experimental economists, as well as from recent attempts by behavioral economists to formulate some of these ideas. But this would be the beginning of a long and hard journey. It would be an exciting journey, in which young theorists of my own generation would be pioneers and explorers; they would be at the front and—importantly for a young researcher's professional ego—retain theory's prestigious status in the profession's food chain. From this point of view, theorists of the "pure," foundational variety would carry the torch of behavioral economists. This was the mentality with which I arrived in Palo Alto.

### Torchbearer or Backseat Passenger?

As it turned out, the summer school's leaders did not share my mentality.

Yes, the summer school was everything it promised to be. It was an extraordinary experience—extremely well-organized, rich in stimulating content, giving students ample opportunity to interact with the teachers and among themselves. But far from putting pure theory on a pedestal, the summer school gave the few "pure" theorists among us a sense that we were backseat passengers, not torch carriers. There was no mention of any need to push the conceptual frontiers of theory, to lay new foundations and forge new formal languages on a par with, say, game theory or Savage's (1954) formulation of subjective expected utility theory. There was no sense that the way forward would be to ignite the imagination of young theorists of the "pure" variety, who would be to the early twenty-first century what David Kreps, Roger Myerson, or Ariel Rubinstein were to the early 1980s.

If anything, the implicit message from Thaler and company seemed to be that the theoretical apparatus for future developments in behavioral economics was already in place: Prospect theory, in the case of decision under risk; the multi-selves model and its "hyperbolic discounting" parameterization, in the case of intertemporal choice; and various utility functions that capture social preferences. In the latter case, some of these utility functions (for example, the one in Matthew Rabin's [1993] paper on fairness considerations in games) borrowed the formalism of "psychological games" developed by Geanakoplos, Pearce, and Stachetti (1989). This formalism was a nice modification of the standard game-theoretic model, which allowed players' utility function to depend on their *beliefs* (including their beliefs about other players' beliefs, as well as higher-order beliefs), and thus enabled behavioral economists to represent preferences that are sensitive to players' *intentions*.

For someone with my background, these theoretical gadgets were anything but avant-garde. They were interesting but rather modest modifications of conventional frameworks. They barely seemed to scratch the surface of the rich psychological phenomena that Tversky, Kahneman, and their associates (including Thaler in the 1980s) had uncovered for economists. But the teachers seemed happy with them. Indeed, they *prized* the fundamental conventionality of these theoretical tools. As far as they were concerned, the future of behavioral economics didn't depend on inventing new theoretical frameworks.

Instead, our summer-school teachers aimed at students with an "applied microeconomics" orientation: those who did empirical work, with or without an element of "applied theory." The vision was that these applied researchers would incorporate ideas from behavioral economics into their investigations. They would make room for "behavioral" explanations of observed phenomena (for example, showing that certain types of economic behavior are a result of systematic mistakes). They would pose empirical questions that are inspired by the ideas of behavioral economists (for example, how changes in the salience of product features affect consumer choices). When estimating a structural model, they would include "behavioral" parameters (for example, those that measure the magnitude of loss aversion or present bias) into the model and estimate them.

This apparent indifference to foundational theory was not self-evident. "Psychology and economics" deals with the most basic aspects of economic behavior. A priori, one might have expected foundational theory to receive greater attention by the movement's leaders. In retrospect, I can speculate about the forces that shaped the theory-lite attitude of the summer school's leaders.

First, most obviously, except for Matthew Rabin, none of them *was* a theorist. But deeper factors were at play as well. Whereas I hailed from a relatively small department having a formidable, outsized theory group, most of the summer-school leaders came from large, balanced departments at the center of the profession. As such, they were in a much better position to sense where it was going in terms of its attitude to economic theory. In chapter 1, I mentioned Colander and Klamer's 1987 article "The Making of an Economist," which was based on interviews with PhD students in top graduate programs. I noted that a primary theme in that article was the "oppression by theory" that many students felt during that peak time of theorists' dominance and influence. In Colander's 2007 book sequel, he and the students he interviewed were relieved to see the waning influence of theorists on the curriculum. Toward the end of the 1990s, when my summer-school experience took place, the "empirical turn" that would soon engulf the economics profession was in its early stages. Perceptive economists at top economics departments could predict that the energy of our profession was about to shift from theory to the empirical side.

This perception may have been strongest in places like Harvard or Berkeley, where a significant share of the summer-school participants (both teachers and students) came from. As a crude generalization, it is probably fair to say that through much of their history, these departments tended to lie on the less enthusiastic side of the spectrum of attitudes to theory. A famous example is Ken Arrow feeling like a fish out of water during his early Harvard years.[5] Behavioral economists flourished and found support in these departments, and it was natural for them to share their view of the role of theory in the scheme of things.

In fact, what I hadn't appreciated at the time was that in the eyes of someone like Thaler, theorists may have represented a vocal pocket of *resistance* to behavioral economics. The positive attitude I experienced in Tel Aviv was possibly the exception rather than the norm. Many theorists acted as conservative defenders of the standard rational-choice modeling framework. They cherished the elegance and completeness of this framework. They also had a good understanding of its adaptability to apparent empirical challenges. In contrast, they regarded behavioral economics as a collection of anecdotes and ad hoc modeling tricks that threatened to replace the unity and beauty of rational-choice modeling with a mess of specific, incongruous models.[6] One might argue that, viewed as a community, theorists weren't friends to behavioral economists, compared with, say, empirical labor economists.

## What Was Behavioral Economics?

Behavioral economics cannot be defined by some distinct methodology or set of tools. Instead, it can be described as a shared commitment to make mainstream economists more open to ideas from psychology, without creating a major disruption of their basic methodologies.[7] Behavioral economics is not synonymous with "incorporating psychology into economics." Economists of different stripes have been trying to do this in various ways and styles. But they weren't all part of the same socio-scientific network as the behavioral economists: they didn't attend the same conferences and didn't cite the same papers. Identifying oneself as a "behavioral economist" meant something else than mere interest in "psychology and economics." What that something else was is what we will try to get a better understanding of in the course of this chapter.

One thing that set behavioral economics apart was its orchestrated-campaign nature, which aimed at the very centers of the profession's mainstream: not foundational economic theory, which is largely viewed as a fringe of the discipline, but "hard-core" fields like finance or public finance. The leaders of the behavioral economics movement wanted to change the sensibilities of practitioners of those fields. To achieve this goal in the medium run, a radical transformation of economic theory was probably not required. Indeed, it might have been an impediment.

In 2019, I published a polemical piece in *American Economic Journal: Microeconomics*, based on the observation that the behavioral economics movement effectively chose a theory-lite style of disseminating and applying its ideas.[8] I argued that this orientation manifests itself in different ways across genres. In "popular-science" pieces that address the general educated public, there is a clear preference for anecdotes over theoretical arguments, however easy it is to transcribe these arguments for the lay reader. In pieces of purely academic writing, there is a tendency toward the most basic, least sophisticated tropes of economic modeling. It is as if whenever there was a choice between different modes of developing or communicating an idea about psychological origins of economic behavior, behavioral economists opted for the "least theoretical" mode possible given the material at hand.

This essay is an attempt to develop the "path of least theory" theme in the "cultural criticism" style of the present book—unlike the style of my 2019 article, which was shaped by its designated venue. I will briefly revisit one of the examples I used to substantiate my case in Spiegler 2019, before delving into a detailed discussion of a new, more central example. The latter example will also give me an opportunity to describe how the "pure theory" community reacted to the theory-lite style of behavioral economics, as exemplified by the "mindless economics" debate that erupted in 2005. Recounting this episode will suggest that the experiences I had in the 1998 summer school were not an idiosyncratic quirk; they reflected conflicting attitudes to the dilemma of how a new, ambitious field like behavioral economics should locate itself on the theory spectrum.

## Phishing for Phools

George Akerlof and Robert Shiller's (2015) book *Phishing for Phools* argues that consumer fallibility should change the way we think about market institutions. Their main thesis is that consumers' deviations from rational choice (their "phoolishness," to use the authors' neologism) makes exploitative transactions ("phishing") an inevitable feature of market interactions.

Akerlof and Shiller make their case with anecdotes of market exploitation. Their exposition is almost entirely devoid of theoretical reasoning. By "theoretical," I don't mean formal modeling, as that would be unusual in a "popular" book (though not *that* unusual, as superb popular physics expositors like Simon Singh or Brian Cox have demonstrated). What I mean is the analogue of explaining the notions of Nash equilibrium or backward induction in a popular game theory book. Even by this soft standard, theoretical arguments are virtually nonexistent in their book. This places *Phishing for Phools* in the large category of popular books on behavioral economics, often written by psychologists and marketing researchers, which to an economist read like an anecdotal "collection of biases." What's unusual about *Phishing for Phools* is that this style is practiced by such eminent academic economists.

I will illustrate my point with a single example from the book. One of the earliest stories in *Phishing for Phools* involves the famous empirical finding of Stefano DellaVigna and Ulrike Malmendier (two star veterans of that 1998 summer school) that health-club customers appear to overestimate their future consumption when choosing a price plan.[9]

Many of those who select monthly subscriptions (with automatic renewal) end up paying more than if they had opted for a by-the-visit plan—they "pay not to go to the gym," as DellaVigna and Malmendier put it in the title of their paper.

Yet, except for two sentences at the end of the book, Akerlof and Shiller remain silent about a simple theoretical argument that DellaVigna and Malmendier themselves made in a companion paper.[10] In their model, two firms play a game in which they simultaneously offer two-part tariffs (a combination of a lump-sum payment and a per-unit price) to consumers with a taste for immediate gratification. In the health-club context, this means that, ex ante, consumers would like to commit to do plenty of physical exercise in the future, but as time goes by their preferences change and they become lazier. Whether or not consumers can predict this future change in their preferences, the two-part tariffs that emerge in Nash equilibrium consist of a large lump-sum payment and a per-unit price below marginal cost. By comparison, if consumers had dynamically consistent preferences, firms would adopt marginal-cost pricing (with no lump sum) in Nash equilibrium.

Why is the omission of this theoretical result remarkable? Because in a later chapter, Akerlof and Shiller present yet another example of market "phishing": the pricing of credit cards. Here, common price plans are a mirror image of the health-club case; they involve no (or effectively negative) lump sum and a high marginal interest rate. DellaVigna and Malmendier's 2004 model offers a simple explanation. Credit cards enable the consumer to enjoy an immediate consumption benefit and defer its cost. In contrast, attending a health club is an investment that pays off in the future. According to the model, this inversion in the temporal distribution of costs and benefits explains the direction of the equilibrium departure from marginal-cost pricing.

The logic behind this result depends on whether the consumer predicts the future change in his preferences (that is, whether he is naïve or sophisticated, to use the terminology we encountered in chapter 3). When he does, he seeks a commitment device to counter his taste for immediate gratification. A high marginal interest rate acts as a partial commitment device that deters excessive use of the credit card, whereas a low per-visit price acts effectively as a partial commitment device that incentivizes health-club attendance. When the consumer underestimates his future taste for immediate gratification, the equilibrium two-part tariff is essentially a *gamble* on the consumer's future consumption. The firm and the consumer entertain different beliefs regarding the consumer's future preferences, and therefore they have a motive to engage in speculative trade, shifting net consumer payoff from the state predicted by the firm to the state predicted by the consumer. The deviation from marginal-cost pricing is a means toward this end. When the firm's belief is accurate, the contract exploits the consumer.

The DellaVigna-Malmendier model thus links two otherwise distinct examples of nonlinear pricing. The model not only links them, but also explains the difference in their departures from marginal cost pricing. Luckily for authors of a popular book, this involves an undergraduate-level argument that can be conveyed verbally to a broad audience. And yet, Akerlof and Shiller refrained from doing so.

As a piece of academic writing, the DellaVigna-Malmendier 2004 paper was itself a piece of "applied style," "low-brow" theory, which was nevertheless pregnant with follow-up questions for "pure style," "middle-brow" theorizing. What kind of price plans would firms offer if they were not confined to two-part tariffs—in particular, can we explain real-life examples of more complex nonlinear pricing? How would firms design a menu of price plans if they did not know the consumer's ability to predict future changes in his preferences? What is the effect of market competition on consumer welfare?[11]

So why did Akerlof and Shiller ignore this aspect of DellaVigna and Malmendier's work? After all, they belonged to the same milieu. The most plausible explanation is that Akerlof and Shiller placed low weight on the need to thicken their plot with a theoretical argument, even an elementary one that could help them link together two apparently different anecdotes. This modus operandi was consistent with how other leaders of the behavioral economics movement acted: whenever possible, follow the path of least theory.

## The "Applied-Theory" Style in Behavioral Economics

It is easy to dismiss the example from *Phishing for Phools* as unrepresentative because of its "popular-science" context, where authors are always concerned that every additional equation will lower sales by 50% (to use Stephen Hawking's famous quip). However, we can find the theory-lite tendency in more "properly" academic outputs of behavioral economics.

Even when behavioral economists tried to engage with economic theory, they typically followed a protocol codified by Rabin (2013): postulate a functional form that captures a psychological force parametrically, then incorporate it in an "applied-theory" exercise or confront it with lab or field data. (A particularly desirable property of such paramet-ric modification is its "portability"—namely, the ability to apply it to a large domain of economic problems.) This methodology tends to appeal to economists with an "applied" orientation more than to the "pure theory" crowd.

Rabin did produce a few works in a "pure theory" style during his mature period as a behavioral economist. Interestingly, these works were in the "paradoxical" mode we encountered in chapter 2; their stated objective was to highlight absurd predictions of rational-choice models. In Rabin (2000), he presented his famous "calibration theorem," which showed that if we use standard expected utility—defined over *absolute wealth*—to explain realistic levels of risk aversion over *small* stakes, the curvature of the utility function this requires also implies unreasonably extreme levels of risk aversion over *large* stakes.

In another beautiful paper, Eyster and Rabin (2014) revisited the stan-dard model of "social learning," in which each player takes an action after observing a private signal regarding a state of nature, as well as the actions of some subset of his predecessors. The definition of this subset for each player constitutes the game's "observability structure." Each player's payoff is only a function of his own action and the state. Eyster and Rabin used a standard payoff specification, under which a player's optimal action coincides with the probability he assigns to one of two possible states. The crucial feature of social learning models is that while they include no direct payoff externalities between players, they exhibit informational externalities: each player can draw inferences about the state from the actions he observes. Nash equilibrium analysis implies that these inferences are based on Bayesian updating and correct knowledge of previous players' strategies. Eyster and Rabin showed that for some observability structures, Nash equilibrium implies a coun-terintuitive "anti-imitation" pattern: if the players you observe take a higher action, sometimes you will respond by taking a *lower* action.

It appears that "pure theory" was a muscle that Rabin enjoyed flexing for the sake of lobbing grenades at the rational-choice model. When he was spreading behavioral economics gospel, his revealed preference was for the more "applied" style.

## Hyperbolic Discounting

Since economists regularly work with parametric functional forms to describe preferences or technology but rarely use them to describe beliefs, it is not surprising that the "applied-theory" style of behavioral economics made the biggest splash in the modeling of preferences, rather than in the modeling of beliefs or cognition in general. The greatest success story of the big wave of behavioral economics around 2000 involved the modeling of intertemporal preferences. Let's turn to this story.

DellaVigna and Malmendier's 2004 model made use of a utility function known as "hyperbolic discounting," originally introduced by Phelps and Pollak (1968) to represent limited intergenerational altruism. In the last two decades, it became a fixture in behavioral-economics models of intertemporal preferences, following seminal papers by Laibson (1997) and by O'Donoghue and Rabin (1999) (a paper we already encountered in chapter 3).

This utility function takes as a starting point the standard model of exponential discounting, which represents the decision-maker's evaluation of consumption streams from some time period $k$ (the period in which the evaluation is made) to some later period $T$:

$$U(c_k, c_{k+1}, \ldots, c_T) = \sum_{t=k}^{T} \delta^{t-k} u(c_t)$$

In this formula, $c_t$ is the decision-maker's consumption at period $t$, $T$ is the time horizon of the model in question, $u$ is his utility function from periodic consumption flows, and $\delta$ is his discount factor, a number between 0 and 1. This is the common tool that economists use to describe decision-makers' preferences over consumption streams. Every economist knows it, and many use it on a daily basis.

The hyperbolic discounting function makes a slight modification in this formula:

$$U(c_k, c_{k+1}, \ldots, c_T) = u(c_k) + \beta \sum_{t=k+1}^{T} \delta^{t-k} u(c_t)$$

The difference is the added parameter $\beta$, which is another number between 0 and 1. This parameter represents "present bias" or a "taste for immediate gratification," as it makes a stark distinction between the evaluation period $k$ and subsequent periods. The rate of intertemporal substitution between periods $k$ and $k+1$ is $\beta\delta$, whereas the rate for any subsequent pair of consecutive time periods is $\delta$. Since $\beta\delta < \delta$, this captures the "present bias" motive—that is, the idea that getting something *now* has special importance.

To illustrate how this formula is plugged into economic applications, consider the DellaVigna-Malmendier 2004 model: the consumer chooses a price plan at period 0, then makes a consumption decision at period 1, and this decision has implications for his consumption at period 2 (due to an implicit budget constraint).

The hyperbolic discounting formula performs a "parametric tampering" with a standard utility function. This is a common "applied-theory" trope. The researcher takes a familiar utility/cost/production function. He forms an immediate, intuitive grasp of what each of its components represents. In the standard exponential discounting formula, the discount factor $\delta$ intuitively represents impatience—the preference to frontload benefits and backload costs. Looking at the standard exponential discounting functional form, it is natural to incorporate present bias by adding a special parameter that creates a wedge between the evaluation period $k$ and all subsequent periods.

Because it is so close to the standard model, the hyperbolic discounting formula invites applications. Indeed, numerous papers in the last quarter century used this formula to study the implications of present bias in various economic settings. The formula is particularly convenient in models that involve a long (or infinite) time horizon.

Describing the hyperbolic-discounting model entirely in terms of the utility function is incomplete. The reason is that the hyperbolic discounting utility function induces dynamically inconsistent preferences: ask the decision-maker at period 0 for his preferred consumption plan starting at period 1, then ask him again at period 1, and you'll get two different answers. Since the decision-maker's rate of substitution between consumption in periods $t+1$ and $t+2$ changes when the evaluation period changes from $t$ to $t+1$, so will his favorite allocation of consumption between periods $t+1$ and $t+2$.

As a result of this dynamic inconsistency, one cannot perform utility maximization unambiguously to analyze the behavioral implications of hyperbolic discounting. As we saw in chapter 3, the standard resolution has been to use the multi-selves approach, treating decisions made at different periods as if different players make them, and (when the decision-maker is considered to be "sophisticated") essentially analyzing subgame perfect equilibria in the resulting game—with a subtle difference in the treatment of indifferences. One could come up with alternative approaches, but this is the one that stuck (along with the naivety variant that we encountered in chapter 3).

Following an "applied-theory" style, most expositions of the hyperbolic discounting model place this general modeling approach in the background and the utility function at the fore, even though the multiselves methodology is at least as essential to the workings of the model as the utility function. When economists think about hyperbolic discounting, they have the utility function in mind, not the solution concept that turns it into an unequivocal model of choice.

Behavioral economics has seen few innovations in modeling intertemporal choice since the late 1990s. The $(\beta, \delta)$ formula became "canonical," and since then it has been a matter of *applying* it rather than challenging it—at least as far as researchers who identify themselves as behavioral economists were concerned. From time to time, creative theorists did find ways to perform interesting "pure theory" exercises using the hyperbolic discounting formula. To take a recent example, Paul Heidhues and Philipp Strack (2021) examined whether the model can be refuted by observed choice behavior in a task-completion setting like the one we examined in chapter 3, albeit with random payoffs. But by and large, hyperbolic discounting hasn't inspired purely theoretical work, and it hasn't served as a springboard for new models of intertemporal choice.

**Self-Control Preferences**

Alternatives to hyperbolic discounting were mostly proposed in the *decision theory* literature, initially in a spirit of antagonism toward behavioral economics. Chief protagonists in this development were the top theorists Faruk Gul and Wolfgang Pesendorfer, who presented a different approach to modeling decision-making in the presence of limited self-control.

Gul and Pesendorfer (2001) examined a two-period setting, in which the decision-maker chooses a choice set (a "menu") in the first period and an element from this menu in the second period. For a vivid image, consider a diner who chooses a restaurant in the morning, and a dish from the restaurant's dessert menu in the evening (assume the entree and main course are fixed). Skipping dessert can be modeled as an additional element in the menu. However, for the sake of the example, let us assume that this is not an option. The setting in the DellaVigna-Malmendier 2004 model fits this two-period model: the choice of a two-part tariff in period 0 is like the choice of a menu, and the choice of how to allocate consumption between the two following periods is like the choice from a menu.

The main innovation in Gul and Pesendorfer's model from a *behavioral* point of view is the idea that an element the decision-maker *doesn't* choose can nevertheless exert a bad influence on his well-being because of self-control problems. For instance, suppose that the diner in our parable is dieting. If the dessert menu of some restaurant consists of a fruit platter and a chocolate mousse, he prefers the former. However, the presence of the latter lowers his well-being relative to a situation in which the dessert menu consisted of nothing but the fruit platter. The reason is that not choosing the mousse requires the diner to exert *self-control*, which he finds mentally costly and would therefore prefer to avoid.

More generally, when the consumer ends up consuming alternative $x$ from a menu $A$, his utility according to the Gul-Pesendorfer model is

$$U(x, A) = u(x) - [max_{y \in A} v(y) - v(x)]$$

In this formula, $u$ and $v$ are two utility functions defined over the space of consumption alternatives. The interpretation is that $u(x)$ is the decision-maker's "commitment utility" from $x$; $u$ is a utility function that captures the decision-maker's long-term perspective. In contrast, the function $v$ is a "temptation utility" that measures how tempting alternatives are at the time of consumption. When the decision-maker chooses an alternative that is not the most tempting in $A$, he incurs a cost of self-control, defined as the difference between the $v$-values of the consumed alternative and the most tempting alternative in $A$. If $A$ is a singleton $\{x\}$, then $U(x, \{x\}) = u(x)$—that is, no self-control costs are incurred because the decision-maker doesn't face an actual choice in the second period.

The Gul-Pesendorfer utility function U can be rewritten as

$$U(x, A) = u(x) + v(x) - max_{y \in A} v(y)$$

When faced with the menu $A$, the decision-maker will choose the element $x$ that maximizes $U(x, A)$, such that his utility will be

$$V(A) = max_{x \in A}[u(x) + v(x)] - max_{y \in A} v(y)$$

This is a natural candidate for the decision-maker's indirect utility from the menu $A$. It represents how the decision-maker compares menus. Indeed, what Gul and Pesendorfer did in their 2001 paper was to posit a *preference relation over menus* that describes the decision-maker's first-period choice: he ranks $A$ above $B$ if $V(A) > V(B)$. Gul and Pesendorfer referred to the preferences over menus represented by $V$ as "*self-control preferences.*" One motivation for the focus on first-period preferences over menus is that an outside observer may have access to these choices but not to the second-period choices from menus. This makes sense in some settings. For example, we can see the gaming plan that a consumer selects without seeing his utilization of the selected plan.

To illustrate these preferences, consider two elements, fruit and mousse. Define the commitment and temptation utilities $u$ and $v$ such that

$$u(\textit{fruit}) + v(\textit{fruit}) > u(\textit{mousse}) + v(\textit{mousse})$$
$$v(\textit{mousse}) > v(\textit{fruit})$$

This means that when the menu is {fruit, mousse}, the decision-maker will choose fruit from the menu. At the same time, mousse is more tempting than fruit. Therefore,

$$V\{\textit{fruit}\} > V\{\textit{fruit, mousse}\} > V\{\textit{mousse}\}$$

The decision-maker's ideal menu is {fruit}, because this enables him to consume according to his commitment preference without incurring self-control costs. The second-best menu is {fruit, mousse} because the decision-maker consumes the item that maximizes his commitment utility but suffers the cost of self-control in the presence of the more tempting element. This menu is better than the singleton menu {mousse}.

This pattern of preferences over menus is impossible under the multi-selves approach that is commonly applied to the hyperbolic discounting model: a tempting element can lower the decision-maker's evaluation of a menu only if he succumbs to the temptation, in which case he would be indifferent between this scenario and being *forced* to consume this tempting element.

Gul and Pesendorfer imposed a few axioms on the decision-maker's first-period preference relation over menus, and showed that these axioms pin down the representation V. This placed their theoretical exercise in the decision-theory tradition of axiomatizing a preference relation. More specifically, they were drawing on a smaller tradition of axiomatizing preferences over menus in the context of two-period decision problems, which David Kreps (1979) started and Eddie Dekel, Barton Lipman, and Aldo Rustichini (2001) were reviving at the same time.

To get their representation theorem, Gul and Pesendorfer made a few moves that have "abstract decision theory" written all over them.

First, they defined consumption alternatives to be *lotteries*, such that the space of consumption alternatives is the set of all lotteries over some finite set of *prizes*. This is standard operating procedure in decision theory, but serves to remove the modeling exercise from natural economic situations. Sure, people often choose between random prospects, but has anyone outside a casino ever been tempted by a *lottery*? Does being tempted by having chocolate mousse with probability 70% and a fruit platter with probability 30% sound natural to you? It's the sort of thing that one must entertain in order to get a utility function that (essentially) uniquely represents the preference relation, but it can alienate economists with a more "applied" orientation.

Second, and relatedly, Gul and Pesendorfer postulated an axiom that bears a formal resemblance to the von Neumann–Morgenstern independence axiom that underlies classical expected utility theory— and indeed reduces to it when we consider preferences over singleton menus. But in non-singleton menus, it ultimately means that the effect of a temptation is linear in its probability. That is, there is a sense in which doubling the probability of chocolate mousse in a menu doubles the intensity of the temptation it presents to the decision-maker.

This is not how Gul and Pesendorfer motivate their independence axiom. They invoke a rationality property of "indifference to the timing of resolution of uncertainty." Whether or not one finds this property normatively convincing, its very normative character seems alien to the context of decision-making under temptations and limited self-control. Why should normative rationality principles govern choice under temptations?

These technical and rhetorical moves place Gul and Pesendorfer's exercise firmly in the tradition of abstract decision theory, while distancing it from the more "applied" community of researchers.

## The "Mindless Economics" Debate

Gul and Pesendorfer presented their work in a spirit of defiance against what they perceived as methodological deficiencies of behavioral economics. The main culprit in their opinion was behavioral economics' apparent disregard for the *revealed preference principle*—namely, the idea that welfare judgments must be based on observed choices in a suitable domain. Their own exercise followed this principle: they posited well-defined preferences over menus, such that these preferences represent both observed choices and welfare comparisons between menus (choices *from* menus are indirectly inferred from the revealed preference relation over menus). They showed that under certain assumptions on these preferences, a particular cost of exerting self-control is implicit in how the decision-maker ranks menus.

By comparison, the behavioral-economics style was to write down a utility function that tries to capture a psychological motive (such as limited self-control) with some parametric modification of a standard functional form, and use that benchmark utility function as an intuitive guide for welfare comparisons. Those are based on setting the new parameter to its benchmark value ($\beta = 1$ in the case of hyperbolic discounting).

Gul and Pesendorfer did not allow their paper to speak for itself: they also wrote a methodological piece, "The Case for Mindless Economics," which ignited a controversy that lasted a while.[12] The hubbub led to a conference that took place at NYU in 2006, in which I had the good fortune to take part. The conference proceedings came out in a book edited by the initiators of the conference, Andrew Caplin and Andrew Schotter, titled *The Foundation of Positive and Normative Economics*.[13] I don't know whether the book will have a long-lasting effect on the philosophy or methodology of economics, but I believe the debate itself was significant for two reasons.

First, it brought up the question of whether economic analysts are "allowed" to interpret agents' observed choices as revealing anything other than their preferences or probabilistic beliefs. In our everyday judgments of other people's behavior, we usually mix an intuitive "revealed preference" criterion with more paternalistic attitudes. Observing someone ordering an extra portion of a dish for dinner, we are equally likely to comment "he must be really hungry" or "he's going to regret this tonight." Before behavioral economics, economists were extreme in their adherence to the former stance, which avoids paternalistic judgments at all costs (academics of the Marxian "false consciousness" persuasion are at the opposite extreme). Behavioral economics helped push economists toward a more balanced mixture of the two attitudes.

This has important implications for the kind of policies that economists may recommend: using "nudges" to manipulate people to save more, taxing high-sugar beverages to reduce their consumption, and so on. These attitudes are controversial, both philosophically and politically. This is one of the things that made the debate over Gul and Pesendorfer's "mindless economics" article significant, because it gave economists an opportunity to locate themselves on this politico-philosophical spectrum.

From this point of view, perhaps the most important article in the conference volume was the one by Botond Kőszegi and Matthew Rabin,[14] who made a clear case for the situations in which economists may want to interpret observed choices as errors rather than conscious preferences. Ariel Rubinstein and Yuval Salant later wrote a nice paper in the "pure theory" style about the problem of eliciting decision-makers' welfare from observed choices when these are known to involve certain systematic errors.[15] Yet this paper hasn't led to a noticeable back-and-forth with the behavioral economics community. The separation between this community and the "pure theorists" was not about political attitudes—it was about the style of doing research.

This is the second important aspect of the 2006 NYU conference. The real clash was not between conflicting approaches to revealed preferences, or between libertarian and interventionist policy instincts. It had more to do with general attitudes to economic theory. On one side, there was the theory-lite attitude of behavioral economics, promoted by Matthew Rabin: write down a utility or belief function that contains a parametric representation of the psychological motive you are interested in, and then apply it or test it against data. On the other side, there was the decision-theory approach of Gul and Pesendorfer, which emphasized axiomatization of preferences over appropriate choice domains. Rabin's style was closer to "applied" theory, Gul and Pesendorfer's committed to "pure," axiomatic decision theory. The behavioral-economics style was technically "low brow" and exhibited sophisticated understanding of experimental psychology. The decision-theory style was technically "highbrow," and its interest in experimental evidence was more cursory. The behavioral-economics style generated little modeling innovation once a handful of functions were "canonized." The decision-theory style generated a lot of innovation, albeit in tightly prescribed frameworks.

Indeed, the decision-theory revival in the years following Gul and Pesendorfer (2001) saw numerous proposals for specific models of preferences over menus (and dynamic decision problems more generally). These models captured various aspects of the psychology of temptation and self-control, or used the same methodology to explore other psychologies (regret, belief distortion, social image, and more).[16] There was plenty of innovation to go around, in contrast to the quick canonization of hyperbolic discounting that seems to have stifled innovative modeling of intertemporal choice in the behavioral economics camp.

At the same time, the innovation was confined to the narrow circle of decision theorists. It was constrained by the incremental style of much of axiomatic decision theory, where innovation proceeds by tampering with some reference set of axioms. Very little of that research spilled over to the more "applied" wings of the theory community, let alone the economics profession at large—again, in marked contrast to the hyperbolic discounting model.

The question of which style led to a greater proliferation of new models should not be confused with the question of radicalism versus conservatism. The Gul-Pesendorfer approach was conservative in a number of ways. First, it didn't invent a new type of decision theory but helped revive an existing one (due to Kreps and Porteus 1978 and Kreps 1979). Second, it insisted on conventionally assuming complete and transitive preferences, even as the new choice domains became increasingly complicated. And third, by doing so, it insisted on identifying choice and welfare in keeping with the revealed preference principle, whereas behavioral economists were happy to dissociate the two. That latter move was behavioral economics' most "radical" and politically charged. However, in terms of methods, behavioral economics was even more conservative than the Gul-Pesendorfer approach: its theoretical methods were closer to bread-and-butter applied theory.

I have always regarded Gul and Pesendorfer's "mindless economics" article primarily as a missive against the "theory-lite" aspect of behavioral economics and a call to pursue "psychology and economics" in a "high theory" style. But since they lumped this call with a specifically conservative conception of such a style and a doctrinaire commitment to the revealed preference principle (with its paternalism-averse flavor of libertarian politics), they ironically helped crystallize the narrative that lumped the radical elements of behavioral economics with its indifference to "high theory."

## The Dilemma

Like all narratives, the one that pits Rabin-Thaler against Gul-Pesendorfer is simplistic and distorts reality. For one thing, there are card-carrying behavioral economists (like Erik Eyster and Botond Kőszegi, two prominent theorists from my own generation, both longtime collaborators of Rabin) who have produced admirable pieces of behavioral "pure theory."[17] In addition, there have been "pure theory" approaches to "psychology and economics" (including my own work) that do not fall into the axiomatic-decision-theory mold.

What my narrative doesn't distort, in my opinion, is the "path of least theory" that behavioral economics, viewed as a whole, has taken. It is an area of academic activity that effectively kept itself at a remove from foundational, pure theory—even though its subject matter is the most fundamental building block of the economics discipline. This orientation was consistent with the general professional zeitgeist: Thaler (2016) referred to behavioral economics as an aspect of the profession's empirical turn.

The success of this orientation is undeniable. It maximized behavioral economics' medium-term impact. Thaler's 2017 Nobel Prize was the highest official recognition of this achievement. But is it possible that it also entailed a loss for the economics discipline in the *long* run? This is an example of a larger dilemma: Is it possible for a new field in economics to take a "wrong turn" in terms of how foundational it chooses to be? This question cuts both ways: it is fair to ask whether, for example, the abstract, axiomatic style of decision theory has been a "wrong turn" in the opposite direction.

I should clarify that I am not a conspiracy theorist (just a theorist): I don't think that the leaders of the behavioral economics movement sat in a smoke-filled room and planned a theory-lite strategy. I don't think the field would have looked very different today if Thaler or Laibson had attended more theory seminars. Instead, the behavioral economics community and its surrounding culture somehow made the "joint decision" to navigate away from the "pure theory," foundational style. It is interesting to ask whether that move, its success notwithstanding, also had a cost.

### Incomplete Contracts

A similar dilemma presented itself to students of the theory of the firm in the 1980s and 1990s. During these decades, "incomplete contracts" emerged as a frontier subject that occupied some of the best minds of our profession. Chapter 2 gave us a glimpse into this literature. Jean Tirole's 1994 Walras-Bowley lecture may be a good entry point into this fascinating, now rather neglected, field, because it came near the end of the subject's period of ascendance, and it has some overlap with my present discussion.[18]

The basic observation underlying this field is that real-life contracts and other legal arrangements (such as laws or constitutions) are simpler and less exhaustively detailed than what might appear optimal from a standard mechanism-design point of view. One example that Tirole (1999) gives is the institution of patents, which rewards the winner of an R&D race with inefficient monopoly. A more efficient alternative would be not to use the allocation of property rights as an instrument for encouraging innovation, but instead design a contest mechanism, whose winner receives a monetary reward.

The question of why such arrangements appear in reality despite their apparent suboptimality is of key importance for several fields in economics. Most of the research into incomplete contracts examined the problem in the more specific context of the design of organizations. Grossman and Hart (1986) and Hart and Moore (1990) are the seminal papers in this literature; they tried to explain aspects of the organization of firms as a consequence of contractual incompleteness.

From the start, researchers had conflicting ideas about the terms of this investigation. To quote from the opening paragraph of Tirole (1999):

A methodological divide may have developed in our profession in recent years between those who advocate pragmatism and build simple models to capture aspects of reality, and others who wonder about the foundations and robustness of these models, and are concerned by the absence of a modeling consensus similar to the one that developed around the moral hazard and adverse selection paradigms in the 1970s.

The Grossman-Hart-Moore approach was to assume specific, exogenously given restrictions on the space of feasible contracts, and to examine the contracting process under these restrictions. The primary motivation for these restrictions was "unforeseen contingencies": it is hard for economic agents to imagine and then put into words the numerous future scenarios that may affect the future outcomes of this or that contractual arrangement.

This line of inquiry was the dominant one in the literature. It had an "applied-theory" style: once researchers were satisfied with imposing prior restrictions on what is feasible, they probably also had fewer inhibitions regarding additional special assumptions, such as functional forms or the order of moves in a game. Or is this merely a matter of correlation and selection—namely that researchers who feel temperamentally comfortable with ad hoc restrictions of contracts and mechanisms are also going to feel comfortable with the type of additional special assumptions that characterize the "applied-theory" style?

The alternative approach to incomplete contracts tried to be more foundational. Rather than assuming incomplete contracts, researchers in this wing tried to *derive* incomplete contracts from assumptions they considered more primitive, such as difficulty to imagine future contingencies (Lipman 1992) or the complexity of long contracts (Battigalli and Maggi 2002). This literature was relatively small. Of course, the classification is not airtight. Some works that asked questions of a foundational nature often had an "applied-theory" look (for example, Kathryn Spier's (1992) paper, which argued that signaling motives may deter negotiators from proposing complete contracts).

The dilemma was similar to the one over behavioral economics. Is the best way to make progress with the subject matter to treat it as raw material for "applied theory"? Or should we regard it as a foundational problem that demands new modeling frameworks? Between 1985 and 1995, the profession gave a clear preference to the former approach. (However, I don't recall the interaction between the two approaches as being as conflictual as in the case of behavioral economics. The paragraph from Tirole [1999] that I quoted above ends with the (parenthetical) sentence: "I personally have sympathy for both viewpoints.")

This phase more or less ended when Tirole and Eric Maskin circulated a paper that set out to shatter the unforeseen-contingencies hand-waving defense of the "applied-theory" approach to incomplete contracts. The paper made a big splash in the mid-1990s, and eventually was published in a landmark special issue of the *Review of Economic Studies*, which contained other seminal contributions to the field.[19]

According to my reading, Maskin and Tirole argued that the usual defense for the standard incomplete-contracts exercise was inconsistent. Although researchers in this literature used unforeseen contingencies to motivate contractual restrictions, they kept assuming that economic agents are rational and forward-looking, and in particular able to perform backward induction. In other words, agents were able to imagine and calculate the future *payoffs* that result from any contractual arrangement. Maskin and Tirole showed that if we maintain this rationality assumption, then in many environments agents can circumvent an inability to describe contingencies by cooking up a mechanism that only presumes the ability to calculate future payoff consequences of current decisions.

Maskin and Tirole effectively put a mirror in front of incomplete-contracts researchers. If you want to keep doing what you are doing, you'd better drop the unforeseen contingencies motivation (or at least think harder about whether it fits your setting). But if you think that unforeseen contingencies are relevant to the problem of incomplete contracts, then you'd better start thinking about the bounded rationality that may prevent agents from imagining and calculating the future consequences of their current decisions. However, that will force you to drop the "applied-theory" style and start doing the more foundational, "pure theory" type of work.

Whether or not by coincidence, the incomplete-contracts literature dwindled shortly after 1999, and it is now unofficially dead, even though to my taste its deepest questions still merit close investigation.

As with behavioral economics, the medium-term payoff of the "applied-theory" style was considerable, culminating in a Nobel Prize to Oliver Hart in 2016. But the thought that the field may have ended in a state of exhaustion rather than fulfillment raises the question of whether it missed an opportunity of a "longer, richer life" by largely evading a more foundational style.

## The Story of Market Design

The field of "market design" offers an illustration of the kind of sustained verve that early investment in "pure theory" can bring. Its origins were in beautiful contributions of theorists like David Gale, Herbert Scarf, Lloyd Shapley, and Martin Shubik to the study of two-sided matching and other models of markets for indivisible goods. For a long time, the area of inquiry firmly belonged to the "pure theory" category. Al Roth and Marilda Sotomayor's (1990) authoritative textbook synthesized the theoretical literature. However, at the same time that Roth was developing the pure theory of two-sided matching, he began linking it to concrete economic settings (for example, in his famous exploration of the market for medical interns [Roth 1984]). The field exploded around 2000 when theorists gave it a more determined "applied" color by arguing that its tools can help solving real-life design problems (such as systems of school choice).[20] This move turned the field into a brand of "economic engineering." Nowadays, it is still very much alive, with a diverse community that includes theorists, computer scientists, and empirical economists.[21]

I believe that the continued liveliness of the field, sixty years after its beginnings, is in large part thanks to its deep theoretical roots. It is one of the reasons talented researchers with diverse backgrounds and skills continue to find interest in this area. A building with deep foundations may take longer to build, but the deeper the foundations, the taller the building one can erect on their bases.

## The Textbook Test

A simple litmus test of the kind of long-run impact that awaits behavioral economics is to look at economics textbooks. The game theory revolution led to a complete rewriting of graduate-level microeconomic-theory textbooks.[22] Nothing of the sort has happened with behavioral economics. And where are the graduate-level textbooks devoted entirely to behavioral economics, other than as an aspect of experimental economics? I am not talking about surveys, pamphlets, handbooks or autobiographies, but about pedagogical texts that an instructor in a PhD program can follow closely (like the Roth and Sotomayor 1990 monograph I referred to in my abridged history of market design).

And what about graduate-level textbooks in other fields? Despite the "theory dethroning" trend that I described in chapter 1, economic thought is still largely carried by *models*. When you enter a new field in economics, you typically navigate it with the aid of a few models. Sometimes the models are simple, and sometimes they are elaborate. Sometimes you will spend a lot of time with the models, and sometimes this journey is brief and you soon switch to empirical work. But the models will be in the background and shape your thinking. Has any major field in economics seen a thorough "behavioral" overhaul of its basic collection of models? Have macroeconomists realized that they need to revamp their textbooks in light of behavioral economists' insights into people's formation of expectations or the role of fairness considerations in labor relations? If Jean Tirole wrote a new edition of his magisterial *Theory of Industrial Organization* textbook,[23] would behavioral economists' ideas about consumer psychology force him to rethink the book's overall organization? Or would he settle for adding a "behavioral industrial organization" chapter toward the end of his book?

From this perspective of influencing technically oriented, graduate-level textbooks, the success of behavioral economics appears limited. Compare this with the unmitigated success it has had in this regard with *experimental* economics: a graduate-level textbook in this field is inconceivable without a massive behavioral-economics dose. And compare it also with the growing influence of behavioral economics on nontechnical, *undergraduate*-level textbooks (for example, the treatment of social preferences in the CORE team's [2017] introductory textbook).[24]

The textbook test confirms the intuition that the long-run impact of behavioral economics has been an enrichment of the basic attitudes that economists absorb in early stages of their education, rather than a fundamental change in their technical, graduate-level education. To the extent that this accurately describes the outcome, is it also an accurate description of the original ambitions of the movement's leaders? Is this a "happy ending"?

**Crowding Out?**

The reader may wonder why I am framing the "theory content" dilemma in either-or terms. Why can't a field of inquiry open itself to multiple styles of doing theory, and let a thousand flowers bloom? I agree that, in an ideal world, that would be the case. However, economics being the type of science that it is, it lacks a clear mapping from substantive economic questions to the spectrum between foundational and applied work. Historical accidents and the predilections of a field's pioneers determine its early orientation on the pure-applied axis. The "pure" and "applied" styles move at different paces, they demand different kinds of rhetoric, and they have different notions of what it means for the outcome of a research project to be a success. Ultimately, they compete for journal space, professional prestige, and the peaks of professional fashion cycles.

When a substantive economic question becomes associated with a particular theoretical style, the practitioners of this style will be the gatekeepers who determine what kind of work gets access to the central stage. The simple fact is that the "applied" style has a bigger short-term payoff and a bigger audience, and therefore it tends to overshadow the "pure" style—just as forward soccer players almost always beat defenders at the Ballon d'Or. As a result, when the "applied" style dominates the early development of a new theoretical subfield, this is likely to have a lasting effect on its character. Whether this is a gain or a loss is something that economists will disagree on.

# 5     Rational X

## Statistical Discrimination

In the tumultuous summer of 2020, when Twitter was boiling over with threads on race relations in America, my attention was drawn to an interesting side discussion about the treatment of ethnic discrimination in economics. Not how economists as people exercise various kinds of discrimination (there was a bit of that, too), but how their *research methods* lead to biased or blinkered intellectual treatment of the role of ethnicity in social interactions.

Although the discussion was largely about empirical research, some of the arguments were at least tangential to economic theory—more specifically, the theory of "statistical discrimination." When economists talk about discrimination, they traditionally distinguish between two models, known as *taste-based* and *statistical* discrimination. The former means that the decision-maker treats differently two otherwise-identical people who belong to different social groups, only because he likes people who belong to one group better than people who belong to the other. Becker (1957) introduced this concept into economic modeling and argued that a perfectly competitive market will eradicate sellers or employers who exhibit this type of discrimination.

Phelps (1972) and Arrow (1973) contributed the "statistical discrimination" model. The idea is that the decision-maker is not interested in a person's social group per se but in an *unobservable*, economically relevant characteristic (such as latent productivity). The decision-maker draws a statistical inference about this characteristic from the *observed* social group to which the person belongs. The inference is based on "rational expectations"—that is, correct knowledge of the joint distribution of the observed and unobserved characteristics, coupled with correct application of Bayesian updating. According to this theory, for differential treatment to take place, there must be intergroup differences in the unobserved variable of interest.

You can see why this is political gunpowder. Statistical discrimination says that the reason different groups are treated differently is that they are actually different in ways that "legitimately" matter to other people. Applications of the theory often take these differences to be exogenous without offering an account of how they came into being. Sometimes the analyst endogenizes the difference: individual members of one social group anticipate receiving worse treatment and therefore they do not incur a costly investment in a desirable skill; as a result, members of this group are less desirable to other decision-makers who therefore give them worse treatment. Individual agents are too small to affect this inference unilaterally and must take it as given. This argument regards the social group as a "sunspot"—an arbitrary device for coordinating expectations, and therefore it is silent about why one specific group ends up getting the raw deal.

Some outside observers found this troubling. They argued that the explanatory framework of statistical discrimination has the rhetorical effect of *normalizing* stereotypical thinking. Here is Sonja Starr, a law professor who has published in leading economics journals. In June 2020, she fired a tweetstorm, from which I quote selectively (with slight editing, mainly replacing abbreviations with full terms; the emphases are as they appear in the origin):[1]

Although criticizing statistical discrimination has been a theme of my work . . . some of my own economics papers nonetheless discuss why what we found seems to be stereotyping or taste-based discrimination. This is such a core concern of the field that it has seemed unignorable. It is one of the first questions at every seminar. We do emphasize that what economists label statistical discrimination would be equally bad and illegal, and say we are just exploring mechanisms. . . . Recognizing that does not require *defending* statistical discrimination. . . . But I worry that "understanding mechanisms" isn't the only reason so many papers contain such a discussion. It is also because some (not all) economists will not think discrimination findings reveal a *problem* unless there is evidence it is not "just" statistical discrimination. . . . And in contexts where it *is* relevant or useful to parse mechanisms, it would help to come up with a better name for "statistical discrimination." Maybe "racial profiling"?

In other words, the rhetoric of "statistical discrimination"—not least its very *title*—effectively sanitizes a problematic social practice, and as such creates a bias within the world of academic economics—including economic theory, to the extent that it uses statistical discrimination models uncritically.

The rhetoric of statistical discrimination is sneaky in other ways. Taken literally, "statistical discrimination" doesn't mean that the statistics are done *correctly*. A decision-maker can engage in statistical discrimination while committing errors of statistical inference. Or he could perform the statistical inference on the basis of a wrong subjective model. For example, his wrong model can include a presumption that agents who are identical in everything except their ethnicity can have different "ability." The assumptions of his model could also be self-serving in a way that blurs the distinction between taste-based and statistical discrimination. None of these examples of "statistical discrimination" would have the soothing rhetorical effect that Sonja Starr complains about. It is fundamental for the rhetorical power of the "statistical discrimination" title that the audience links it with rationality and rational expectations: agents have "legitimate" preferences, and they are merely doing what they always do in standard economic models: forming beliefs based on correct priors and Bayesian updating according to their imperfectly informative signals.[2]

This discussion of statistical discrimination broaches the big question of whether economic theory has inherent political biases. This is a weighty subject that I am *not* going to discuss in this chapter. My objective with this example was different: to remind readers that the "rationalizing" mode of explanation that is second nature to economists doesn't always go as smoothly down non-economists' throats. This in turn generates another question, which is in principle independent of politics: Could it be that our basic fondness for rational explanations makes us less critical of their surrounding rhetoric? Are there other ways in which rationalizing explanations filter effortlessly through our economist's consciousness, without facing the walls of resistance we would mount in response to other modes of explanation?

### I'm Sure There's a Perfectly Rational Explanation for This . . .

Our eagerness to make every kind of human behavior under the sun consistent with some maximizing model is a key feature of the culture of economic theory. Many economists, Gary Becker the most well-known among them, *define* economic analysis as the "relentless," "unflinching" attempt to explain behavior as a result of some kind of utility maximization subject to some constraint. By "some kind," what I mean is that economists feel free to play with the utility function, the domain over which it is defined and the constraints that the economic agent faces, as long as the "max $u(x)$ subject to the constraint that $x$ is in $B$" explanatory framework remains. This mode of explanation also assumes rational *expectations*: decision-makers have a correct understanding of the causal and statistical regularities in their environment.

At its extreme, this methodology takes a type of behavior that we would normally think of as irrational, impulsive, emotional, or self-destructive and nevertheless fits it into the maximizing framework. Pick an apparently irrational behavior X, add a prefix like "rational," "Bayesian," "statistical," or "optimal," et voilà: you've got yourself a rationalization of supposedly irrational behavior. Gary Becker earned his legendary status in economics partly because he was the absolute master of this *rational X* approach. He took criminal behavior or romantic attachments, which people hadn't imagined to be part of either economics or rational behavior, and found a fruitful way to model them as some form of constrained utility maximization, thus bringing them into the purview of economic inquiry.

Naturally, the rational X category lacks a precise definition. I wouldn't use it to describe every attempt by economists to rationalize observed behavior. For example, Herbert Simon (1956) famously examined the realistic "satisficing" choice procedure, according to which the decision-maker searches through her choice set in some order until she finds an alternative that is "good enough," and stops there. Although this description differs from utility maximization at the algorithmic level, Simon showed that it is consistent with rational behavior (as long as we take the search order as given). I wouldn't refer to this type of rational explanation as "rational X" because satisficing doesn't strike us as irrational in the everyday sense of the word. Indeed, Simon himself referred to it as an example of *procedural* rationality. In contrast, phenomena like addiction or self-delusion, which I cover in this chapter, belong intuitively to the category of the irrational. This is partly what made the rational X program so provocative and appealing: if economists can rationalize *that* . . . well, there is no limit to what they could accomplish.

However, when one tries to mash up two radically different visions of human behavior—the rational and the irrational—this marriage is not going to be without its frictions. How do economists respond to these tensions? Does our love of "rational explanations" make us gloss over them? What rhetorical devices do authors employ to preempt potential reservations?

This chapter reflects on these questions by looking at a few examples of "rational X" exercises in the literature, speculates about the sources of their rhetorical power, and points out how, in order to work, they sometimes distort the description of the phenomena in question or the notion of rationality they involve. Although these examples do not always fall squarely into what we nowadays classify as economic theory, they are fundamentally theoretical. Even if Gary Becker is not anyone's idea of a contemporary theorist in the sense that Ken Arrow is, the ideas he presented were theoretical in nature.

## Rational Addiction

In 1988, Becker and Kevin Murphy presented a model that offered a rational-choice account of addictive behavior.[3] In their model, the decision-maker chooses how much to consume from a certain product at each time. The decision-maker is conventionally forward-looking: he evaluates a stream of consumption by the discounted sum of future periodic utility flows.

Becker and Murphy's model operates in continuous time. The decision-maker's instantaneous utility flow at time $t$ is $u(y(t), c(t), S(t))$, where $y(t)$ is the consumption quantity of a "regular," nonaddictive good; $c(t)$ is the consumption quantity of an *addictive* good; and $S(t)$ is a state variable that represents a "stock of past consumption" of the addictive good. This stock depends on the history of consumption of the addictive good—a property that enables Becker and Murphy to model the good's addictive qualities. Its rate of change at time $t$ is given by the formula

$$\dot{S}(t) = c(t) - \delta S(t) - h(D(t))$$

If only the first term existed, $S(t)$ would be the mere integral of the addictive good's past consumption. The second term represents "exogenous" depreciation, which weakens the history-dependence that creates addiction-related effects.

The third term in the formula for $\dot{S}(t)$ represents what Becker and Murphy call *"endogenous depreciation."* It is a more dubious object. Becker and Murphy don't say much about it, and settle for the laconic statement that $D(t)$ captures expenditures on nonconsumption measures that the decision-maker takes in order to affect the stock variable ($h$ is some function of this expenditure). For most of their paper, they set the third term to zero. Let us therefore set $h = 0$ and revisit this term later.

The past-dependence of consumption utility gives Becker and Murphy many degrees of freedom for expressing assumptions that correspond to salient features of addictive goods. For example, they can express the "reinforcement" property that higher past consumption increases marginal utility from current consumption. They can also capture "tolerance"—namely, the property that larger past consumption of a good lowers the decision-maker's utility from a given level of current consumption.

In the best Beckerian tradition, the model takes a plausible basic motive—yes, even addicts might perform intertemporal trade-offs, and their desire to consume the addictive good is comparable to the "ordinary" consumer's desire to eat bigger portions at a restaurant or drive a bigger car—and then pushes it to an extreme that an economist with lesser faith wouldn't dare. Becker and Murphy's relentlessness pays off because it produces results that we didn't associate with the behavior in question before setting our eyes on the model. For example, the model predicts that an anticipated future increase in the price of the addictive good will lead the decision-maker to lower his current consumption of the good. The reason is that a higher future price raises the cost of becoming addicted. This prediction has limited theoretical interest, as it is not specific to addictive goods. Nevertheless, it underscores Becker and Murphy's claim that even the consumption of addictive goods responds to the pressures of forward-looking intertemporal substitution.

Part of the rhetorical effect of rational addiction is the brash, unapologetic manner in which the authors present their stance. The opening words of Becker and Murphy (1988) paper almost taunt the skeptical reader:

> Rational consumers maximize utility from stable preferences as they try to anticipate the future consequences of their choices. Addictions would seem to be the antithesis of rational behavior. Does an alcoholic or heroin user maximize or weigh the future? Surely his preferences shift rapidly over time as his mood changes? Yet . . . we claim that addictions, even strong ones, are usually rational in the sense of involving forward-looking maximization with stable preferences. Our claim is even stronger: a rational framework permits new insights into addictive behavior.

So, you thought addiction was irrational? We'll show you that not only is the rational-choice model compatible with addiction, but it also does a better job explaining it than anything else you might have in mind.

Yet, the curious thing about the rational-addiction model is that it is so easy to *falsify*. The very rationality it assumes means that the decision-maker will *never* want to limit his options. The decision-maker maximizes a stable utility function and hence he is dynamically consistent:

if he forms a plan for future consumption at some period $t$ (the plan can be contingent on random future events), he never wants to deviate from it at any subsequent period. And he is never made worse off when we expand his choice set. Yet, a major aspect of addictive behavior is the addict's occasional attempts to *limit his options* as a means for fighting the addiction: checking himself into a rehab center where his actions are controlled, or avoiding enjoyable social interactions because they offer consumption opportunities that may trigger a relapse.[4] The most basic premise of the rational-addiction model excludes such a defining feature of the experience of anticipating and dealing with addiction.

I find it remarkable that this very basic observation wasn't considered a good enough reason for economists to discard the model and adopt an alternative. The opposite is the case: Becker and Murphy's model has become *the* benchmark model for (mostly empirical) economic studies of the consumption of addictive goods.

Like the model of statistical discrimination, the Becker-Murphy model is politically sensitive. Since it follows the revealed-preference tradition of equating choice with welfare, it rules out self-destructive behavior from the outset, and produces a welfare analysis that interprets the addict's choices as welfare-improving *by definition*. Therefore, according to the model, curtailing the availability and affordability of addictive products can never benefit the decision-maker. Paternalistic interventions are needless because the decision-maker is rational and knows what he is doing. As in the case of statistical discrimination, the rational-addiction model sanitizes behavior that we usually regard as problematic (when not wearing our economist's hat).

## Rebuttals

Let us consider two counterarguments against my claim that the model's inability to accommodate a taste for limiting one's options would normally hand it a major blow.

*What is the alternative?* We can grant the criticism that the rational-addiction model gets some things wrong, but it does get other things right. In the absence of an alternative, why can't we accept it as a useful, provisional model?

*Reply*: There *are* alternatives. Gruber and Kőszegi (2001) presented a version of the Becker-Murphy model that incorporates dynamic inconsistency, using the "hyperbolic discounting" parameterization we discussed in chapter 4. This model assumes forward-looking behavior and therefore shares the feature that anticipated price changes affect current consumption, but it also implies that the decision-maker may prefer to limit his options. The relative conventionality of the hyperbolic discounting model makes it handy for applications and empirical work, as Gruber and Kőszegi demonstrated themselves.

There is more. Gul and Pesendorfer (2007) extended their modeling approach, also described in chapter 4, to consumption of addictive goods. Laibson (2001) and Bernheim and Rangel (2004) contributed other models. Neither abandons the rational-choice paradigm. In particular, Gul and Pesendorfer's model—as we saw in chapter 4—reconciles a preference for limiting options with maximizing behavior by *redefining the domain* of the decision-maker's preferences to be the space of dynamic choice problems. This is another common expression of economists' taste for "rational explanations."

The point is that although forward-looking behavior and past-dependence of preferences over current consumption are building blocks in a reasonable approach to modeling addiction, going the extra distance of assuming a stable preference over streams of consumption may be a step too far. The fact that observed behavior is consistent with some aspects of the Becker-Murphy model (that are shared by other models) doesn't mean that it lends support to the Becker-Murphy model in its totality.

*Doesn't the "endogenous depreciation" term address the preference to limit one's options?* For example, checking oneself into a rehab center is a non-consumption activity that reduces future addictive behavior.

*Reply*: The "endogenous depreciation" term strikes me as a mostly rhetorical device. As mentioned above, Becker and Murphy hardly discuss it and set it to zero for most of their paper. Its role seems to be precisely to shush the criticism that their model rules out self-handicapping. If the term is supposed to correspond to certain observable actions like checking oneself into a rehab center, then why aren't those actions part of the *domain* over which the rational addict's preferences are defined? And if "endogenous depreciation" is meant to capture the effect of unmodeled activities on future preferences, then doesn't the model cease to be one with stable preferences over consumption streams? In other words, is it really "rational" in the sense that Becker and Murphy implied?

In the end, the dubious term obfuscates the model's answer to the following simple question: Will the decision-maker ever prefer to limit his future consumption options? Without this term, the answer is clear: no, never! The endogenous-depreciation term only creates ambiguity about what the formal model actually assumes. Therefore, I regard it as a patch that serves a rhetorical purpose; interpretation of this term would imply that the decision-maker doesn't have stable preferences over consumption streams after all, belying his "rationality."

The Becker-Murphy model has drawn fire over the years, mainly over its substantive conclusions about the nature of addiction and how public policy should address it.[5] This is not the place for a survey of these critiques. What I want the reader to take from the present discussion is the observation that despite an obvious limitation of the model, it has captured the imagination of so many economists. Such is the rhetorical power of the rational X approach in the hands of a master practitioner.

## Interlude: What's in a Name?

The very title of rational X models—rational addiction, statistical discrimination, and so on—is part of their rhetorical appeal. Successful names have a way of short-circuiting our critical faculties and lulling us into acceptance of their underlying message.

My favorite example in this regard is the auction-theoretic notion of *the winner's curse* (encountered in chapter 3). In its simplest form, it means that in an auction for a commonly valued object in which each bidder has some private signal regarding the object's value, a bidder's valuation of the object conditional on her private information *and* the event of winning the auction is lower than the valuation that only conditions on her private information. In other words, winning the auction is "bad news." The reason is that if bids are positively correlated with bidders' private signals (as they naturally are), the highest bid will tend to come from the bidder who received the most optimistic signal regarding the object's value. By definition, this signal has an upward bias.

What is the relevance of this bias for bidding behavior? In the absence of externalities, bidders care about the object's true value *only* when they win the auction. Therefore, all they should care about is the object's expected value conditional on the hypothetical event of winning the auction. Consequently, they need to incorporate the winner's curse into their bidding strategy.

But how *should* the bidder incorporate it? According to Wikipedia, "Savvy bidders will avoid the winner's curse by bid shading, or placing a bid that is below their ex ante estimation of the value of the item for sale."[6] Well, this is not quite right. One can easily construct examples of a common-value, second-price auction (the format alluded to by the quote; in a first-price auction, shading is optimal even in the absence of common-value effects), in which a Nash-equilibrium bidding strategy will involve *raising* the bid above the nonstrategic benchmark for a range of signal values. The reason is that the winner's curse has both "extensive" and "intensive" margins. The extensive margin is the one we described above: for a given bid, winning the auction is bad news. The intensive margin means that raising the bid will make the news *less bad*, because the higher one's bid, the weaker the adverse informational content of winning the auction. For a range of signal values, the intensive margin will outweigh the extensive margin and lead the bidder to overbid rather than underbid.[7]

Why, then, did the Wikipedia entry commit such a basic error (and this is but one out of several examples one can find on the web)? My theory is that the phenomenon's very name bears significant responsibility. If winning the auction is a "curse," then one should definitely try to avoid it, which means lowering one's bid. As sexy and attention-grabbing as the name "the winner's curse" is, it distorts our perception of the phenomenon by highlighting its extensive margin at the expense of the intensive margin. How theorists choose to name their models or theoretical effects has an impact on how their audiences perceive them. Such is the case with rational X models.

## Rational Inattention

In 2003, Christopher Sims presented a model of decision-making under uncertainty that was meant to account for what he (as a macroeconomist-econometrician) perceived as economic agents' sluggish response to macroeconomic shocks.[8] He envisaged a decision model in which agents do not process all available information because of limited information-processing power or limited attention. He called his model "rational inattention."

The model is simple to describe. The decision-maker has a prior belief $p$ over some set of states of nature. Before the state is realized, she can choose a signal function, which assigns a probability distribution over some set of signals to every state. This is known as a "Blackwell experiment," after the great statistical theorist David Blackwell. Importantly, the set of available signals is "rich": there are no constraints on the signal function that the decision-maker can choose.

Given a prior belief, a signal function can be represented by a probability distribution over posterior beliefs. For example, suppose there are only two states, $A$ and $B$, such that $p$ is identified with the probability of $A$. Consider the following signal function. There are two possible signals, $a$ and $b$. When the state is $A$, the two signals are equally likely. When the state is $B$, the signal $b$ is realized with certainty. The resulting distribution over the posterior belief $q$—identified by the posterior probability of $A$—is as follows. With probability $p \cdot 0.5$, the posterior is $q = 1$, and with probability $1 - p \cdot 0.5$, the posterior is

$$q = \frac{p \cdot 0.5}{p \cdot 0.5 + (1-p) \cdot 1}$$

These posteriors are associated with the signal realizations $a$ and $b$, respectively.

Thus, given the prior $p$, the signal function can be identified by this distribution over posterior beliefs. What "richness" means is that *every* distribution over posteriors $q$ whose mean is equal to $p$ is feasible. Any other distribution is infeasible because it violates the Martingale property of Bayesian updating (which we encountered in chapter 3).

After the state is realized and the decision-maker observes the signal, she chooses an action. At this stage, the decision-maker maximizes expected utility with respect to the posterior belief $q$. This enables us to conventionally define an indirect utility function $V(q)$: it is the maximal expected utility the decision-maker can get when her posterior belief is $q$.

So far, we have merely set the stage. The main assumption is that given the prior $p$, the decision-maker chooses a signal function (equivalently, a feasible distribution over posterior beliefs $q$) that maximizes the expectation of $V(q) - C(q, p)$.[9] What is this new object $C$? It is a function of the decision-maker's prior and posterior beliefs. Sims went further and imposed a particular functional form on $C$: it is proportional to the reduction in the *entropy* of the posterior belief $q$ relative to the prior belief $p$.

The entropy of a probability distribution was defined formally by Claude Shannon in the canonical paper that gave birth to information theory.[10] The mathematical definition of the entropy of $p$ (where $p(s)$ is the probability of the state $s$) is

$$H(p) = -\sum_s p(s)\log(p(s))$$

A distribution $p$ that reflects larger uncertainty has higher entropy. In particular, the uniform distribution has the highest entropy. A degenerate distribution that assigns probability 1 to a single state has zero entropy. The difference $H(q) - H(p)$ is the change in entropy when moving from $p$ to $q$. This difference can be positive or negative. However, when a distribution over $q$ arises (via Bayesian updating) from some signal function that the decision-maker obtained when her prior was $p$, the difference will be negative in expectation. That is, when the decision-maker acquires information, she lowers the entropy of her belief on average.

Sims assumed that $C(q, p)$ is proportional to the entropy reduction $H(p) - H(q)$. When the decision-maker chooses a signal function to maximize the expectation of $V(q) - C(q, p)$, she trades off the expected increase in $V$ (information is generally valuable as far as $V$ is concerned) against the cost of information as captured by the expected entropy reduction.

By the way, what I have just described is not literally Sims's original model, but a slightly modified version. Sims didn't assume a cost function that is proportional to entropy reduction, but a *constraint* on the set of available signal functions, quantified by the maximal feasible entropy reduction. For a fixed static decision problem, the two formulations are mathematically equivalent because $C$ can be viewed in terms of the shadow cost of the constraint in Sims's formulation.

### What Is the Interpretation?

In the large literature that followed Sims (2003), the interpretation of the rational-inattention model has been remarkably fluid. The model rubs shoulders with three distinct interpretations, without firmly attaching itself to any of them. I believe that this ambiguity was a major source of the model's rhetorical power and ultimately one of the reasons for its success.

One take is that it is a model of *costly information acquisition*. The decision-maker arrives at the scene with a prior belief $p$, and chooses an information source (from a "rich" set) in a way that trades off the value of information (captured by the expectation of $V(q)$) and its physical cost (captured by the expectation of $C(q, p)$). This sounds like a standard, indeed "rational" cost-benefit calculus. The terminology of costly information acquisition brings to mind activities like asking for a tip about a stock, consulting an expert, or spending time on a search engine. But do we think of the cost of such information sources as a function of one's prior *belief*? How is the cost of asking an expert a function of my current belief?

It should be clear that from the costly-information-acquisition point of view, writing down $C$ as a function of beliefs is not meant to be interpreted literally; it is a *representation*. When the decision-maker performs a Blackwell experiment, this entails a certain physical cost. For this cost to be represented by the function $C$, it should be equal to the expectation of $C(q, p)$, calculated according to the probabilities derived from the prior $p$ and the experiment. However, such a mapping between $C$ and physical information-acquisition costs, if it exists, is not transparent. It is hard to evaluate the plausibility of any given cost function $C$—let alone the specific entropy-based function—as a description of the physical costs associated with acquiring information. We will return to this problem later.

### The Inattention Interpretation

Sims himself didn't think of the function $C$ as representing the physical cost of acquiring information—at least not in his original 2003 paper. Instead, he proposed more "psychological" interpretations, including the eponymous interpretation of *costly allocation of attention*.

Although this interpretation was very good at calling attention to the model (pun unintended but unavoidable), it is unclear how the model captures the psychology of limited attention. How does choosing a distribution over posteriors in a way that trades off the value of information and its entropy reduction map into our basic intuitions about attention? Doesn't it leave out a whole lot in this regard? The rational-inattention model focuses on the decision-maker's ability to control how she allocates her scarce attention. Moreover, the richness assumption—which means that *any* signal function the decision-maker ends up with is a result of her own choice—means that the rational-inattention model leaves *no* room for external manipulation of one's attention.

But isn't vulnerability to external manipulation a key feature of attention? Where do we see in the rational-inattention model anything corresponding to other parties' ability (and indeed constant attempts) to divert our attention? Where are the annoying distractions? Isn't a big chunk of the advertising business devoted to manipulating people's attention?

Of course, one can argue that at some "evolutionary" level, the susceptibility of our attention to external manipulation is itself part of some optimization: if you are not easily distracted by that vague noise emanating from the grass, that tiger will eat you alive. But that is a far cry from optimization with respect to the objective stochastic process that characterizes the decision-maker's *current* economic environment given by the economic model at hand.

A model of inattention that doesn't account for external manipulation of attention is like a model of addiction that disregards the self-handicapping motive. In both cases, the "rational explanation" approach distorts our view by pushing key aspects of the phenomena in question out of the scope of inquiry. It exaggerates decision-makers' agency and underestimates their vulnerability. This has a "sanitizing" effect similar to the one we observed in the statistical discrimination model.

We live in a time of information overload, when attention-deficit disorder is a common diagnosis in affluent societies, and when the mobile phone in our pockets is perceived by many as a direct assault on our simple ability to concentrate.[11] In this context, adding the "rational" prefix to the phenomenon of inattention is as much a provocation as the notion of rational addiction. This makes Sims's model an honorary member in the rational X category.

## The Information Processing Interpretation

Sims's other "psychological" interpretation is *costly information processing*. This is similar to the costly information acquisition story, except that the costs are *internal* to the decision-maker. This interpretation is attractive because information processing is about transforming an input into an output, and indeed $C(q, p)$ is a function of the input $p$ and the output $q$. The bigger the distance of $q$ from $p$, the more thorough the processing and therefore the more mentally taxing it is. The rational-inattention model describes a decision-maker who optimizes over this allocation of her cognitive information-processing resources.

Does entropy reduction capture this type of costly information processing? It is easy to come up with concrete mechanisms of human information processing that can be described neatly in terms of entropy reduction. For example, suppose the decision-maker's uncertainty is over the value of bits in a binary string. Information processing corresponds to a series of classifications of specific bits into 0's and 1's. The more bits one figures out, the more thorough one's information processing.

However, the fact that *some* concrete information-processing procedure has an intuitive cost that corresponds to entropy reduction doesn't lend *universal* appeal to the entropy-reduction function. First, for a fixed interpretation of the bits, the bit-classification procedure cannot mimic the assumption of a *rich* space of signal functions. Second, in many economic environments, agents don't receive information in the explicit form of bits. Of course, information can always be *redescribed* in terms of bits. However, we are looking for a direct interpretation, not an "as if" argument. We want to be able to *see* the cost of information from the *literal* form in which it arrives. Hand-waving about how consuming more bits of information is more time-consuming and therefore more costly won't do. Indeed, the contrary is often the case: I can easily recall spending a lot of precious time on long, poorly written papers that conveyed little information, and relatively little time on short papers that were packed with valuable information.

If we find a particular information-processing procedure convincing, then we can make it a cornerstone of our decision model and relegate entropy reduction to the status of a technically convenient representation (when it actually *is* a valid representation). But that is different from making entropy reduction the very *language* we use to describe the model.[12]

## A Cobb-Douglas Function for the Twenty-First Century

As the discussion above suggests, the inattention and information-processing stories were probably not meant as literal, one-to-one interpretations of the formal model. The decision-maker's "costing" of distributions over posterior beliefs by their associated expected entropy reduction doesn't map directly into an actual psychological process of allocating attention or processing information. Neither the practitioners of the rational-inattention model nor their audience seem to have expected this from the model. Instead, they probably accepted these stories as an "as if" routine. What they saw was an interesting, suggestive cost function with rich, nontrivial mathematical properties. It is not entirely standard because of its belief dependence, but it gives the model the shape of a nice constrained optimization problem. The following passage from a review article by Maćkowiak, Matějka, and Wiederholt (2023) conveys this spirit:

> While we do not intend to argue for a universal application of entropy, we think that entropy is an appealing benchmark, similar to the Cobb-Douglas production function. The main reasons for that are: (i) entropy allows for tractability, (ii) most of its qualitative properties are reasonable (more precision at a higher cost), and thus many qualitative implications of the model are independent of this particular choice, (iii) the foundation of optimal coding and also the axiomatic foundations of entropy suggest that it is a suitable function for processing of available information.

Exactly. Practitioners of rational inattention have approached the entropy-based cost function in the same way that applied economists approach the Cobb-Douglas production function in the textbook theory of production, where output is a log-linear function of production factors. (And note how deftly the authors attach the concept of entropy to information processing, even though Shannon developed it for the distinct problem of *communicating* information.)

There was practical wisdom in this approach. Entropy is a such a deep, elegant function, with a history of being relevant to many things, that astute theorists could sense the model's potential. Indeed, when talented theorists decided to look into it, they produced valuable results. To take just one very nice example, Matějka himself (in joint work with Alisdair McKay) showed how the observed behavior induced by the model maps into a subtle variant on the familiar "logit" model of random choice.[13]

Still, one might have thought that in the age of behavioral economics, theorists would develop a taste for models of limited attention or information processing that strive at a closer, more direct correspondence with actual psychological processes. But no, it turns out we prefer our early twenty-first-century models of individuals to look like our mid-twentieth-century models of the firm.

### The Rhetoric of "Micro-Foundations": Rational Inattention and Wald Sampling

Well, this is not a complete description. A number of leading theorists have in fact explored specifications of the rational-inattention model that went beyond the entropy-based version—especially in the context of trying to substantiate the costly-information-acquisition interpretation.

Stephen Morris and Philipp Strack (2019) is an example of such an attempt. It is worthwhile to give this impressive paper a close look, because it will teach us something about the rhetoric of successful rational X research programs. I should add that, at the point of writing, the paper hasn't been published yet, and it is possible that future versions will modify the paper's rhetoric. Nevertheless, the 2019 version has already enjoyed word-of-mouth circulation, received citations, and in general made an impact that is worth discussing in the context of this chapter.

Morris and Strack consider an explicit costly information acquisition model. Moreover, it is a classical one that dates back to Wald (1945). Suppose there are two states of nature. At every period, the decision-maker can acquire an independent signal of exogenously given accuracy, or she can stop and make a decision. A sequential-sampling strategy specifies a stopping decision for every history of signal realizations. When the decision-maker stops the sampling process, she chooses an action that maximizes her expected utility given her belief at the moment she stopped. For a rational decision-maker, the history of signal realizations per se doesn't matter for her decision; only her current belief over the two states does. Therefore, we can restrict attention to sampling strategies that specify a decision whether to stop as a function of the decision-maker's current belief.

To complete the model, we need to specify the cost of sampling. Wald's original model makes the simple assumption—which later became standard in the economics literature—that the cost is constant. Each time you want to get another independent signal, you incur the same cost. (To be more precise, Morris and Strack analyze a continuous-time version of this model, in which the decision-maker's belief during the sampling phase evolves according to Brownian motion with drift.)

Morris and Strack obtain an interesting result. First, building on earlier work in probability theory that goes under the name of *Skorokhod embedding* (which Strack's earlier work had put to good use in other economic problems),[14] they establish that every distribution over the decision-maker's posterior belief when she stops and makes her decision can be generated by some sampling strategy. This means that the space of sampling strategies in the Wald model is a "rich" signal space in the sense of the rational-inattention model. Second, they show that the expected cost associated with a sampling strategy can be expressed as a function of the decision-maker's prior and posterior beliefs. However, this cost is not proportional to expected entropy reduction, but the expected change in the expected *log-likelihood ratio*. To see the difference, recall that in the case of two states, the entropy of a belief (identified by the probability $q$ it assigns to one of the two states) is

$$q \cdot \log(q) + (1-q) \cdot \log(1-q)$$

By comparison, the expected log-likelihood ratio of the belief is

$$q \cdot \log\left(\frac{q}{1-q}\right) + (1-q) \cdot \log\left(\frac{1-q}{q}\right)$$

Thus, when we collapse the dynamic two-state sampling model into a static model of information acquisition, we can retrieve the rational-inattention model, with the difference that the cost function is not entropy reduction but expected-log-likelihood reduction.

Morris and Strack generalize this result in various ways. First, they extend it to more than two states of nature, deriving a more complicated version of the log-likelihood formula. Second, they show that if we insist on deriving the entropy-reduction function, we need to modify the original Wald model by assuming that the cost of acquiring an individual signal changes in a particular way with the decision-maker's current belief. They generalize this observation: *any* cost function C can be justified by the extended Wald model, provided that we are willing to accept the idea of a belief-dependent sampling cost.

Ok, that's an impressive collection of results. But how should we relate it to the rational-inattention model? Strack and Morris's foundation for the entropy-reduction function hinges on the notion of belief-dependent periodic sampling cost. Does this make sense? We were willing to tolerate the concept of an information cost function C that depends on the decision-maker's prior belief because we thought of it as a *representation* of some underlying model of costly information acquisition. The Wald model is exactly one such model, but here the belief-dependence should have disappeared. How can the physical cost of a sample have anything to do with one's belief? If we interpret it as an opportunity cost of time (as the decision-maker delays his decision) or as a monetary cost of a draw from an urn, these physical costs are orthogonal to one's belief.

It follows that as an attempt to provide a costly-information-acquisition foundation for Sims's original model, the Wald sampling model actually *fails*: it doesn't derive the entropy-reduction function but some other function. And lest we dismiss this failure on account of the superficial resemblance between the two functions, Strack and Morris point out an important difference. Under the log-likelihood model, when the decision-maker's belief is close to certainty, the cost of additional information explodes and therefore the decision-maker will never acquire perfect information (as long as the benefit of information, given by the function $V$, is bounded by a finite range of values). This is not the case with the entropy function. Furthermore, unlike the two-state case, the specification of $C$ that is consistent with belief-independent Wald sampling costs for general state spaces is substantially less elegant than the entropy-based specification. It is hard to imagine that this specification would have generated the same level of excitement had Sims introduced it from the outset.[15]

Yet, this is not how Morris and Strack pitch their results. Their delivery of the result that links the entropy-reduction function to belief-dependent sampling leaves the impression of a "foundation" rather than a "critique." Their rhetoric is positive (emphasizing that essentially every $C$, including the entropy-based version, *can* be derived from a Wald model with some *belief-dependent* sampling cost function) rather than negative (emphasizing that almost every $C$, including the entropy-based version, *cannot* be derived from a Wald model with *belief-independent* sampling costs).

This doesn't seem to be a purely subjective impression of mine. The word-of-mouth spread of this beautiful paper (indeed, its beauty was a main driver of this spread) has been carried by the simple meme: "Morris and Strack (2019) provided a foundation for the rational-inattention model." This meme is already finding its way into the footnotes of written papers. It reflects the research community's interest in a "micro-foundation" for the rational-inattention model, and gets support from Morris and Strack's positive rhetoric.

### In Search of the Model's "Core"

We have identified a number of ambiguities in the rational-inattention model. The first is whether it invites a "rational" interpretation (costly information acquisition) or a "psychological" one (limitations on attention or information processing). The second concerns the validity of a particular rational interpretation (Wald sampling). A third ambiguity concerns the model's "core." In particular, how fundamental is the entropy-reduction cost function?

As mentioned earlier, I believe that these ambiguities actually *contributed* to the rhetorical power of the model and enabled its influence to grow—partly by inspiring a literature that tried to *resolve* these very ambiguities. Interpretative ambiguity allowed the model to be attached to different stories. None of them is a perfect fit, but they are all close enough to give the model rhetorical support. Not committing to a clear interpretation and being ambivalent about the rationality of the behavior captured by the model enabled its practitioners to appeal to various audiences having different predilections.

Let us pause on the third ambiguity regarding the role of the entropy specification. On the one hand, it has been a major reason for the model's appeal—partly because of the general fascination that the concept of entropy holds for people with a scientific background, and partly because entropy *is* a beautiful concept. On the other hand, proponents of the model often hedge over whether our assessment of rational inattention should involve absolute commitment to the entropy function. This ambivalence is apparent in Maćkowiak, Matějka, and Widerholt (2023), from which I have already quoted. When they describe applications, they do not always clarify which of them rely on the entropy specification and which do not. Here is another quote:

This [the entropy-based cost function] assumption is not crucial, and can be relaxed. While the model [which includes the entropy function] is the "pure form" of rational inattention, models with cost functions other than mutual information and models with some restrictions on available signals can also be viewed as rational inattention.

Departures from the entropy-based cost function can be seen in theoretical exercises that perform revealed-preference analyses of preferences over Blackwell experiments. Sometimes, these exercises axiomatize more general $V - C$ representations.[16] Sometimes they set aside the $V - C$ representation altogether and define the cost of information directly for Blackwell experiments.[17] Virtually all the exercises I am aware of do not allow the decision-maker's prior belief $p$ to vary, thus effectively assuming it is fixed. One exception is Denti, Marinacci, and Rustichini (2022), who examine what happens in a variable-prior model when we replace entropy with a more general function $H$ that shares some of its properties, such that the formula $V(q) - C(p, q)$ can be written as $V(q) + H(q) - H(p)$ (this representation is referred to as "uniformly posterior separable"). They allow the prior $p$ to vary and show that in this case, the formula generally fails to be a proper representation of profiles of prior-dependent preferences over Blackwell experiments.

This one-paragraph mini-survey is not meant to be exhaustive, but to suggest several observations. First, the methodology of axiomatic revealed-preference exercises tends to generate departures from the entropy specification (and the uniformly posterior separable representation in general), because it is often hard to come up with elegant, compelling axioms that will characterize highly specific functional forms. Second, these exercises usually disambiguate the interpretation of the rational-inattention model and converge on the strict costly-information-acquisition view. Third, although these exercises typically do not end up endorsing the entropy specification, it continues to play an important role in the motivation behind them. It is almost always one of the main examples that authors provide, and I believe it is one of the reasons that this subliterature will attract an audience outside the coterie of axiomatic decision theorists.

Thus, the entropy specification has been essential for the appeal of the rational-inattention enterprise, even when theorists end up moving away from it. In a similar "bait and switch" manner, the psychological motivations for the rational-inattention model continue to attract theorists even when axiomatic characterizations end up suppressing these motivations in favor of the more traditional costly-information-acquisition interpretation—which probably would never have generated the same level of excitement in the first place.

The above quote from Maćkowiak, Matějka, and Widerholt (2023) raises a fourth ambiguity: Is the assumption of a "rich" signal space fundamental to the rational-inattention model? Although it makes the $V - C$ representation the tractable workhorse model that it is, the authors preemptively claim jurisdiction over models that relax it.

The ambiguities over the interpretation and scope of rational inattention thus offered rhetorical retreat strategies in the face of criticisms, as well as an impetus for foundational work. The central ambiguity about whether the model is "rational" or "psychological" was a strategic asset in the age of behavioral economics. It aroused curiosity and gave theorists a broader audience.

Like rational addiction, the case of rational inattention demonstrates that economists' commitment is not necessarily to a particular normative notion of rationality, nor to faithful description of behavioral phenomena. In rational X exercises, the behavior we model is not exactly X and not exactly rational. The true commitment is to utility maximization as a modeling strategy. The challenge is to find interesting problems of this type and to pull off the rhetorical maneuvers that make these problems appear behaviorally and economically relevant.

## Optimal Expectations

For our last dish in the rational X feast, let us turn to Markus Brun-nermeier and Jonathan Parker's (2005) model of "optimal expectations," which addressed the important psychological phenomena of self-delusion and wishful thinking. Following everyday observation and research by academic psychologists, Brunnermeier and Parker observed that people's risk-taking behavior is often affected by wishful thinking, but tempered by their realization that taking a fantasy too seriously may lead to ruin.[18]

In a simple version of their model, a decision-maker is equipped with a material utility function $u(a, x)$, where $a$ is her action and $x$ represents a state of nature. There is a probability distribution $q$ over the states of nature, which represents the objective uncertainty that the decision-maker faces. The decision-maker chooses $a$ and a subjective probabilistic belief $p$ to maximize the following objective function:

$$\alpha \cdot \sum_x p(x)u(a, x) + (1 - \alpha) \cdot \sum_x q(x)u(a, x)$$

subject to the constraint that $a$ maximizes the first term. The idea is that the decision-maker chooses both how to act and what to believe, trading off the *anticipatory utility* from the distorted belief $p$ (the first term in the objective function) against the *material utility* based on the undistorted belief $q$ (the second term). The exogenous parameter $\alpha$ determines the weights of these two considerations. The constraint is that the decision-maker cannot suffer cognitive dissonance: the action must be materially optimal given the distorted belief.

The Brunnermeier-Parker model is a fascinating example of the rational X program. On the one hand, it is written as a straightforward constrained-maximization problem, and in this sense fits squarely into the standard paradigm. On the other hand, it doesn't get more irrational than when people *choose* what to believe. After all, being able to distinguish between what is feasible and what is desirable is a defining feature of rationality.

In fact, despite the outward conventionality of the maximizing model and the rhetorical effect of referring to the decision-maker's expectations as "optimal," the choice behavior that the Brunnermeier-Parker model induces is *not* rational according to the textbook definition. In Spiegler (2008), I gave an example in which the Brunnermeier-Parker decision-maker violates the classic independence-of-irrelevance-alternatives (IIA) axiom. This axiom requires that if an element is chosen from a set and contained in some subset, then it will also be chosen from the subset. When the choice set consists of a safe option and a positively skewed, risky option (consisting of a likely small loss and an unlikely large gain), the Brunnermeier-Parker decision-maker may prefer the latter even if it is inferior in terms of material expected value. This is the effect that Brunnermeier and Parker emphasize in their paper: positively skewed risk allows decision-makers to indulge in fantasies of winning the jackpot, and therefore enhances their risk seeking. But now add a negatively skewed, ultra-risky option (including a huge and not unlikely loss). The decision-maker may now switch to the *safe* option (which already belonged to the small set), thus violating IIA.

The reason behind this effect is that the decision-maker will choose the positively skewed option from the small set only if he convinces himself that the chances of a "good state" are sufficiently high. But once we add the third option, such an optimistic belief that nearly ignores the "bad state" makes him go for the new, negatively skewed option. The material consequences of this choice are so dire that indulging in fantasy becomes too costly. As a result, the decision-maker prefers to switch to a realistic belief that impels him to choose the safe option. He loses the anticipatory utility "kick," but at least he doesn't find himself ruined.

This is an interesting effect, and a highly suggestive one. But it shows that the choice behavior induced by the Brunnermeier-Parker model is not rational; that despite the title "optimal expectations," the beliefs that the decision-maker chooses and their resulting behavior can be "irrationally" sensitive to "irrelevant" alternatives. The soothing rational X rhetoric gives a wrong impression about the nature of this beast.

So, optimal expectations aren't really "rational." But do they at least describe the phenomenon of interest, namely self-deception and wishful thinking? A hallmark of self-deception is conflicted attitude to information. On the one hand, decision-makers value information because it helps maximize material payoff. On the other hand, information means the possibility of bad news that depresses anticipatory utility. Decision-makers may avoid information sources that are likely to present an "inconvenient truth"—the term itself reveals the wishful thinking that underlies this common attitude to information.

Brunnermeier and Parker are silent over the issue of attitudes to information. Since their model describes only how people choose between lotteries, one has to extend it in order to address this issue. In Spiegler (2008) I showed that the most obvious and conventional extension of

the model is disappointing: as long as we restrict attention to signal
functions that never rule out states of nature for sure, the decision-
maker's attitude to information will be entirely standard: he will
weakly prefer having more information. It is not clear how we should
extend the model if we want to escape this conclusion. But a model of
wishful thinking that is unable to address information avoidance is
limited, like a model of addiction that leaves out self-handicapping, or
a model of limited attention that leaves out external distractions.

**The Power of Rational X**

The list of examples in this chapter is not exhaustive. I have deliberately
focused on some of the most famous examples in the rational X tradition. One prominent example I left out is Bayesian persuasion (Kamenica and Gentzkow 2011), which we already encountered in chapter 3.
This model (which is conceptually and technically related to rational
inattention) reduces the phenomenon of persuasion to simple Bayesian
updating.

    Most of economic theory can be viewed as one big "rational explana-
tion" campaign, trying to conquer more and more areas of human
behavior and bring them under the wings of the maximizing paradigm.
What I referred to as "rational X" are simply the most daring instances
of this program. They take types of behavior that people usually assign
to the irrationality category and find a way to reconcile them with maximizing behavior of some sort. Yet, as I concluded from the examples,
the reconciliation is partial: it leaves important aspects of the phenomenon out of the theory's reach, and it also has to compromise the
rationality of the behavior it attributes to the decision-maker. The
blanket of utility maximization is not as wide as we imagine it to be.

    The "imperialism" of the rational X program is an important reason
for its success. Consider the behavioral and social phenomena we have
covered in this chapter: ethnic discrimination, wishful thinking, addiction, attention deficit. These are such important and fascinating objects
of study. If we look at wishful thinking alone, it seems relevant to voter
behavior, provision of health information, media consumption, mana-
gerial behavior, and other social and economic arenas. The rational X
approach gives us a sense that we've got these phenomena "figured
out," and that we're carrying the great tradition of economics forward
rather than undermining it. It lets us play with models that deviate

from the norm far enough to make the problem novel and nontrivial, but not too far to deter most theorists from joining the endeavor.

Interestingly, the models I have discussed here were originally proposed by authors who are not card-carrying or full-time microeconomic theorists. Were these economists more comfortable juggling the elements of maximizing models without feeling inhibited by the traditional revealed-preference methodology, which would have exposed the tensions between these models and normatively rational choice behavior?

My description of several highly successful examples of the rational X genre may create the impression that there is a *recipe* for writing a successful rational X paper. First, identify a problematic or pathological type of individual or group behavior—ideally, one that has been studied by another academic discipline. Next, formulate a maximizing model to describe the phenomenon. Make the utility function mathematically nontrivial yet tractable. If the behavior that comes out of your model isn't exactly rational, be ambiguous about whether you intend this to be a proper rationalization of the phenomenon. If the model is silent over a key aspect of the phenomenon in question, be silent, too.

This impression would be wrong: sorry, there is no surefire recipe. Observe the caliber of the economists whose work we have examined in this chapter! Part of the genius of economists like Becker or Sims is their deep understanding of their professional culture. They are like master storytellers with a keen intuition for the suspension of disbelief they can wring from their audiences. Analyzing their rhetoric and speculating about the sources of its success doesn't mean that any economic theorist could pull it off—just as being able to explain how the shower scene in Hitchcock's *Psycho* sends shivers down our spine doesn't mean that any film director could duplicate this feat. If I knew how to write successful rational X papers, maybe I would do it instead of writing essays about them. That's the thing with the "cultural criticism" genre: it can make even an admirer come across as a sourpuss.

Whatever the ultimate reasons for the success of rational X models, it seems that, as economists, we have such an insatiable taste for "rational explanations" that we are willing to overlook their limitations. We are less likely to extend this benefit of the doubt to other modes of explanation of human behavior.

# 6   Appendicitis

## SOAP

The culture of economic theory, like any other, is constantly evolving. Active theorists like me have trouble spotting big cultural changes in real time. We are little particles, swept in big cultural currents with little sense of where they are going. One heuristic for getting a broader understanding is to try looking at surface details of our culture. These seemingly superficial features may be signs of deep cultural trends. This chapter is devoted to one of these features: the *supplementary online appendix* (SOAP henceforth).[1]

The SOAP is a section of an article that is physically separated from its main body. It is entirely absent from the article's print version. In the online version, it appears as a distinct link that can escape the reader's first glance.[2] When you perform a Google search to find the paper, it'll take you to the main file, but you won't always have an independent link to the SOAP. If you want to get to the SOAP you will, but access is not always easy.

What goes into SOAPs of economic-theory papers? Usually, you will find additional examples, results, or applications that demonstrate the scope of a model, as well as variations on the paper's main model. Some of these variations are intended as "robustness checks" that examine whether the paper's main theoretical conclusions survive certain tweaks of the main model. Recently, more and more SOAPs include mathematical proofs of formal results that appear in the print version.

The proliferation of SOAPs in economic-theory papers is a recent phenomenon. Of course, they only became possible when journals went online. When we look at the period since 2005, the picture we see is figure 6.1.

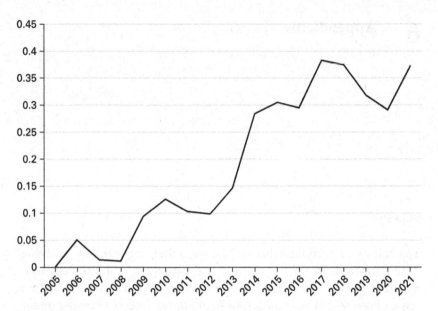

**Figure 6.1**
Share of papers with SOAPs in *JET*.

Figure 6.1 gives one illustration from the *Journal of Economic Theory* (*JET*). I deliberately chose a theory field journal, where the phenomenon is supposedly uncontaminated by considerations that apply to "general readership" journals. I also chose *JET* because by 2005 it was an established journal with an illustrious history.[3]

While it may be reassuring these days to see an increasing graph that is *not* exponential, the rise is impressive. In 2005–2008, virtually none of the papers published in *JET* had a SOAP. By 2015, the share of published papers with SOAPs had risen to 30%, and has stayed above this level since then.

SOAPs are an example of "two-tier communication," which involves a clear separation between "front" and "back" material. This structure can be found in various cultures. In the corporate world, we are familiar with the combination of an executive summary and a technical report. In the world of science, prestigious journals (*Nature, Science*) adopt a similar format: the official publication is a short and relatively accessible piece that is backed by longer technical appendices.

However, two-tier communication is not a sweeping norm. Publications in math journals, for instance, don't have SOAPs. Moreover, as we will see, the form that two-tier communication has taken in economic theory is very different from the *Nature/Science* model. What does it say about the culture of economic theory that two-tier communication in the form of SOAPs has become so ubiquitous in so little time? Is it a superficial development of no importance? Or does it have something interesting to tell us about our current professional culture?

## The Great Inflation

Before we get there, we need to look at the forces that led to the rise of the SOAP. The obvious proximate reason for the proliferation of SOAPs in economic theory is that papers have become increasingly long. Returning to our *JET* data, in 2020 the average number of pages in published papers with a SOAP was fifty-seven (including the SOAP), compared with an average length of thirty-three pages for papers without a SOAP.

So, papers with SOAPs are long. Let us go a bit deeper (but not too deeply) into the question of long papers. The gradual increase in the length of economic-theory papers is one of the dramatic changes in our field in recent decades. Commentators already wrote about this trend twenty years ago: from a world in which fifteen to twenty pages per article had been the norm, we moved to a world in which thirty to forty pages were a new normal. And these days, papers whose total length (including all appendices) exceeds sixty pages are increasingly common. In light of the proliferation of SOAPs, official data about length of published papers in economics journals are highly misleading if they focus on the print version and ignore the SOAP.

Why have economic-theory papers become so long? The evolution of the dimensions of creative works is a fascinating subject that pertains to various scientific and artistic cultures and merits a separate inquiry. To give just one example, from 1950 and 1965, the average length of *feature films* went up from 90 minutes to 120 minutes.[4] In the context of economic theory, a key factor is probably that as the field matured and its pace of conceptual innovation slowed down, the natural development has been to add complexity to existing classes of models, rather than invent simple versions of new ones. Complicated models take longer to present and demand longer proofs. Whether this is a healthy development or a sign of an ossifying culture is a matter for debate. Two decades ago, Glenn Ellison (2002) documented the trend toward longer papers and a slower publication process and tried to explain these phenomena with a simple model of the "natural" evolution of professional standards.

I do not wish to challenge this perspective here, nor to probe deeper into the intrinsic forces that have led to the inflating dimensions of economic-theory papers. In keeping with the spirit of this book, I focus on factors behind the trend that owe to the growing *external* influence of the "applied" culture on the theory culture.

## Robustness Checks

A common presentation of a theoretical exercise begins by proposing a basic model and analyzing it, and follows by considering various extensions, generalizations, or variations. This sometimes serves a pedagogical purpose: it is easier for the reader to absorb a simple instance of the relevant class of models before delving into more elaborate specimens.

Authors used to present extensions quite regularly even in the "old days." However, it seems that, over the years, the expectation from authors to pack their papers with extensions and variations has become firmer. These are no longer regarded as free exploration of nearby models, but as mandatory *"robustness checks."* Their purpose is to establish which conclusions from the basic model survive natural variations. This subtle shift in the status of extensions and variations is important. If one regards an extension as voluntary exploration of a natural variation on an interesting model, then one can be happy with relegating it to a separate paper. But if the exercise is meant to *validate* the basic model, then the expectation that it will be part of the submitted paper becomes understandable.

The "robustness checks" approach to extensions and variations has spilled over from the "applied" economics culture, where it seems to make sense. An empirical study makes a claim against the background of objective data. Since different methods for processing or interpreting data may lead to different conclusions, the reader is rightly interested in the role that these choices by the researchers played in their analysis.[5]

By comparison, a theoretical model lacks a comparably clear objective reference. Several layers of abstraction separate the model and whatever slice of reality it aims to capture. Every economic model involves many unstated assumptions. Unpacking the implications of these assumptions could be a lifetime mission. The decision of which of them to put under a "robustness check" is largely driven by convention. For example, in papers that involve a repeated-game model, authors are never asked to reanalyze their model under various assumptions about how players aggregate temporal payoff flows because exponential discounting has become an unshakable norm in this literature.

In the case of many classic papers, natural extensions are deep problems in their own right, which were developed later (often much later) by different authors. Asking Roger Myerson to extend his classic paper on optimal auctions to multiple objects,[6] or demanding that Ariel Rubinstein check whether the immediate-agreement result of his 1982 alternating-offers bargaining model survives an extension to heterogeneous prior beliefs regarding players' bargaining power—these would be ludicrous requests. Indeed, later authors devoted impressive papers to these very extensions.[7]

For all these reasons, I find the "robustness checks" culture dubious when it comes to economic theory. Yet it explains a big chunk of the inflated dimensions of theory papers.

### General Reader

The verbal exposition of economic-theory papers has become fattier over time. Introductions have grown longer. Presentations of the formal model are thick with rhetorical gyrations in defense of its assumptions. Discussions of the economic significance of theoretical results have become more elaborate.

The reason behind this trend appears to be the increasing importance of the top-five journals in our profession (as we discussed in chapter 1). These journals pitch themselves as "general readership" venues.[8] As a result, theorists are encouraged to double down on arguing the relevance of their exercises for non-theorists, which inevitably adds mass.

This pressure generates subtle ripple effects. First, if publishing a paper in a "high five" journal becomes more important for theorists' careers, they will try more of these journals before giving up and turning to a lower-ranked, theory-oriented field journal. Each rejection from a top-five journal begets a revision that tries to appease the referees of the rejected version (who are likely to be summoned again for subsequent submissions). From rejection to rejection, the authors produce more robustness checks and more applications. As time goes by, the authors keep thinking about their project and spontaneously generate new results, and so they contribute additional, unsolicited material. After the paper finishes its journey in top-five purgatory and reaches field-journal hell, authors rarely rewrite their paper specifically for the more specialized journal. The "general reader" gambit has a long-lasting effect even when this reader is no longer relevant even as a fiction.

There are additional positive feedback loops. When a paper becomes longer, it is harder for readers to navigate through it. This requires more foreshadowing and repetition, which makes the paper even longer. It also intensifies the defensiveness that characterizes academic writing in general. With a long paper, referees are more likely to make up their mind and "check out" before the paper has served its main dish. Anticipating this, the author engages in preemptive rhetorical warfare at the beginning of the paper. Excessive length begets excessive length.

## Scarcity?

In response to the inflation trend, economics journals have been placing length constraints on published papers. Sometimes the constraints are rigid.[9] Sometimes they are soft and negotiable. Historically, the scarcity that motivated length constraints was physical—namely, the size of printed journal volumes. For a long time now, this has ceased to be a relevant consideration, as the vast majority of readers rely on the online publication. If some economists still rely on printed journals, it makes sense to prepare an abridged version that meets their physical space constraints. Claiming that these constraints represent the relevant scarcity that motivates length limits amounts to putting the cart in front of the horse. To all intents and purposes, the published paper's "real" location is online. Whatever motivates journal editors to impose length limits on economic-theory papers, physical scarcity it is not.

To understand what it is, then, and how the SOAP fits into all this, we need to contend with three alternative conceptions of what an economic-theory paper *is*.

## The Aesthetic-Pedagogical Conception

Now, that is a fancy term! What do I mean by it? Not judgments of beauty—at least not directly. Instead, what I have in mind is that when authors, readers, referees, and editors evaluate the paper's length and overall organization, they think about the prospective readers' experience. For some, this experience consists of committing a certain attention span to the paper, with the hope of satisfying professional curiosity. Enjoyment from the paper's prose and rhetoric, the ingenuity of its modeling strategies, the elegance of its proofs—all these are essential to this experience. Others read the paper with the purpose of preparing a lecture, and therefore they are attuned to the paper's pedagogical qualities—practically speaking, how difficult it is going to be to translate the paper into an effective lecture. If the former example is like listening to a piece of music, the latter is analogous to the experience of a conductor perusing the score of a musical composition toward a live performance.

It is easy to tell when a theory paper puts a large weight on the pedagogical dimension: just try making lecture notes out of it. The less you need to tamper with the paper, the clearer it becomes that the paper was written with pedagogical considerations in mind. Otherwise, you will find yourself searching for formal assumptions amid surrounding rhetoric; developing a simple illustrative example because you can't find one in the paper; concluding that the illustrative example that the paper *does* contain is misleadingly simple and actually needs complication; or finding the notation too cumbersome because the author aimed at greater generality than what is needed pedagogically.

In principle, the aesthetic and pedagogical dimensions are distinct; in practice, I believe they have near-perfect overlap, which is why I am lumping them together. When we think about the paper in these terms, the quality of a reader's experience takes the front seat. Readers' *attention* is the scarce resource. The paper is a claim on their attention; effective, economical writing makes the claim worth their while. From this point of view, it is clear why length can be an issue: a longer paper usually entails a larger claim on the reader's attention.

I should clarify that I am not talking here about the margin between twenty and thirty pages. Some authors prefer terse verbal exposition, others prefer more leisurely turns of phrase. Some authors abhor repetition, others feel it is useful pedagogically. Some authors prefer skeletal proofs in order to make their structure easier to perceive, while others feel that skipping steps makes the proof harder to follow.

But when the paper exceeds, say, fifty pages, the question is whether its overall organization can sustain an effective aesthetic experience. There is such a thing as a natural scale of an economic-theory paper— just as there is a natural scale for novels, films, or symphonies. The typical novel will not exceed 400 pages, the typical film will not exceed 150 minutes, and the typical symphony will not exceed 40 minutes. The rare instances that transgress these limits are an exception that proves the rule. The inordinate length then becomes part of the specialness of the piece, and provokes a special reaction. In a similar manner, if we think of the economic-theory paper from the aesthetic point of view that regards the paper as an invitation for the reader to commit a span of her scarce attention, there are natural limits to how long the paper can be. A paper that is as long as a quarter of a textbook lies well beyond those limits. And it is not just readers who strain under excessive length: most *authors* will find it hard to maintain a consistently high level of formal and verbal exposition.

From the aesthetic-pedagogical point of view, there is no free disposal: every part of the paper counts because every part is a claim on the reader's attention. The author is not free to add variations, extensions, and examples just because she has them under her wraps. Prioritization and selection are essential decisions for the author when she thinks of her paper from the aesthetical-pedagogical point of view— just as a film director will sometimes cut scenes to enhance the audience's watching experience. It is hard to imagine a moviegoer leaving the theatre before the film is over and concluding that she has had a satisfying experience. Likewise, if the reader of a six-section theory paper doesn't get past section 3, her reading experience cannot be deemed a complete success from an aesthetic point of view.

## The Store-of-Knowledge Conception

Another conception of the economic-theory paper is that it is a *store of knowledge*. The paper is the sum of its findings. It functions as a reference: if you are interested in a certain result, you can consult the paper and learn the result and the reasoning behind it. From this point of view, it seems that readers *can* exercise free disposal: if the paper contains $n$ results but you only care about $k < n$ out of them, nothing prevents you from reading only those $k$ results and ignoring the rest—as long as the paper is well organized and the results are retrievable. When we view a theory paper as a store of knowledge, large dimensions aren't a problem if they don't create difficulties for the paper's efficient organization. To take an extreme example, an encyclopedia is not meant to be read in one breath; it should be a well-organized store of knowledge.

The store-of-knowledge conception does not preclude aesthetic judgments. One might think that papers about equilibrium existence theorems would be the most typical specimens of the store-of-knowledge category. And yet, one of the most beautiful lectures in my recollection was one that Phil Reny gave about existence of pure-strategy Nash equilibria in Bayesian games.[10] Yet, it is telling that I remember the experience from a *lecture*, where the audience is "forced" (at least in the pre-Zoom era) to sit in the seminar room for an allotted amount of time, and expects to be entertained in return. The live-lecture format invites a more purely aesthetic response, compared with the written paper.

The main problem that long papers create for the store-of-knowledge view is that they strain the paper's *validation* process. This is presumably the most important function of the peer-review publication system. And yet, when a theory paper exceeds fifty pages (with proofs taking, say, twenty pages), can we still trust that the referees gave these pages the same level of scrutiny that they would have given a paper half the length?

Editors handling long submissions are concerned that referees will become exhausted and skip key parts. To compensate for this antici-pated deterioration in the quality of refereeing, the editor may enlist additional referees. This in turn generates free riding because, when a referee knows that she is one out of many, she may feel less pressure to expend energy on the task. To mitigate this free-riding effect, the editor may try to "surprise" referees by soliciting even more reports: if a referee calibrated her effort to an expectation of $n$ additional referees, having $n + 1$ referees will be an effective counterweight. Although this unraveling dynamic is a purely theoretical speculation, it is consistent with observable facts. In the not-so-distant past, two to three referees per submission were the norm. Nowadays, top-five journals often recruit four to five referees for theory submissions (six referees are not unheard-of). More referees generate more comments, more requests for applications, more robustness checks, more preemptive rhetoric.

## The Legal-Document Conception

The third salient conception of an economic-theory paper is that it makes a substantive argument and therefore needs to validate it with support-ing "evidence." This conception is particularly relevant for applied-theory papers, which make a direct claim about reality. Since these papers typically lack serious empirical sections, the supporting "evi-dence" is more theory, in the form of extensions and variations of the basic model. This is the "robustness checks" culture I discussed earlier.

The proliferation of "robustness checks" in economic-theory papers can be likened to a discovery process in US civil law. Indeed, there is something *legalistic* about the view of a theory paper in terms of staking a claim and backing it up with supporting evidence. According to this legal-document conception, the more arguments the author can muster, the better. This is in marked contrast to the "less is more" aesthetic-pedagogical perspective.

If we adopt the legal-discovery metaphor and push it to a grotesque extreme, we may wonder whether all those variations, extensions, and robustness checks are actually meant to be read. Or are they part of the author's litigious warfare with referees and editors? Is their mere *existence* a "proof by intimidation" posture that dares the skeptical reader? This turns the "free disposal" argument we invoked earlier on its head. Not only can the reader skip parts of the paper, but their very proliferation creates "choice overload" that may *encourage* him to do so—bringing to mind the famous "jam experiment."[11] If we had empirical data about the number of read pages as a function of the paper's total number of pages, are we sure that this function would be monotonically increasing?

**The Basement**

We have thus mapped three ways of thinking about what an economic-theory paper is. They all imply different attitudes to long papers. The aesthetic-pedagogical perspective is averse to long papers, because it regards the theory paper as a claim on readers' scarce attention. The store-of-knowledge perspective is indifferent to length, insofar as it doesn't jam the editorial validation process—because it views the consumption of a theory paper as being similar to consulting an encyclopedia. The legal-document perspective is favorable to inflating papers as part of their discovery-like process of "robustness checks."

When theory papers tended to be shorter, there was little tension between the aesthetic-pedagogical and store-of-knowledge views. However, as papers became longer—partly as a result of the growing popularity of the legal-document conception—tensions became harder to reconcile. Authors, readers and journal editors had to start making choices.

This is where SOAPs came to the rescue, as a *compromise* between the conflicting motives. An author could split her paper into a modest-size print version that could be experienced "aesthetically," and a SOAP that would act as a basin that absorbs the rest of the material and thus fulfill the paper's store-of-knowledge and legal-document functions. This compromise has served the field for the past fifteen years.

Is this a successful compromise? To my taste, there are a number of reasons not to be satisfied with it. First, the split naturally hurts the aesthetic-pedagogical value of the material that falls into the SOAP. I likened the SOAP to a basin that absorbs material that cannot fit the print version's straitjacket. But perhaps the basin image isn't quite apt. For a more accurate metaphor for what the SOAP solution looks like in practice, imagine the parent of a child who is bombarded with toys, runs out of storage space in the child's playroom, and moves some toys to the basement. But how different the two toy collections are! In the playroom, they are dusted and carefully placed on a shelf within the child's reach. In contrast, the toys in the basement are a pile of dusty, barely retrievable objects.

This *Toy Story* scene strikes me as a decent metaphor for the contrast between the print version and the SOAP. The peer-review process amplifies this contrast. The print version is subjected to numerous expositional comments by the editor and the referees, and the author is highly incentivized to care about the organization of the material in the print version. By comparison, I don't recall ever seeing a referee report that commented on the SOAP's expositional quality. The amount of attention to typos and mathematical errors seems to share this asymmetry. In some journals, SOAPs are not typeset—the analogue of dust in my *Toy Story* metaphor—symbolizing the journal's lack of interest in the SOAP's aesthetic qualities.

The gap between the expositional qualities of the paper's two parts leads to an ambiguity about whether the standards that we apply as authors, readers, referees, and editors to the print version extend to the SOAP. Is the SOAP relevant for evaluating the paper's contribution? Or is it a random assortment of miscellaneous stuff that only the author and a few die-hard fans might find interest in? To reuse our basement metaphor, think of a certificate that proves you are the rightful owner of your house. This certificate validates your hold on the property. If it's buried in some long-forsaken box, you're never going to be able to find it. Can we then say the certificate fulfills its validation function?

## The Declining Status of Mathematical Proofs

The other problem with cutting long papers into an "aesthetically pleasing" print version and a legalistic, store-of-knowledge SOAP is that this surgery is not always clean. Remarkably, SOAPs have increasingly taken on the role of absorbing mathematical proofs of the paper's formal results. It often happens that a formal result is stated in the main body of the paper, a sketch of its proof is also given in the main body, most of the steps in the formal proof are given in a "regular" appendix in the print version, and some intermediate steps are deemed less important and sent to languish in the SOAP. Navigating back and forth between these many parts, the reader's experience is quite far from the image of a linear proof.

This is a momentous development. Many theorists, if not most of them, used to regard proofs as a prime conveyor of the argument that an economic model makes. Throw the proof, and you've thrown the baby with the bath water. The classic Hotelling "high street" model, which is familiar to many of us from our undergraduate economics education, offers a good illustration. In this model, two vendors choose where to locate their shop along a real interval. Their objective is to maximize their market share. Each consumer chooses the nearest shop to her own location, which is continuously distributed along the interval. In Nash equilibrium, both vendors choose the median consumer location. The economic significance of this result is that this form of market competition generates no product differentiation. But real appreciation of the result comes from its simple proof. For any other choice of locations by the vendors, at least one of the following deviations would be profitable for any of them: moving toward the other shop (in case the vendors are located at different points) or moving toward the median consumer (in case they are located at the same spot). These deviations tell us more about the workings of the model than its ultimate "solution."

Of course, cutting-edge theory papers involve far more complicated arguments. Yet, the principle that proofs transmit the essence of the theoretical argument remains. The relation between the proof and the result is analogous to the relation between a novel and its synopsis. Reading the latter is no substitute for reading the former.

So how did proofs get kicked to the rear office? There are several reasons. First, complex proofs of results in mature fields have "routine" parts. Editors feel that moving these out of sight does little harm. From this point of view, the relegation of proofs to SOAPs is a symptom of the advanced state of many branches of economic theory. (One difficulty with this justification is that a step in a proof may be "routine" for a seasoned theorist, but not for a graduate student who is a newcomer to the field. Smuggling the step to an "undisclosed location" interferes with the natural flow of the proof, and thus makes it less readable for the newcomer.)[12] Second, a proof that cites an established mathematical result and refers the reader to the relevant math journal or textbook is arguably no different than relegating parts of a proof to a SOAP. In both cases, the proof as it appears in the print version is not self-contained. If we can do the former, why not the latter?

In the "high five" journals, editors prioritize parts that are perceived to be of interest for "General Reader"—the verbal motivation, the applications. Limits on the print version's length leave little room for the proof. Thus, the "general reader" orientation imposes a prioritization of material that departs from traditional priorities in the theory culture. This tension was hidden when papers were short: the published text included the proof, and "general readers" could exercise free disposal. The tension has now come to the fore, when length limits force editors to make the prioritization decisions themselves.

A "purist" or "traditionalist" position of keeping all proofs in the print version meets its most serious challenge in the case of ultra-long proofs. When a proof of a major result of the paper takes thirty pages, it seems impossible to accommodate it in the print version without tearing through the length barriers. (Of course, one can always mechanically shorten a proof by skipping steps. This is not an interesting argument. I am considering proofs that are written at a level of detail that enables most economic theorists to follow them.) This leads authors to identify parts of the proof that are standard or uninteresting and throw them out of the print version. It is this practice that creates three-tier communication of formal results in many economic-theory papers: results are stated in the main body of the print version, then proved partly in its "regular" appendix and partly in the SOAP.

The argument against ultra-long proofs is that no result in economics is so important that it needs such a long proof. The interest in a result is not based entirely on its statement, but also on the quality of its proof. A long proof in economics indicates a certain clumsiness in the theoretical argument. This is especially relevant for game-theoretic models, in which the proof is meant to capture strategic considerations. A complicated proof often means that these considerations are convoluted, which makes them less realistic. Alternatively, the proof may need to consider many cases, each one involving a different strategic consideration, which makes the overall argument less coherent or unified. From this point of view, if strengthening the model's assumptions or restating the result enable a drastic reduction in the length of the proof and a corresponding increase in its elegance and transparency, that is a net gain.

I can offer a simple example for this trade-off from my own experience. In a few papers that belong to the subfield of "behavioral industrial organization," I dealt with mixed-strategy Nash equilibrium in symmetric pricing games among firms.[13] Suppose we want to show that there is a unique Nash equilibrium in mixed strategies, and therefore it must be symmetric (because symmetric games always have at least one symmetric Nash equilibrium, assuming an equilibrium exists). If one restricts attention to symmetric equilibria from the outset, it is fairly immediate that firms' equilibrium strategy involves a *continuous* price distribution. The rest of the proof flows smoothly and conveys the insights that the model was meant to deliver. If symmetry is not imposed from the outset, it is hard to rule out discontinuous equilibrium strategies until the very last steps of the proof. This means that one needs to keep the possibility of discontinuities throughout the proof, carrying a loss of elegance and clarity. Unless one finds a way to isolate the continuity issue from the rest of the proof (which I wasn't able to), one faces a genuine trade-off. It may be better to sacrifice the strength of the result for the sake of a crisper, more transparent proof.

This debate over the meaning of long proofs in economic theory is not easy to resolve. I realize that for some readers, there is no dilemma: the proof is as long as it has to be; its dimensions do not affect our interest in the result; one always prefers a shorter proof but this should not be traded off against modeling choices or the statement of the result. As to the claim that proofs should be accessible because they are meant to capture the reasoning of real-life economic agents, a counterargument is that some results with long proofs are meta-claims about classes of models; as such, they are not meant to represent agents' reasoning within one model. Finally, as mentioned before, a proof is sometimes long because it requires a mathematical lemma that the author wasn't able to locate in the math literature, and so she needs to do it herself. If the result existed, a long sub-proof could be replaced with a single line and a reference. Therefore, length is sometimes a consequence of arbitrary circumstances.

Wherever one stands on the issue of long proofs, one should probably admit that if long proofs imply that part of them is relegated to a SOAP, their status is diminished in the overall scheme of things. If a result is so important that we can't tweak it for the sake of a shorter proof, but then we break the proof into pieces and dump some of them in the dusty basement, can we still argue that the proof is an essential part of the theoretical argument? Will authors treat it with the same care and precision? Will the number of readers who at least skim through the entire proof be the same? Should we regard the disruption of proofs' linear flow as an aspect of their declining importance?

Relegating proofs to the SOAP is both a symptom and a cause of their declining status in economic theory. We seem to be assigning increasing importance to stated results and their economic implications and decreasing importance to the reasoning behind them. From this point of view, the SOAP is indeed an external signifier of a major change in the values that underlie our professional culture.

## Choose Your Adventure

A common defense of SOAPs is that two-tier communication is an effective response to a *heterogeneous* audience. Most readers will not be interested in the paper's themes to such an extent that they will want to read all of its extensions and variations and the entire proofs. Yet others, perhaps a small minority, *will* be interested. The SOAP serves these readers; others can exercise free disposal. This is a *choose your adventure* approach: rather than a compromise, two-tier communication is a product-differentiation device that helps readers sort themselves into groups that differ in their level of interest in the paper.

This is the same rationale we list for two-tier communication in journals like *Nature* or *Science*. Yet there is a vast difference. The published paper in these venues is a very short and relatively nontechnical "executive summary" that deliberately appeals to a wide audience; the appendices are for the specialists. By contrast, the published economic-theory paper (even in "general readership" journals) already targets a relatively specialized audience. Its model section contains a carefully notated formal exposition, replete with Banach spaces and weak-* topologies. If anything, the "executive summary" function is fulfilled by the paper's *introduction*. The print version as a whole is technical and anything but short. Thus, the character and proportions of the print version and the SOAP in economic-theory papers are very different from the *Nature*/*Science* model.

Consequently, I doubt that SOAPs produce effective product differentiation. A better strategy in this regard might be to move material from the SOAP into a *separate* follow-up paper. It is likely that this paper would be publishable in a lower-ranked journal. Yet, if the material is so interesting that the editor of the original paper wants to put a stamp of approval on it, then, a fortiori, the editor of a lower-tier journal should feel the same. A separate paper is easier to retrieve, and it gives the author freedom to explore new expositional gambits.

So why not a separate paper? Because the legal-document conception regards so much of this follow-up material as essential for the main paper's validity. But I believe that another culprit is the huge premium that our profession puts on publishing in top journals. Authors find the task of rearranging the SOAP into a separate paper not worth the effort if the paper is not published in a lucrative venue. Some go further and argue that an additional publication in a so-so journal lowers the "market value" of the author's publication list. Once again, the "top-five" culture appears as a key driving force behind the appendicitis phenomenon.

## Aesthetics and Politics

My conclusion is that far from a superficial phenomenon, the rise of the SOAP reveals important trends in the professional culture of economic theory: the growing influence of the "applied-economics" culture, the "tyranny of the top five," the diminishing status of mathematical proofs, and the growing tendency to sacrifice aesthetic-pedagogical values for other considerations.

As mentioned earlier, when we apply the aesthetic-pedagogical perspective to pieces of economic theory, we essentially have prospective readers in mind. Instead of writing the paper litigiously to appease grumpy referees (who were *assigned* to read the paper), an aesthetically minded author tries to edify curious readers (who *chose* to do so). Having *prospective* readers in mind: that is the simple meaning of viewing papers through an "aesthetic" lens.

But do we still think about prospective readers when we write economic-theory papers? Do we write for readers or for referees? The distinction itself is bizarre—shouldn't we think of referees as a subgroup of readers? But do referees put themselves in the shoes of future readers and try to predict their future *enjoyment?* Or do they spend most of their energy *litigating* the paper's "case"?

It has become commonplace to say that no one reads published economics papers anymore. This is usually traced to the massive slow-down in the publication process. By the time the paper gets published, it has been circulating for a number of years and its immediate impact is complete: no one needs to bother reading it. We saw that, at least in the case of economic theory, the dynamic that has led to this state of affairs is more complex: the publication slowdown itself has a number of driving forces, one of which may well be a shift from an aesthetic conception of theory papers to a legalistic one.

We have thus reached an equilibrium in which effective communication, at least in the top echelons of our professional culture, takes place less through written papers and more through *oral* presentations in seminars and conferences. This brings to mind the recent decline in the importance of the recorded album in popular music and the rising importance of live performances. If written communication is becoming less important, no wonder less effort is spent on making it aesthetically pleasing, effectively treating it as a burial site of accumulated results.

Assuming my diagnosis of a shift from written to oral communication is correct, it raises a few interesting questions. First, does it mitigate the *long-run* impact of theory papers? In principle, the written word is more permanent and has more staying power—but not if people no longer read it.

Second, which of the two forms of communication is more *democratic*, in the sense of being open to a diverse set of authors? I am mainly thinking of geographic diversity, but one can think of other kinds. Do journal publications make it easier for the voice of a theorist with a provincial academic affiliation to be heard? Or is the seminar and conference circuit better in this regard? With the shift from written to oral communication in our culture, is it becoming more or less democratic?

I began this chapter with the superficially trifling matter of supplementary appendices, and now I am ending it with the democracy and diversity of our profession.

# 7  Cover Versions

## Patents and Royalties

Every economic theorist dreams of being *the first*: the first to explain an economic phenomenon, the first to formulate a decision model, the first to define a domain of problems (and maybe even solve one of them). The few pioneering works that manage to attract a following earn their due credit (putting aside issues of obscure precedents and overlapping discoveries). This chapter is about what happens *next*. How do we regulate the evaluation and assignment of credit for follow-up research? Do our norms in this regard generate some kind of "market failure"?

Since we are dealing here with the management of intellectual innovation, perhaps it is instrumental to invoke some jargon from the economics of intellectual property. Two metaphors come to mind: patent protection and royalties.

"Patent protection" limits entry into the area of inquiry defined by the original pioneering work. The enforcers of this protection are editors and referees (often including the pioneers themselves and their early disciples), who set the terms for publishing follow-up research in the area.

My impression is that our professional culture is quite generous with the patent protection it showers on pioneering work. We reward economists for "being the first to talk about X." Theorists who happen to be the first to offer *some* formal model of an economic phenomenon get to exert considerable influence on the direction of subsequent research.

"Royalties" are not about limiting entry, but rather about the sharing of the "surplus" that the pioneering work made possible: making sure the follow-up work acknowledges its debt to the pioneer.

The patent-protection and royalty modes are not mutually exclusive: we tend to apply both when regulating follow-up work. At stake for both is the issue of "protection breadth": how widely the net that protects the pioneering work is cast.

### Extensions, Applications, and Foundations

When a pioneering work establishes a new research area, follow-up work usually takes one of three forms.

**Extension.** This type of follow-up work may prove additional or more general results for the same domain of problems that the pioneering work defined. Alternatively, it may enrich the original model with new dimensions and thus enlarge its domain.

**Application.** In some cases, the pioneering model is relatively abstract and leaves many key details unspecified. It is not so much a model as a modeling framework or an approach to analyzing a class of models (game-theoretic solution concepts or utility representations in decision theory fall into this category). An application completes these specifics in order to fit a more concrete economic situation, and uses the additional details to derive further results.

**Foundation.** In other cases, the pioneering model treats a certain component as a black box or a just-so assumption. The follow-up study derives it from a more elaborate model that is perceived as more fundamental (for example, showing that a behavioral rule that the pioneering model introduced can be obtained as a solution to a maximization problem with a "conventional" friction).

Extensions, applications and foundations are "certified" modes of follow-up work. They never put the original work's "patent protection" in doubt. They respect its primacy, extend its reach, and deepen its roots. They are consumers, distributors, and maintenance providers for the original product, rather than competing producers.

### Remodeling

A fourth follow-up category consists of *alternative formulations* of the pioneering work. These are remodeling exercises, which take the same ideas of the original piece and offer different ways to formalize them. The economic ideas and basic modeling strategies are not meant to be new. However, enough modeling choices are different to make this a distinct exercise that cannot be identified with the original. A remodeling exercise makes no pretense of a genuinely new idea. Rather, it suggests a different way to realize an existing one.

Reformulations of economic-theory pieces can take various shapes: from different yet mathematically equivalent versions of the original model to models that modify the original's ancillary assumptions. A remodeling exercise is a variation on the original model, but not in a sense that falls under the "extension" category. It is a different way of telling the same story.

I liken remodeling exercises in economic theory to *cover versions* of pop songs. A cover version is not a new song, but a new take on an existing song. The artist who records the cover version is expected to pay royalties to the creators of the original song. It is not rare for listeners to find the cover version superior to the original (try googling "cover version better than original").

Where can we find such cover versions in the economic-theory literature? Is their supply "efficient"? If not, what can this "market failure" teach us about the culture of economic theory?

## Loss Aversion and Optimal Pricing

I started thinking about these questions when I was busy writing my behavioral industrial organization textbook.[1] I wanted to include a chapter on optimal pricing when consumers are loss averse, based on interesting ideas introduced in a series of papers by Paul Heidhues, Botond Kőszegi, and Matthew Rabin.[2] The basic economic question is natural and simple. Suppose consumers are loss averse as in Kahneman and Tversky (1979), broadly construed—that is, they record outcomes as gains or losses relative to a reference point, and they overweigh losses relative to gains. How would a monopolist set product prices in response to supply or demand shocks, when faced with such consumers? Can consumer loss aversion explain real-life pricing phenomena?

To develop a model of pricing with loss averse consumers, one has to address several questions. First, while the original Kahneman-Tversky model dealt with unidimensional monetary outcomes, market outcomes are multidimensional. At the very least, they have two dimensions: money spent and quantity consumed. How should we handle this multidimensionality? Should we aggregate the two dimensions into a single net value, and then record gains and losses along this synthetic dimension? Or should we record outcomes for each dimension separately, and aggregate them only after they have been weighted as gains or losses in their respective dimensions? If so, should we assume the same intensity of loss aversion for the two dimensions?

Second, when the environment is stochastic (as it would be, say, when cost shocks lead to price fluctuations), will the consumer's reference point be fixed? Or should it fluctuate as well, reflecting the randomness of his environment? For example, considering the price dimension alone, when the price fluctuates, how should we model the formation of the reference price and how should we model the way it is integrated into the consumer's utility calculations? Moreover, should the prices that inform the reference point be the firm's stated prices or transaction prices (which can be lower due to discounts)? If no one ever buys the product at the stated price, can it serve as a reference point?

As we can see, there is a multitude of modeling choices to be made, even for the seemingly basic setting of monopoly pricing with loss averse consumers. Let this refute any claim that doing "psychology and economics" is mere plug-and-play insertion of psychologists' experimental findings into economists' models. However rich and established one's "psychological evidence" may be (and it doesn't get better than loss aversion), incorporating such evidence into the simplest models of economic behavior requires the theorist to make modeling choices that lack a straightforward empirical validation.

Heidhues, Kőszegi, and Rabin resolved these modeling dilemmas by applying Kőszegi and Rabin's (2006) now-canonical model of reference-dependent preferences. Since their analysis generated valuable insights into pricing phenomena, I was eager to devote my textbook chapter to their models. Yet, as I was trying to implement this plan, I noticed that I kept modifying the authors' modeling choices. Why? Different tastes, different intuitions about the formation of reference points in stochastic environments, and pedagogical considerations (which naturally matter more when one writes a textbook). Whatever the reason, my version of their model ended up different. Same basic ideas, different execution: a "cover version."

Since this cover version generated more material than I could fit in a textbook chapter, I decided to make a paper out of it. On one hand, the paper had very little new economics relative to the Heidhues-Kőszegi-Rabin papers. On the other hand, I felt that the different modeling choices were significant enough to justify a separate paper. But this paper did not fall into any of the three standard categories: it wasn't a foundation, an extension, or an application, but a pure remodeling exercise. Accordingly, I subtitled my paper "A Cover Version of the Heidhues-Kőszegi-Rabin model." I submitted it to a top theory journal. The editor rejected the paper, but also wrote that the decision was made after consultation with the other coeditors because he felt that, independent of the paper's quality, its unusual "cover version" genre demanded a decision of principle: Does a pure remodeling exercise merit publication as a regular paper in a top theory journal? The journal editors concluded it does not and duly rejected the paper. This was a very sensible decision, and the paper was later accepted at a respectable theory journal.[3]

This episode raises the following question: How should we regard papers that primarily reformulate existing theory exercises? The question may seem esoteric because we don't see such papers floating around. However, as I will argue, this impression is misleading. Yes, there is a low supply of "cover versions" seeking the light of day. However, the remodeling exercises themselves are *not* infrequent. They sometimes appear as by-products of research papers that largely follow the established modes of extension, application, and foundation. For example, a theorist may adapt an existing model in order to make it better suited for an extension she has in mind. A common outlet for remodeling exercises is textbooks, as in my own story. Most importantly, many remodeling exercises probably languish in theorists' drawers, in the form of lecture notes that they share with their graduate students but not with the community of theorists at large.

Is this a problem? If so, what is the explanation for its persistence? How can we address it? These are the questions I tackle in this chapter, starting with the first question: Is an undersupply of cover versions a problem?

## Motorcycles and Reactors

In his great autobiographical book *Disturbing the Universe*, the physicist Freeman Dyson recounts his involvement in an attempt to invent safe, efficient nuclear reactors (Dyson 1979, chap. 9). His working group's endeavor failed, and Dyson concludes the chapter with a sense of disillusionment with the direction that the nuclear-power industry had taken. He argues that large, bureaucratic organizations took over and crowded out the romantic, entrepreneurial spirit that typified the field in its early days. As a result, Dyson claims, fewer risks were taken, and too few reactor models were tested for significant breakthroughs to occur.

Dyson contrasts this with the historical development of motorcycles (inspired by Robert Pirsig's famous *Zen and the Art of Motorcycle Maintenance* [Pirsig 1974]):[4]

When my father was a young man, he used to travel around Europe on a motorcycle. . . . In those days every rider was his own repairman. Riders and manufacturers were together engaged in trying out a huge variety of different models, learning by trial and error which designs were rugged and practical and which were not. It took thousands of attempts, most of which ended in failure, to evolve the few types of motorcycles that are now on the roads. . . . This is why the modern motorcycle is efficient and reliable.

The accuracy of Dyson's technological history is not my concern here: I am interested in it purely as a *metaphor* for remodeling exercises in economic theory. The early motorcycle is the analogue of a pioneering economic model. Subsequent tweaks of motorcycle design were not "extensions": they did not add major new functionalities to the original motorcycle. In the same manner, remodeling exercises in economic theory are not meant to add new dimensions to the original model: they simply offer different ways to realize the original inventors' vision. In Dyson's history, inventors and users of the early motorcycles were incentivized to tinker with their design and thus produced more efficient versions. By this analogy, if the professional culture of economic theory incentivized theorists to tinker with interesting new models, we would have better-working versions of these models, and their eventual impact would be enhanced.

Instead, my impression is that too often we let the first version of an interesting model be its final version, because we lack a reward system that encourages theorists to tinker with existing models and share the fruits of their tinkering with the rest of the theory community. The "patent protection" we provide for the pioneering model encourages us to apply, extend, and "microfound" them—not to remodel them. As a result, our models may sometimes resemble Dyson's elephantine nuclear reactors rather than his agile motorcycles.

The claim I am making here is that the path of innovation in economic theory may be suboptimal because of insufficient tinkering with models' initial version. Tinkering *does* take place in the classroom— where instructors come up with pedagogically useful versions of interesting new models. However, the products of this tinkering are not made public.

This claim is difficult to substantiate. If the state-of-the-art version of an interesting economic model is suboptimal, then improvements should be feasible. Therefore, to demonstrate my claim, I should present a sufficiently long (and sufficiently distinguished) list of such models. In fact, such a list would have to be duplicated: each model would come in its current version as well as in an improved cover version of my own design. This is an ambitious exercise that greatly exceeds the boundaries of the present essay. Clearly, I am unable to meet this high substantiation standard. Instead, the remainder of this chapter is devoted to a few examples, which hopefully provide the *beginning* of such substantiation. I will also use the examples to illustrate various kinds of remodeling exercises and their diverse roles.

## Local Optima

Before I jump into the detailed examples, I wish to clarify that in all of them, the cover versions' targets are absolute classics in the economic-theory canon, which most readers of this essay will be familiar with. This expositional strategy enables me to escape the duplicated presentation I alluded to above. Yet, there is a larger point here: even our best and most frequently used models are "local optima" that have limitations. It's just that these local optima are so good and have been around for so long that we rarely think about trying to improve on them.

Take a few examples. In the theory of repeated games, the dominant specification is that players use discounted expected utility to evaluate streams of payoffs. Furthermore, in almost all applications of the model, the discount factor is the *same* for all players. In some settings, this is a plausible assumption: if we think of periodic payoffs as monetary flows and regard the discount factor as representing an interest rate, then a common discount factor can mean that all players have access to the same competitive credit market. But this is a special, often irrelevant justification, which narrows the scope of investigation. Compare this with bargaining theory, where heterogeneity in discount factors is a major factor that determines equilibrium allocations (as in Rubinstein 1982).

However, allowing for heterogeneous discount factors in repeated games complicates the analysis considerably. For example, Ehud Lehrer and Ady Pauzner (1999) showed that merely thinking about the feasible set of payoff profiles, let alone their sustainability in equilibrium, becomes much more complicated when players have different discount factors (that are not arbitrarily close to one). The upshot is that the canonical repeated-game model with its common discount factor is a local optimum: it has difficulties addressing long-run relationships between diversely patient players.

A more specific modeling gadget is the ubiquitous quadratic loss function. For example, in many applications of Crawford and Sobel's

(1982) cheap-talk model, the state of nature and the receiver's action are real numbers. Each player's payoff loss is the squared distance between the action and some ideal point that is determined by the state. The attraction of this specification is that the receiver's optimal action against her belief is simple: she wants to match the action to the expected ideal point according to her belief. The quadratic loss function is merely reverse engineering: we assume it so that we can get that simple choice rule as the consequence of expected utility maximization.

However, the quadratic loss function carries additional implications. It is a concave function. Therefore, if we extend the model by allowing the receiver to take a prior action before the cheap-talk game begins, we are bound by the risk aversion that the concave utility function represents. But maybe we didn't sign up for risk aversion! What if we wanted risk-neutral players? Sorry, that's the price we have to pay if we want to "rationalize" the behavioral rule that matches the action to the expected ideal point. If we want to break the association between the two, we have to look for alternative modeling gadgets.

The point is that even our best modeling devices have weak spots that could use an occasional tweak. The need for remodeling exercises is not the sole province of faltering first steps in a modeling agenda; even established classics can use them.

## Trees and Histories

Every student of game theory encounters the formalism of extensive-form games with perfect information: a model of strategic interactions that unfold over time, where players always observe all prior moves (including exogenous moves by "nature").

Extensive-form games are highly intuitive objects because they can be visualized as trees. Indeed, their only difference from decision trees is that different players having idiosyncratic preferences may act at different decision nodes. This is why the easiest way to impart the model to students is to draw game trees. However, this ceases to be convenient when the tree is large (or infinite). And, in any case, pictures are not enough if we want to state and prove general mathematical results about behavior in extensive-form games. Harold Kuhn (1953) provided a mathematical formulation of extensive-form games that explicitly used the language of trees.

To my taste, the tree formalism is a mouthful, compared with the elegance and transparency of the picture itself. Even if this is a minority taste, I believe that a non-negligible segment in the "market for extensive-game modeling" has latent demand for a cover version.

In their game theory textbook, Martin Osborne and Ariel Rubinstein (1994) responded to this demand and offered a mathematically equivalent reformulation of extensive-form games. Drawing inspiration from the theory of repeated games, Osborne and Rubinstein used the language of *histories* to define the primitives of the model. A history is a sequence of actions (or profiles of actions in the case of simultaneous moves). The key primitive is a set of *terminal* histories: all the possible unfoldings of the dynamic strategic interaction. A terminal history corresponds to a terminal node in the tree formalism. Accordingly, players' preferences are defined over the set of terminal histories. The notion of a terminal history induces an intuitive notion of a nonterminal history: it is a subsequence that starts like the terminal history and stops before the end. If a terminal history is like the complete telling of a story from beginning to end, a nonterminal history is akin to telling the story and stopping before it reaches its end. The "player function" assigns a player (or a collection of players, in the case of simultaneous moves) to every nonterminal history.

And that's it. I find the history language more efficient and elegant than the tree language. When I teach the subject, I use trees to visualize the model and histories to present it formally. Some instructors follow this pedagogical strategy, while others prefer to use the language of trees in the formal exposition. That is fine. As with Dyson's motorcycles, when it comes to formal exposition of an economic model, we should let many flowers bloom and allow different users to pick their favorite formulation.

For my current purposes, the key observation here is that the history formalism is nowhere to be found prior to Osborne and Rubinstein's 1994 textbook. Even if they hadn't written their textbook, their reformulation would probably have found an audience. They could use it themselves in graduate courses; some students could absorb it and later put it to use in their own game theory teaching. This is an example of "oral" cultural transmission. Some theorists could pick up the formalism and sneak it into *written* papers, where they would use it to state and prove results about extensive-form games. However, in the absence of an "authoritative" reference, they would have to reinvent the wheel each time and fight referees for permission to speak an unconventional language. Some would decide that this is not worth the trouble and resort to the conventional tree formalism, even when they personally find it less efficient.

## Retelling Akerlof's Lemons Story

An interesting chapter in the modern history of economic thought consists of game-theoretic retellings of models that were formerly rendered in other languages. Enthusiasm for Cho and Kreps's (1987) seminal paper on signaling games was partly generated by its ability to retell Spence's (1973) signaling model in a game-theoretic language. Likewise, early enthusiasm for Rubinstein's 1982 bargaining model was partly based on the realization (reported by Binmore, Rubinstein, and Wolinsky 1986) that a minor tweaking of his model could offer a "foundation" for the Nash bargaining solution. Other noteworthy examples include Gul's (1989) noncooperative game-theoretic derivation of the Shapley value, and Netzer and Scheuer's (2014) noncooperative foundation for the model of competitive screening, which we will encounter later in this chapter. The chapter devoted to "information economics" in Mas-Colell, Whinston, and Green's (1995) ubiquitous microeconomictheory textbook is almost entirely a fastidious game-theoretic retelling of the classic models of markets with adverse selection.

Given the transformational energy behind these exercises, it would be misleading to call them "cover versions." Indeed, their authors often regarded them as *foundations*. By comparison, the following is an example of a far more modest remodeling exercise in this genre, which can be classified as a cover version.

George Akerlof's (1970) classic model of the "market for lemons" was originally presented in the context of the competitive-equilibrium model (with rational expectations, in the presence of asymmetric information). When I teach game theory, I always want to include the all-important idea of how market interactions can break down due to adverse selection. But since I do not want the methodology to be out of step with the rest of the course (which is, after all, about game theory), I use a simple game that captures the economic essence of Akerlof's model.

The game is probably familiar to instructors of game theory. To my knowledge, its earliest appearance is in a 1984 experimental working paper by William Samuelson and Max Bazerman.[5] Their motivation was not to recast Akerlof's model in game-theoretic terms. Instead, their paper was a series of explorations of whether actual participants in bargaining games internalize the logic of adverse selection. Nevertheless, the authors were aware of the Akerlof connection. In an endnote, they wrote, "Version 3 [the game in question here] is an adaptation to the bargaining setting of Akerlof's (1970) well-known example of adverse selection in a market for 'lemons.'"

The game's protagonists are a privately informed seller and an uninformed buyer. The seller's valuation of his object is $v$. The seller knows $v$. The buyer's prior belief is that this value is drawn uniformly from the interval $[0, 1]$, and he receives no additional information. The buyer's valuation of the object is $1.5v$. That is, it is common knowledge that the buyer always values the object 50% more than the seller. Therefore, trade is always efficient. The buyer makes a take-it-or-leave-it offer to the seller. Trade takes place at the buyer's stated price, as long as the seller agrees to the offer.

The standard game-theoretic analysis of this game goes like this. The seller will only agree to sell when $p \geq v$. Anticipating this, the buyer realizes that conditional on trade taking place at a price $p$ in $[0, 1]$, the seller's valuation of the object is uniformly distributed over the interval $[0, p]$. Therefore, on average, the value is $0.5p$. The buyer's subjective valuation is 50% higher, implying an expected valuation of $1.5 \cdot 0.5p = 0.75p$. For every $p > 0$, the buyer's expected net profit conditional on trade is $0.75p - p < 0$. Therefore, his optimal bid is $p = 0$, which the seller accepts with zero probability because $v > 0$ with probability one. That is, market interaction breaks down completely, even though trade is always mutually beneficial. This is a stark illustration of how market agents' enthusiasm to trade is chilled by their gloomy inference from other market agents' hypothetical willingness to trade at the market price.

This is a clean delivery of Akerlof's insight, even though it uses game theory rather than competitive equilibrium. Instead of competition between privately informed, price-taking sellers, we have a monopsonistic, uninformed buyer. Yet, both descriptions capture market forces that shift surplus from the informed side of the market to the uninformed side. The economic reasoning behind the breakdown of market trade is very similar. In Akerlof's rendering, uninformed buyers understand what the competitive market price means in terms of the quality of traded objects. In Samuelson and Bazerman's retelling, the buyer introspects about the seller's reasoning. The translation is close, and it enables a teacher of a game theory course to convey Akerlof's important economic insight without straying away from the course's unifying methodology. To me, the modesty of this act of translation makes it a worthy member of the cover-version family. I wouldn't regard it as a "foundation."

Again, what is important for my present purposes is that the translation as such was not the focus of the Samuelson-Bazerman paper. Recall that it was an *experimental* paper. It focused on how experimental subjects behave as buyers in this game, taking the seller's conditional best-reply as a given. The authors' objective was to explore whether the subjects of their experiment internalized the logic of adverse selection (spoiler: meh).

From a pedagogical point of view, the Samuelson-Bazerman game is important, even if we completely set aside the published experiment and treat it as a classroom thought experiment. Yet, without the actual experiment, there would have been no paper. No game theorist would have bothered to publish a little game, whose only raison d'être is to make the lemons model suitable for a game theory course.

I am confident that some game theory teachers would have come up with this example on their own. Nevertheless, without Samuelson and Bazerman's experimental paper and in the absence of a textbook that includes this example, its dissemination would have relied on word of mouth. As with the example of extensive-form games, efficient transmission of a pedagogically valuable cover version needs a scaffold that has an independent or larger motivation, such as a textbook or an experiment.

If we accept that the Samuelson-Bazerman game is a good thing to have in one's game theory course, then the observation that we might owe its dissemination to it being a by-product of an experimental paper should give us pause. We need to imagine what would have happened if the experimental motivation for the game hadn't existed. We would have had to count on an oral dissemination process for the game to become common currency in the theory community; the publication system would not have been the conduit.

## Competitive Screening

The central example I present in this chapter involves another great classic of "information economics"—the model of competitive screening due to Rothschild and Stiglitz (1976). This is one of my all-time favorites in economic theory. Technically simple yet conceptually sophisticated, motivated by a concrete economic situation yet offering a subtle solution concept that raises foundational questions—it ticks all the boxes for me.

The Rothschild-Stiglitz model concerns market competition in the presence of adverse selection. The main departure from Akerlof's lemons model is that it does not insist on linear pricing. Instead, it allows for two-dimensional contracts (another difference is that it assumes competition among the *uninformed* market agents). The model illuminates how nonlinear pricing enables firms to screen consumers' private information, and highlights the inefficiencies this entails.

For many years, I taught intermediate microeconomics courses at Tel Aviv University and felt that the Rothschild-Stiglitz model should be an integral part of our (unusually long) sequence. The model had been successfully taught at the graduate level, but I reckoned it was also important to pitch it to undergrads. We had already satisfactorily incorporated Akerlof's lemons model into the curriculum. In contrast, the Rothschild-Stiglitz model was typically left for the semester's final week, and my delivery of this material felt pedagogically inadequate (sometimes I had to skip it altogether). After several failed attempts, I concluded that one major difficulty was that the conventional pedagogical treatment of the Rothschild-Stiglitz model followed closely their insurance-market setting, where contracts are defined by a premium and a deductible. Crucially for this setting, consumers are risk averse, which conventionally means that their preferences are represented by a nonlinear utility function over wealth. Linear preferences would mean risk-neutrality, in which case the market would break down for lack of gains from trade.

However, nonlinearity makes it more difficult to offer undergraduate students an *analytic* treatment of the concept of market equilibrium. Sure, we can write down the conditions of equilibrium, but then the nonlinearity of the inequalities that represent consumers' incentive constraints makes it harder for most undergraduate students to perform calculations that would give them a direct feel for the forces involved. What teachers usually do is show everything graphically: they draw indifference curves and iso-profit lines and demonstrate deviations from candidate equilibria on the diagram.

This pedagogical strategy has two downsides. First, while many students find a graphical demonstration more intelligible than an analytical one, others have the opposite preference. Putting all the pedagogical eggs in the graphical basket leaves one segment underserved. Second, the potential supply of problem sets and exam questions gets quite limited when all you have is diagrams. When a subject doesn't lend itself to successful exam questions, there is a sense in which it hasn't really been taught.

Therefore, my objective was to come up with a version of the Rothschild-Stiglitz model with *linear* consumer preferences. Obviously, that meant abandoning the insurance story. I was familiar with a labor-market example in Mas-Colell, Whinston, and Green (1995). In their telling, firms compete in contracts that condition workers' wage on their amount of training. Workers' productivity is their private information. As in Spence (1973), more productive workers have lower training costs. This description can be reconciled with linear preferences. However, as a primary example for undergraduate students, the story has limitations. Explicit contracts that prospectively condition wage on future training are rare, and so the student is invited to interpret the model more abstractly as a norm that governs workers' wage expectations. Nothing wrong with that, but probably not ideal as an *entrée* for undergrads. When presenting such an important subject, one would like to have an example that can be motivated and interpreted with a minimum of hand-waving.

Eventually, I came up with an example of a *credit market* model, in which loan contracts are defined by an interest rate and a collateral. Since this happened shortly after the 2008 financial crisis, I guess I was primed to think of credit-market failures. After the fact, I learned that the basic economic idea had already appeared in an important paper by Helmut Bester (1985). Bester's paper did not have a pedagogical objective in mind—certainly not my objective of finding a compelling example of competitive screening with linear preferences. It appeared when "information economics" was a relatively fresh subject. Bester wrote it in the extension/application mode, showing that the ideas of Rothschild and Stiglitz (1976) (as well as Stiglitz and Weiss 1981) enabled him to illuminate an aspect of credit markets. Bester's model includes more moving parts because it aims at a realistically faithful description. It also addresses the problem of credit rationing, which has no immediate counterpart in Rothschild-Stiglitz's 1976 model. For these reasons, the importance of Bester's paper notwithstanding, I didn't find it suitable for my pedagogical purposes. It was an extension and an application, not a remodeling exercise.

In what follows, I want to transport you back to the mid-1980s. You are enthusiastic about Rothschild and Stiglitz's 1976 model, and you want to teach it. The nonlinearities of their model are a barrier for teaching it to certain groups of students, and you want to reformulate their model with linear preferences. Bester's 1985 paper may or may not exist in this hypothetical scenario. You stumble on the idea of a credit-market model in which credit contracts may include a collateral, and so you proceed with the following example. I present it in some detail, because this gives me an opportunity to share my take on this wonderful gem of economic theory.

## Interest and Collateral

Imagine a population of borrowers who need a loan (whose size is 1) to finance a project. The value of a successful project is $A > 1$. A loan contract is a pair of non-negative numbers $(r, x)$, where $r$ is the interest on the loan and $x$ (a number between 0 and 1) is the (gross) value of the collateral the borrower is required to deposit. The fruits of the borrower's project cannot serve as collateral.

Every borrower is defined by her credit risk: a probability $q$ between 0 and ½ that her project will fail and she will become insolvent. In that scenario, she is unable to repay the loan (neither the principal nor the interest), but the lender can seize the collateral that the borrower deposited. However, seizing a collateral is inefficient: a collateral of value $x$ is only worth $bx$ to the lender, where $b$ is a number between 0 and 1. This constant can reflect the physical costs of realizing the collateral, or the collateral's sentimental value for the borrower (but not for the lender). As a result, every contract with $x > 0$ is inefficient because of the positive probability $q$ of the welfare loss $(1 - b)x$ from seizing the collateral.

Credit risk is not constant. The population of borrowers is equally split into two types, called 1 and 2, whose credit risk levels are $q_1$ and $q_2$. Suppose $q_2 > q_1$—that is, type 2 is riskier.

The credit market is competitive, in the sense that there is a large number of profit-maximizing lenders who can extend any loan contract. Each lender is restricted to offering a single contract. All market agents are risk-neutral.

Consider an arbitrary type with credit risk $q$. This borrower's expected utility from a loan contract $(r, x)$ is

$$(A - r)(1 - q) - qx$$

The reason is that the value of a successful project is $A$, the net payment to the lender in this scenario (which occurs with probability $1 - q$) is $r$, and the net payment to the lender is $x$ when the borrower is insolvent (an event that occurs with probability $q$). If the borrower opts out, her payoff is 0 (because the project is not materialized). It is easy to see from the linear expression that the borrower's subjective rate of substitution between interest and collateral is

$$\frac{q}{1 - q}$$

A higher risk of insolvency makes the borrower more favorable to loan contracts that rely on interest, relative to loans that rely on collateral.

The lender's expected profit from the same contract when it is chosen by this borrower type is

$$r(1-q)-q(1-bx)$$

The reason is that with probability $1-q$ the lender gets his money back plus interest, while with probability $q$, he loses the principal of the loan and can reclaim only a fraction $b$ of the value of the collateral.

In an environment with complete information, the lender's credit risk $q$ is common knowledge, and so there are separate markets for different risk groups. Thus, fixing $q$, a *competitive equilibrium* is defined as a contract $(r, x)$ that satisfies two requirements. First, it generates zero profits for lenders given borrowers' choice between the contract and the outside option. Second, there exists no new contract $(r', x')$ that could enter the market and generate positive profits, given borrowers' choice from among the original contract, the new contract, and the outside option.

Effectively, this means that a competitive-equilibrium contract maximizes the borrower's expected utility, subject to the constraint that the contract generates zero profits for lenders. Plugging the expression for zero profits in the expression for the borrower's expected utility, we obtain

$$A(1-q)-q(1-bx)-qx$$

Since $b<1$, this expression attains a maximum of $A(1-q)-q>0$ at $x=0$. The equilibrium contract is

$$(r,x)=\left(\frac{q}{1-q},0\right)$$

Importantly, the equilibrium contract is efficient: it makes no use of the wasteful collateral. Competition over borrowers is done entirely through the interest instrument, and the interest rate is set such that lenders break even in expectation.

Rothschild and Stiglitz's departure from this competitive benchmark is that a borrower's credit risk is her private information. In this case, lenders are unable to identify the type of borrower that takes a given loan, and therefore cannot explicitly design contract loans for specific types of borrowers. When borrowers enter the market, they can choose from a *set* of available loan contracts. They can also opt out. However, I will take it for granted that $A$ is large enough, such that all borrowers will always prefer any relevant market contract to the outside option. Therefore, we can ignore the outside option.

In this environment, a competitive equilibrium is defined as a collection $C$ of contracts of the form $(r, x)$, such that two conditions hold. First, each contract in $C$ generates zero profits, given the way each type of borrower chooses from $C$. Second, there exists no new contract $c$ outside $C$ that would generate positive profits, given the way each type of borrower chooses from the extended set that adds $c$ to $C$.

This is the notion of competitive equilibrium in contracts that Rothschild and Stiglitz (1976) introduced. One of its key conceptual moves was the idea that every contract is an independent "profit center." This was also one of the concept's more controversial aspects because it ruled out the realistic scenario in which firms offer multiple contracts that cross-subsidize one another. This feature and the (related) possibility of equilibrium nonexistence are generally regarded as deficiencies of the Rothschild-Stiglitz concept. In my eyes, they are a wrinkle that adds to the attraction of the concept. Unlike more popular equilibrium concepts such as Nash equilibrium, which hide their interpretational difficulties behind a veneer of inevitability, this one wears them on its sleeve.

Let us now analyze competitive equilibria. For brevity, I do not present a complete characterization. Instead, I settle for showing the impossibility of "pooling" equilibria, which will also imply the necessary inefficiency of equilibrium in this model.

In a pooling equilibrium, all borrowers choose the same contract. Assume a pooling equilibrium exists, where the equilibrium contract is some $(r, x)$. The expected profit this contract generates for lenders is

$$r(1 - \bar{q}) - \bar{q}(1 - bx)$$

where

$$\bar{q} = \frac{1}{2}(q_1 + q_2)$$

is the average credit risk in the population of borrowers. By the first condition in the definition of equilibrium, the expected profit should be zero. We will now find a contract $(r', x')$ that can invade the market, attract only low-risk (type 1) borrowers, and make a positive profit. In other words, the new contract will satisfy the following inequalities:

$$(1-q_1)r' + q_1x' < (1-q_1)r + q_1x$$

$$(1-q_2)r' + q_2x' < (1-q_1)r + q_1x$$

$$(1-q_1)r' + q_1(1-bx') > 0$$

The first inequality means that for type 1, expected payments are lower under the *new* contract. The second inequality means that for type 2, expected payments are lower under the *original* contract. The third inequality means that when only borrowers of type 1 select the new contract, it generates positive profits.

What would this new contract look like? It will *raise the collateral and lower the interest*: $x' = x + \varepsilon$ and $r = r - \delta$. What are $\varepsilon$ and $\delta$? To see that, rewrite the first pair of inequalities:

$$\frac{q_1}{1-q_1} < \frac{\delta}{\varepsilon} < \frac{q_2}{1-q_2}$$

Since $q_2 > q_1$, it is clear that we can find $\varepsilon$ and $\delta$ that satisfy these conditions. As the inequality makes clearly visible, the incremental shift from interest to collateral (measured by the ratio $\delta/\varepsilon$) exceeds the low-risk borrower's rate of substitution and falls below the high-risk borrower's rate. It therefore deters the high-risk borrower (for whom seizure of collateral is relatively likely) and attracts the low-risk borrower (for whom collateral seizure is relatively unlikely).

The transparency of this observation is made possible by the linear preferences. In the original Rothschild-Stiglitz setting, we would also have to consider the curvature of borrowers' utility function at the relevant wealth levels. This may appear like a minor detail for specialists, but remember we're trying to address *undergrads* (albeit relatively advanced ones): even small technical complications can divert their attention away from the model's conceptual core.

Can we design $\varepsilon$ and $\delta$ such that the new contract is profitable? Recall that the original contract breaks-even when evaluated according to the *population average* credit risk. The new contract prunes the credit pool such that only low-risk borrowers select it. This leads to a dramatic rise in the contract's profitability. If $\varepsilon$ and $\delta$ are small, their exact absolute value pales in importance relative to the risk pool's massive improvement (while only the *ratio* $\varepsilon/\delta$ is relevant for the inequalities that govern borrowers' choice between the two contracts).

Nonexistence of pooling equilibria means that once lenders can use the twin instruments of interest and collateral, market competition forces will lead to discrimination. The further significance of this result is that competitive equilibrium must be inefficient. The reason is that efficiency requires all borrower types to take a loan without collateral, which effectively means that they would all choose the same contract $(r, 0)$ (this would be the contract with the lowest interest among all available zero-collateral ones).

For the sake of brevity, I will not provide here a detailed derivation of the equilibrium (when it exists, which need not be the case). I will only point out that in this equilibrium, the high-risk borrower type 2 gets the same loan contract as in the complete-information benchmark (which involves no collateral). In contrast, the low-risk type 1 gets a loan with positive collateral, and a lower interest rate than in the complete-information benchmark. The contract is pinned down by the requirements that type 2 is indifferent between the two contracts and that the contract generates zero profits for firms (when only low-risk borrowers select it).

## A Market Failure

I have chosen to describe this "cover version" of the Rothschild-Stiglitz model in some detail because in a book like this, giving a verbal yet precise description of a classic of economic theory is part of the package. My primary aim, however, was to convey the pedagogical value of this cover version. Because preferences in my version are linear, many students will find it easier to "see" the marginal substitution effects underlying the proofs—even without the benefit of diagrams. Perhaps some readers of this chapter will find it helpful if, like me, they want to teach this cool stuff to undergraduates and find the traditionally exclusive reliance on diagrams pedagogically limiting. Even the diagrams are easier to draw when everything is linear.

Now remember the setup. I invited readers to imagine themselves back in the 1980s, in an alternative history in which Bester's 1985 paper did not necessarily exist. In this imaginary scenario, your motivation for this exercise is pedagogical: reproducing the Rothschild-Stiglitz model with linear preferences. You don't want to extend their model, apply it, or give it foundations. You just want to tweak it in a way that (at least in your judgment) makes it easier to teach without compromising its economic relevance. The credit-market example satisfies these desiderata.

This is different from the actual history of Bester's paper: his was a "regular" contribution to economic theory in the extension/application mode. Bester showed how to use the ideas of competitive screening to understand the role of interest and collateral in credit markets. Pedagogical considerations were probably secondary to him, and indeed I wouldn't use his presentation of the model as a first introduction to competitive screening.

Yet, it should be clear that, even in the 1980s, the pure pedagogical exercise that I presented here would have been unpublishable. It is a very minor modification of the original model, a tweak that does not aim to create a genuinely new model, but rather do the same model, only slightly differently. Its value is almost purely pedagogical.

The only feasible ways to make this pedagogical contribution available to other theorists would be (1) publish a textbook; (2) write a paper that advances the literature on competitive screening in a "legitimate" direction and introduce the remodeling exercise as a by-product—just as Cho and Kreps (1987) appended their game-theoretic reformulation of Spence's signaling model into a paper that was mainly about something else (refinements of Nash equilibrium in signaling games); or (3) rely on purely oral transmission (sharing the idea with fellow teachers, or passing it to students who will later use it in their own classes).

None of these channels is satisfactory. Pedagogically useful appendages of regular research article are fortuitous. Textbooks are disappointingly rare (a good example is the theory of games with incomplete information; its treatment in the classic game theory textbooks from the 1990s is cursory and doesn't reflect major developments that largely postdated those books, such as the theory of global games we encountered in chapter 2; I am not aware of more modern graduate-level textbooks that address this gap). Finally, oral transmission is sketchy and inefficient. Of course, ideas *are* disseminated orally: that's how we get to know jokes or folk songs. The whole point of literate traditions, however, is that they massively scale up and accelerate the transmission.

To my mind, this is a failure in our little "market of ideas." The way our field progresses is by sharing and refining models—not by making "discoveries" or solving "open problems." It is analogous to the repeated use and refinement of cooking recipes. Yet, in our public written communication, this aspect is subservient to the established modes of extension, application, and foundation. If you want to build and sell a different version of a motorcycle, you have to pretend it is a car. This "market failure" is yet another example of how the contemporary culture of economic theory suppresses pedagogical values.

## The Journal of Cover Versions

We need to find a way for theorists to write down models that tweak existing ones as if those never existed, while at the same time giving those predecessors all the credit they deserve. This is a "royalties" system, not a "patent protection" one. Of course, an honest explanation of the differences and commonalities between the original and the tweak should always be given. But authors shouldn't be incentivized to exaggerate the differences and downplay the commonalities—which is what they are encouraged to do under the refereed-publication system (the incentives are reversed when writing textbooks). As far as the *execution* of the cover version is concerned, the author should not feel constrained by the specifics of the original.

The "top-five disease" that we encountered in previous chapters means that authors give exaggerated weight to publications in top journals and zero (or even negative) weight to publications in minor journals. Clearly, the pedagogically minded remodeling exercises I am discussing here should not be viewed as major contributions. They are etudes, not symphonies. But etudes should have a place in our professional culture; some may have lasting value.

Experimental economists may face a similar dilemma when thinking about how to manage *replications* of previous experiments.[6] Of course, we are often interested in literal replications whose objectives are to provide additional data points about the original experiment and keep experimentalists honest. However, more subtle replications can modify aspects of the original protocol—rephrasing the questions or the instructions to subjects, modifying the graphical interface, changing the order of the various tasks—in a way that can gradually improve experimental design. These tweaks are the experimentalists' version of theorists' remodeling exercises, and it is unclear how well the current publication system nurtures them.

Within the context of economic theory, a specialized venue devoted to remodeling exercises might be the most effective solution to the problem. It would break down the large textbook format into little fragments, and this unbundling could release dozens of interesting cover versions from theorists' drawers. We could call this venue the *Journal of Cover Versions*.

# 8    From Competitive Equilibrium to Mechanism Design in Eighteen Months

## Sea Change

If I had to name one major shift in the sensibilities of economic theorists in the past half century, a prime candidate would be the way we conceptualize markets—from quasi-natural phenomena admired from afar to manmade institutions whose design can be tweaked by economist-engineers.

The traditional image of markets that reigned in the 1950s and 1960s was competitive equilibrium. Standard accounts of the evolution of modern economic thought emphasize the extreme assumptions of the competitive-equilibrium model, which were subsequently relaxed by the information-economics and game theory developments in the 1970s and 1980s. But what is perhaps most striking in the competitive-equilibrium model is its sense of the market as a *natural* phenomenon. No one designs it. No one runs it. It can be defined with no reference to an explicit mechanism. The Walrasian auctioneer is a fiction aimed at those of us who insist on a concrete mechanism, but it is not an intrinsic part of the model. Endowments are like initial conditions of a physical system, and prices react spontaneously to changes in these endowments until they somehow manage to equilibrate this system. Indeed, as historians of economic thought have pointed out, the conscious inspiration for this image was the physical theory of thermodynamics.[1] According to this point of view, economists study markets in a disengaged manner, as if they were observing a natural system. Sure, they can tweak the system's initial conditions, but then they let market processes unwind naturally.

Compare this view with the contemporary "market design" approach, which regards the economist as an "engineer" that designs the details of the market institution. A good guide into this new culture is Al Roth's

popular book *Who Gets What and Why.*[2] A telling sign of the shift is that
in Roth's book, there is a huge emphasis on market institutions in which
prices play no role (for example, assignment of children to schools)—in
marked contrast to the all-important role of prices in the competitive-
equilibrium model.

Another manifestation of the sea change is the declining status of
competitive equilibrium in the *education* of academic economists. Students are seeing less and less competitive equilibrium and more and
more game theory during their basic graduate-level theory training. In
some quarters, teaching competitive equilibrium is taking place in *macroeconomics* courses. The "market design" approach relies on game
theory, which enables us to describe specific market rules and analyze
participants' behavioral response to these rules. Competitive equilibrium cannot get to this level of resolution.

All this is familiar. The question is whether this great methodological
shift affects our attitudes as economic theorists in ways that might be
less salient. My goal in this chapter is to illuminate this question, making
use of a personal experience of mine: a project I pursued in the last
decade with my longtime coauthor, Kfir Eliaz. We started our project
in a spirit of rebellion against the prevailing mechanism-design approach
to the topic we were interested in, but eventually we capitulated to the
prevailing paradigm and rewrote our paper as a mechanism-design
exercise.

Why did we start out opposing the mechanism-design approach?
And how did we end up accepting it as an effective mode for our
exercise? This personal story can teach us a small lesson about the
power that cultural currents in our profession exert over individual
researchers—even those who make a deliberate effort to swim against
the tide. Of course, I will make my best effort to make the reader
curious about the substantive economic question that Kfir and I studied.
But the real interest here is in the conscious trade-offs that we made
between the two styles of research, our initial decision to adopt the
outmoded style and the reasons behind it, and the forces that led to
our eventual surrender.

## What Do I Mean by "Competitive Equilibrium"?

Strictly speaking, the term refers to the classical model of a market (or
a collection of markets), to which agents arrive with endowments or

production technologies and make their individually optimal consumption or production decisions given market-clearing prices.

I have in mind a looser conception of the term, which describes an attitude to modeling rather than a specific set of models. This category includes the 1976 Rothschild-Stiglitz model of competitive screening in insurance markets that we encountered in chapter 7. In this model, market equilibrium is defined by a collection of insurance contracts, such that all contracts generate zero profits given consumers' behavior, and there is no scope for profitable entry of a new contract. This is quite different from the traditional formulation of competitive equilibrium. Nevertheless, the formalism is close in spirit. In particular, it eschews game theory: there is no clearly articulated protocol of trade. The competitive pressures that insurance companies face have the status of an "invisible hand"—they are in the background, captured by the zero-profit condition. By contrast, in game-theoretic models of market competition, intensity of competitive pressures is determined by the "rules of the game."

So, this is what I mean by a competitive-equilibrium approach: the "reduced form" manner in which the definition of market equilibrium captures an underlying competitive force. It offers a bird's-eye perspective into the market situation at hand. The culture of economic theory has grown rather hostile to this bird's-eye, "invisible hand" approach—favoring the game-theoretic, mechanism-design approach, with its explicit description of the "market protocol."

After this prologue, now to the story itself.

## Can "the Market" Simulate an Ideal Search Engine?

Around 2008, keyword auctions were the rage in parts of economic theory. After years of operating without a clear method for monetizing its incredible search engine, Google had converged on "sponsored search" as a viable business model. Google maintained its so-called organic search engine, where answers to a user's query are determined by the engine's algorithm. However, side by side the organic search, Google started auctioning a chunk of the user's screen space to paying advertisers.

For economists interested in auction theory, the auction-design problem was novel. In this setting, the auction designer aims to allocate multiple "positions" on the user's screen. Different positions have different degrees of prominence. They differ in their ability to attract the user's attention, hence in their value for advertisers. Moreover, unlike traditional advertising, the search engine can partly monitor users' attention, by observing whether they click on ads. This means that the advertiser's bid and payment can be defined "per click." In 2007, Ben Edelman, Michael Ostrovsky, and Michael Schwarz published an influential paper that studied a specific auction format in this environment, known as the "generalized second-price auction."[3] This paper created a buzz in the auction theory community as well as in the subfield known as Econ-CS, which mixes researchers from economic theory and computer science. An important chunk of this multidisciplinary interaction has been taking place under the auspices of new research labs founded by internet giants.

The avalanche of papers in the wake of Edelman et al. (2007) was firmly in the mold of auction theory, itself part of the mechanism-design tradition. When Kfir and I became interested in search engines around 2008, we felt a need to try a different approach, which would abandon mechanism design toward a competitive-equilibrium approach.

Our starting point was the observation that the primary function of search engines is to bridge the gap between what users want and their limited ability to put it in words. When a consumer is perfectly able to describe a product she wants, all the search engine needs to do is provide a list of sellers that provide this product. These alternatives need not be identical; they may differ in price, quality, or certain idiosyncratic details that can be detected only by inspection. But this is not where search engines shine best. It is when they manage to take a vague query like "a tall, handsome Israeli economist" and spit out "Rani Spiegler" in reply, or suggest that when someone spells "Kefir Elias" he is really looking for Kfir Eliaz, that they take the search experience to the next level. Kfir and I referred to this function as "vocabulary expansion." Yet, all the papers that Kfir and I had seen in the literature on keyword auctions ignored this key aspect of search engines. They assumed that the user's query unambiguously defines the set of relevant objects, such that the search engine's job is merely to serve them to the user in a particular order.

Kfir and I posed the following question: Can a "sponsored search" engine, based entirely on the incentives of competing advertisers, mimic the vocabulary expansion performed by an ideal "organic" search engine? In other words, if Google ditched its stupendous algorithm and relied entirely on sponsored search, would the competitive forces that shape advertisers' bidding for keywords lead to a search environment that is as effective in fulfilling the vocabulary-expansion role?

As it happens, Google founders Sergei Brin and Larry Page had considered a similar question ten years before us, in an appendix to the famous 1998 paper that introduced their search engine:

Currently, the predominant business model for commercial search engines is advertising. The goals of the advertising business model do not always correspond to providing quality search to users. . . . We expect that advertising funded search engines will be inherently biased towards the advertisers and away from the needs of the consumers. . . . We believe the issue of advertising causes enough mixed incentives that it is crucial to have a competitive search engine that is transparent and in the academic realm.[4]

Kfir and I have been unaware of this quote until very recently. What Brin and Page asserted back in 1998 (and ironically ignored when they later adopted the advertising business model), Kfir and I were asking from a purely academic point of view. Can "the market" offer "quality search" to users?

### Why Competitive Equilibrium?

History is written by the victors, as the cliché goes. So are lecture notes and textbooks. The narrative that the currently dominant mechanism-design culture offers nowadays is that the "reduced form," "bird's eye," "invisible hand" aspects of the competitive-equilibrium paradigm make it inferior to the mechanism-design approach. The graduate-level microeconomic-theory textbooks by Kreps (1990) and Mas-Colell, Whinston, and Green (1995) were key moments in this development.

An extreme manifestation of the new culture is the intermediate microeconomics course that the leading theorist Jeff Ely has developed (building on the work of his former Northwestern University colleague, Kim-Sau Chung). In traditional courses, competitive equilibrium takes center stage. In contrast, Ely's course strictly adheres to the mechanism-design perspective, which he regards as more basic, leaving the competitive-equilibrium model (which he regards as more specific) to the very end of the course. As he writes on the website that presents his approach:[5]

The goal is to study the main themes of microeconomics from an institution—and in particular market-free approach. To illustrate what I mean, when I cover public goods, I do not start by showing the inefficiency of market provided public goods. Instead I ask what are the possibilities and limitations of any institution for providing public goods. By doing this I illustrate the basic difficulty without confounding it with the additional problems that come from market provision. I do similar things with externalities, informational asymmetries, and monopoly.

All of this is done using the tools of dominant-strategy mechanism design. This enables me to talk about basic economic problems in their purest form.

Even if this is an extreme pedagogical approach at the moment, it may well anticipate the near future of economics pedagogy. It is an impressively unapologetic demonstration of power by the new, self-confident culture.

Like Ely, Kfir and I came of age intellectually when this new culture began its ascent. New graduate textbooks in the 1990s emphasized game theory at the expense of competitive equilibrium. Consequently, I feel more at home in Ely's radical course than in the old-style courses that place competitive equilibrium at the forefront. And yet, when Kfir and I wanted to study sponsored search engines, we were concerned about certain aspects of the mechanism-design approach.

First, when one formulates and analyzes a mechanism-design problem, one tacitly adopts the designer's point of view. But who is this designer and why should we empathize with him? For example, in a principal-agent model of the relationship between an employer and its worker, the theorist effectively identifies with the employer. The principal has a clear objective (maximizing profits or the worker's effort, attaining an efficient allocation), and the theorist finds herself pursuing it single-mindedly. In contrast, if the theorist abandons the designer's perspective and looks at the situation from a more disinterested point of view, she is more likely to explore the economic interaction from multiple perspectives and evaluate its outcome according to a more diverse set of criteria.

This distinction is not clear-cut. For example, Myerson and Satterthwaite's (1983) classic impossibility result employs the mechanism-design approach to obtain a result about the inefficiency of bilateral trade in Nash equilibrium under asymmetric information, which applies to arbitrary trading mechanisms, and regardless of the designer's motivations. Thus, on one hand, it is firmly in the mechanism-design tradition, yet on the other hand, it does preserve something of the outside perspective that I associated with the competitive-equilibrium tradition. However, the Myerson-Satterthwaite paper is an exception in this regard. The typical mechanism-design exercise does not pretend to describe a situation from a disinterested position; it aims to solve a problem. And typically, it is the specific problem of a specific economic agent (an employer, a seller). The single-mindedness of this endeavor can blind the analyst to other aspects of the situation. The analytical identification with the designer risks becoming an emotional one. In the context of the sponsored search problem, it meant identifying with Google and its objectives. And Kfir and I didn't want to act like unpaid Google employees.

Second, the single-minded pursuit of the designer's objective usually comes with fierce determination to relax any constraint on the instruments at the designer's disposal, even if this leads to artificial mechanisms. From this perspective, every limitation on the space of feasible mechanisms feels ad hoc. When theorists carry out a mechanism-design exercise, they tend to have fewer inhibitions when introducing unrealistic instruments, compared with descriptively motivated theoretical exercises. A classic example is the role of integer games in Eric Maskin's (1999) canonical Nash-implementation mechanism.[6] In contrast, the competitive-equilibrium approach is more at ease with restricting contract spaces. The most obvious example is the classic textbook model, which restricts itself to linear prices without trying to derive this restriction from first principles.

To summarize, focus on a single objective and reluctance to limit contractual instruments are two characteristics of the mechanism-design approach. Kfir and I felt that when trying to understand whether "the market can attain quality search," these two characteristics would derail us from our mission and blind us to interesting aspects of the problem. We found competitive equilibrium's disinterested "bird's eye" mentality more fitting. Or was it no more than a childish reaction to the "Econ-CS" papers that gave us the impression that their authors were about to the enter the executive suite of some internet giant (some did)?[7]

And so now I'll tell you the story of our research, how we were determined to follow the competitive-equilibrium style, how we failed, how we ended up adopting the mechanism-design language, how our initial motivation did leave its imprint on the final product (published as Eliaz and Spiegler 2016), and why I think there are general lessons to be learned from this otherwise idiosyncratic experience.

Our theoretical argument can be conveyed with a simple example, so I'll stick to it throughout the chapter, resisting the temptation to explain how much more general our exercise really is. (I should add that my presentation here cheats a little bit; I have tweaked the formal exposition relative to our original working paper, for the sake of clarity.)

## Mozart or Stravinsky

Suppose our search-engine users are interested in classical music. They heard a piece of music on the radio while driving, or possibly as part of a film soundtrack. Having liked the piece, they would like to retrieve it. Unfortunately, they don't know the name of the piece; they can barely hum it. They will recognize it if they get to hear it again, but they cannot describe it.

However, our users are not all helpless. Some of them know the *name* of the piece's composer. For the sake of our example, suppose the universe of classical-music composers consists of only two, Mozart and Stravinsky. Some of our users are looking for a Mozart piece, while others are looking for a Stravinsky piece. Within each group, some can name the composer of the piece they are looking for. Accordingly, there are four types of users:

1. Type (Mozart, MOZART): The composer of this type's favorite piece is Mozart and the user can name him, and therefore he submits the specific query "MOZART."

2. Type (Stravinsky, STRAVINSKY): The composer of this type's favorite piece is Stravinsky and he can name him, and therefore he submits the specific query "STRAVINSKY."

3. (Mozart, CLASSICAL MUSIC): The composer of this type's favorite piece is Mozart but he can't name him, and therefore he submits the generic query "CLASSICAL MUSIC."

4. (Stravinsky, CLASSICAL MUSIC): The composer of this type's favorite piece is Stravinsky but he can't name him, and therefore he submits the generic query "CLASSICAL MUSIC."

I am using capital letters to indicate queries and lowercase letters to indicate the composer of the piece our user is looking for. I will also use the terms "queries" and "keywords" interchangeably.

The economic allocation problem is thus to give each of these types access to a "search pool" from which they can repeatedly sample specimens until they find what they are looking for. Formalize an "ideal search engine" as a function that assigns such a search pool to each query. Note that the search engine cannot distinguish between types 3 and 4 because they submit the same query. Therefore, there will be only three search pools, one for each of the queries MOZART, STRAVINSKY, and CLASSICAL MUSIC.

How does the user navigate inside his assigned search pool? Take the simplest model in the textbook: *random sequential search*. The user samples specimens in random order, until he finds what he likes. (Since we will deal with search pools that contain an infinite number of any given type of seller, the distinction between sequential search with and without replacement is irrelevant.) A user whose favorite composer is Stravinsky will repeatedly sample pieces of music from the pool. He will never choose a Mozart piece; and conditional on drawing a Stravinsky piece, there is some constant probability $q$ that he will select it and terminate the search.

This image is quite different from Google search, where alternatives are presented in a certain order, which affects the order by which the user inspects the alternatives. In this sense, the modeling approach I am describing here does *not* aim at a faithful description of Google search. Instead, it starts from the abstract notion of an "ideal search engine" as a function that assigns a search pool to search queries. It then looks at the simplest textbook model in the search theory literature: random sequential sampling in a stationary environment. This is a difference between "applied theory" and "pure theory" sensibilities.

Given the user's behavioral model, a search pool is fully described by its shares of Mozart and Stravinsky pieces. An ideal search engine will choose a composition for each search pool in a way that *minimizes the user's expected search time*.

The optimal search pool in response to the query MOZART will consist of Mozart pieces only. Likewise, the optimal search pool in response to the query STRAVINSKY will consist of Stravinsky pieces only. Recall that when a user encounters a piece by the right composer, he stops the search with probability $q$. The user's expected search time in either of these two pools will be

$$q \cdot 1 + q(1-q) \cdot 2 + \cdots = \frac{1}{q}$$

What about the search pool that the search engine designs in response to the generic query CLASSICAL MUSIC (I'll use CL as a convenient abbreviation for this query)? This pool should include pieces from both composers. The optimal composition will minimize the expected search time of users who submit this query:

$$\Pr(Mozart \mid CL)\frac{1}{q \cdot Share(Mozart)} + \Pr(Stravinsky \mid CL)\frac{1}{q \cdot Share(Stravinsky)}$$

In this formula, *Share(x)* means the fraction of $x$ pieces in the search pool, and $\Pr(x \mid w)$ is the probability that the user wants $x$ conditional on him submitting the query $w$. Solving this minimization problem is straightforward. The solution satisfies:

$$\frac{Share(Mozart)}{Share(Stravinsky)} = \sqrt{\frac{\Pr(Mozart \mid CL)}{\Pr(Stravinsky \mid CL)}}$$

This is a key observation. When the user submits the generic query, the ideal search engine faces uncertainty regarding the user's taste. To minimize the user's expected search time, the search engine should design a search pool in which the share of a composer is proportional to the *square root* of the fraction of this composer's fans in the population of users who submit the query. In particular, this means that the minority taste group in this population should be *overrepresented*. For example, when the fraction of Stravinsky fans among the users who submit CLASSICAL MUSIC is 20%, the share of Stravinsky pieces in the pool should be *one-third*:

$$\sqrt{\frac{20}{80}} = \frac{1/3}{2/3}$$

## A Competitive Market for Keywords

Suppose there are many sellers of Mozart pieces and *just as many* sellers of Stravinsky pieces. (We can think of a seller as a group of musicians who made a recording of a particular piece of classical music.) Each seller can serve any number of customers, but no seller can provide both types of product. The value of a successful transaction is 1 for all sellers.

The allocation problem is to assign sellers to search pools. This is a many-to-many allocation: multiple sellers are admitted to a given pool, and a given seller can be assigned to multiple pools. The allocation determines the composition of each search pool. For example, if 75% of Mozart sellers and 50% of Stravinsky sellers are allocated to the search pool corresponding to the query CLASSICAL MUSIC, then this pool will consist of 60% Mozart (because $75/(50 + 75) = 0.6$) and 40% Stravinsky.

We want to conceptualize a "sponsored search" engine that performs the allocation task via some kind of "competitive market." For every query there is a market price that a seller needs to pay if she wants to enter the search pool associated with this query. The price can be defined as a fixed entry fee, or equivalently—in the spirit of real-life sponsored search—as a *price per impression* that the seller will pay each time she is examined by a user in the pool she was admitted into. (The search engine cannot monitor whether an impression results in a transaction. Therefore, a price-per-transaction is infeasible.)

A *market equilibrium* consists of a price-per-impression for each keyword and a decision for each seller as to which keywords to pay for (recall that paying the price of a keyword is a necessary and sufficient condition for entering its associated search pool). There are two conditions for this pair to constitute a market equilibrium. First, all sellers earn zero profits. Second, no seller can earn strictly positive profits by paying equilibrium prices for some other bundle of keywords.

The zero-profit condition captures the intense competition among sellers as they attempt to enter search pools. The definition doesn't ask who receives the sellers' payments. We can assume it is the search engine, but the definition is silent on this issue. This is unlike the mechanism-design approach, which puts the designer at the forefront.

Kfir and I thought of this kind of definition as belonging to the tradition of competitive equilibrium. Not because there are clearly articulated supply and demand. Neither did our model introduce an explicit scarcity that presumably calls for a market allocation. The scarce resource is the users' time, but it lies in the background. Like the 1976 Rothschild-Stiglitz concept that served as our inspiration, the definition captures in "reduced form" the competitive pressures that sellers experience when trying to enter users' consideration sets.

An immediate consequence of the two conditions is that we can apply the zero-profit condition to each query separately. The equilibrium price-per-impression of each query is equal to the *conversion rate* experienced by the sellers who are admitted into the query's pool—namely, the probability that an impression in that pool will result in a transaction.

Kfir and I focused on *symmetric market equilibria*. In a symmetric equilibrium, all sellers of a given type make the same choices. Asymmetric equilibria were less appealing in our model, as they could "weaponize" the zero-profit condition to obtain results that disappear with various perturbations of the model.

### A First Welfare Theorem?

Does market equilibrium induce an optimal composition of the search pools associated with the various queries? If so, this would be a "first welfare theorem" specialized for our "market for keywords" setting, and sort of a theoretical "yes" to Brin and Page's 1998 question posed above.

The answer is trivially affirmative as far as the specific queries MOZART and STRAVINSKY are concerned. Users who submit these queries are homogeneous: all users who submit MOZART are looking for a Mozart piece, and all users who submit STRAVINSKY are looking for a Stravinsky piece. We can therefore allocate Mozart sellers to the MOZART pool and Stravinsky sellers to the STRAVINSKY pool. The market price-per-impression that induces zero profits for these sellers is $q$ for each of the two queries. No Stravinsky seller wants to pay this price for MOZART because the conversion rate it will experience in the MOZART pool is zero. Likewise, no Mozart seller wants to pay the market price of STRAVINSKY. So, the equilibrium conditions hold for the specific queries.

The situation is different with the generic query CLASSICAL MUSIC. The optimal search pool associated with this query must include both types of sellers. If we focus on *symmetric* equilibria, then *all* sellers should be in the pool, such that the fraction of Mozart sellers in it will be 50%. This will almost never be the optimal composition.

For the sake of the argument, suppose we *did* allow for asymmetric equilibria, such that not all sellers of a given type act the same. In particular, suppose that $m$ Mozart sellers and $s$ Stravinsky sellers choose to pay the market price of CLASSICAL MUSIC and thus enter its search pool. The conversion rate that each seller experiences in this pool should be equal to the market price. Let us see what this entails.

The random-sequential-search assumption means that every seller in the pool gets the same number of impressions. In order for all sellers' conversion rate to be the same, the number of transactions that each of them completes must be identical as well. Let's calculate this number for each type of seller. Suppose that the total number of users who submit the query CLASSICAL MUSIC is $n$ (m, s and n are all large numbers). Then, a Mozart seller gets the following number of transactions:

$$\frac{n \cdot \Pr(Mozart \,|\, CL)}{m}$$

Likewise, a Stravinsky seller gets the following number:

$$\frac{n \cdot \Pr(Stravinsky \,|\, CL)}{s}$$

The requirement that these numbers are identical translates to the following equation:

$$\frac{m}{s} = \frac{\Pr(Mozart \,|\, CL)}{\Pr(Stravinsky \,|\, CL)}$$

But the ratio $m/s$ is exactly the ratio between the shares of Mozart and Stravinsky sellers in the pool. That is,

$$\frac{m}{s} = \frac{Share(Mozart)}{Share(Stravinsky)}$$

We see that $Share(x)$ must be *proportional* to the fraction of $x$ fans in the population of users who submit CLASSICAL MUSIC. But recall that an ideal search engine requires $Share(x)$ to be proportional to the *square root* of this fraction. In other words, if $m$ and $s$ were selected to implement the optimal pool composition, Mozart sellers would be earning more than Stravinsky sellers, because the latter would be overrepresented in the pool relative to their fan base. Competitive forces would then lead Mozartians to crowd out the Stravinskians.

The conclusion is that a competitive market equilibrium cannot sustain the search pool that an ideal search engine would generate—even if we allow for asymmetric equilibria. We can't get our first welfare theorem. There is a fundamental tension between search-time minimization and the zero-profit condition that dictates competitive allocation of sellers into search pools.

## Broad Match

Let us now tweak our competitive market for keywords, by redefining the entitlement that paying for a keyword gives. Suppose that when a seller pays the market price for the keyword MOZART or STRAVINSKY, she is also granted *probabilistic entry* into the search pool CLASSICAL MUSIC.

This indirect access is in the spirit of the "vocabulary expansion" function of search engines, bridging between supply and users' imperfectly described demand. When someone submits the query CLASSICAL MUSIC, there is some probability that what he is looking for is a Mozart piece. Just as when someone Googles "Kefir Elias," there is a good chance that he is actually looking for material on Kfir Eliaz. It is therefore helpful to form some linkage between the query "Kefir Elias" and the objects that are more obviously associated with the query "Kfir Eliaz."

Linkages of this sort are known in the industry as "broad match." Let us hijack this term and apply it to our model of a competitive market for keywords. This means adding the following component to the model: a function that assigns to every pair of queries $w$ and $v$ a number

$b(w, v)$ between 0 and 1. The interpretation is that if a seller pays the market price for $w$, she is admitted into the search pool of query $v$ with probability $b(w, v)$.

This is the only change in the model: an extended definition of what paying the market price of a keyword entails in terms of admission into search pools. Under the original definition, a seller is admitted into the pool associated with a query if and only if she pays the market price for that same query. The broad match function means that a seller can enter a search pool associated with one query even if she pays the market price of a different query.

For example, suppose that all Mozart sellers pay the market price for MOZART and CLASSICAL MUSIC, whereas all Stravinsky sellers pay the market price for STRAVINSKY only. Then, the fraction of Stravinsky sellers in the search pool of CLASSICAL MUSIC will be (using abbreviations for the three queries):

$$\frac{b(STR, CL)}{b(STR, CL) + b(MOZ, CL) + b(CL, CL)}$$

The remaining fraction will consist of Mozart sellers.

The definition of market equilibrium remains the same: sellers must earn zero profits, and they should not be able to find a more profitable bundle of keywords. The only thing that changes is the entitlement that paying the market price of a keyword gives. This modified entitlement is defined by the broad match function $b$. In this sense, the broad match function is analogous to the endowments in the classical exchange-economy model.

## A "Second Welfare Theorem"?

The introduction of broad match into the model raises a question in the spirit of the second welfare theorem: Is there a specification of the broad match function $b$ for which the optimal composition of the ideal search engine can be sustained in *symmetric* market equilibrium?

The answer turns out to be—it depends. More precisely, the following inequality is a necessary and sufficient condition. Suppose that in the general population of users, there are more Mozart fans than Stravinsky fans. Then, this is what the inequality looks like:

$$\frac{\textit{Share of Mozart fans}}{\textit{Share of Stravinsky fans}} \cdot BC \leq 1$$

$$(*)$$

The first term on the left-hand side is clear: that is the ratio of Mozart and Stravinsky fans in the general user population. But what is BC? This is a measure of the similarity between the query distributions that characterize Mozart and Stravinsky fans. It is known as the *Bhattacharyya Coefficient*, following Bhattacharyya (1943)—hence the abbreviation BC—and defined as follows:[8]

$$\left(\sum_{w}\sqrt{\Pr(w\,|\,Mozart)\Pr(w\,|\,Stravinsky)}\right)^{2}$$

In this definition of BC, $w$ is a query; $\Pr(w\,|\,x)$ is the probability that a user who wants $x$ submits the query $w$. BC takes values between 0 and 1. It increases with the similarity between the query distributions of Mozart and Stravinsky fans. Put differently, BC measures how informative users' queries are of their preference type. For example, when the query is fully informative, $\Pr(w\,|\,Mozart)=0$ or $\Pr(w\,|\,Stravnisky)=0$ for every $w$, such that BC is zero. At the other extreme, if the query is entirely uninformative, $\Pr(w\,|\,Mozart)=\Pr(w\,|\,Stravinsky)$ for every $w$, such that BC becomes

$$\sum_{w}\Pr(w\,|\,Mozart)=1$$

The BC formula applies to any conditional query distribution. In our simple example, BC is reduced to the simple product

$$\Pr(CL\,|\,Mozart)\cdot\Pr(CL\,|\,Stravinsky)$$

Inequality (*) conveys the following lesson. If users' queries are sufficiently informative about their preferences, and if the preference distribution is not too skewed, then the search pools that an ideal search engine would devise can be sustained in symmetric market equilibrium, provided that we design the broad match function appropriately. In this sense, we have a qualified second welfare theorem.

The reason broad match can help is that it dissociates the considerations that dictate the optimal composition of search pools from the competitive pressures that govern sellers' access to the pools. Recall that the former consideration requires overrepresentation of Stravinsky sellers in the CLASSICAL MUSIC pool. Stravinsky sellers who pay for STRAVINSKY and enter the CLASSICAL MUSIC pool thanks to broad match give the necessary boost to the representation of Stravinsky in that pool. At the same time, the conversion rate that these sellers get from STRAVINSKY is lower than in the previous, "narrow match" case because now they also encounter Mozart fans who submitted the query

CLASSICAL MUSIC. If there are too many of those users, then Mozart sellers, exploiting broad match, will become too eager to pay the market price for the keyword STRAVINSKY. As a result, they will disrupt the optimal allocation by diluting the STRAVINSKY pool. Inequality (*) prevents this scenario from materializing.

Kfir and I went further and constructed the broad match function and the equilibrium prices-per-impression of all queries in the market equilibrium that sustains the optimal search pools, when inequality (*) holds. For example, we showed how BC enters the equilibrium price formula: as users' queries become more informative, the price-per-impression of keywords rises across the board.

A happy ending?

## Primitives and Solution Concepts

Only as far as Kfir and I in our "research lab" were concerned. But in the summer of 2013 came the time to tell other people about it in seminar or conference talks, as well as in ten-minute personal chats over coffee.

This proved to be not so happy. Time and again, we found it hard to communicate our model and our findings. The market equilibrium concept itself was difficult to get across. Not because it is formally complicated; it is in fact quite simple to describe, as we saw earlier. It is certain that our written exposition back then was muddled. But we had enough experience with seminar presentations and one-on-one chats to be able to explain what we were doing in an intelligible manner. Yet, unlike other occasions with other papers, we felt we were failing at that.

Of course, this is not interesting by itself, but I believe our communication failure had a broader significance. The difficulty in getting the message across efficiently—"twenty five words or less," as the villainous movie producer Griffin Mill demands from screenwriters who try to pitch him a story in Robert Altman's fabulous 1992 film *The Player*— seemed to lie in economic theorists' guarded attitude to any theoretical exercise that involves a nonstandard solution concept.

Most economic models have two built-in parts: a description of the model's *primitives* and the *solution concept* that one applies to these primitives. The culture of economic theory welcomes a proliferation of primitives but dislikes a proliferation of solution concepts; it prefers to take solution concepts off the shelf. If a paper wants to introduce a new solution concept, it must make a big fuss around it. The concept is expected to apply to a general, abstract class of models. As a result, the paper ends up being *about* that solution concept. Casually introducing a new solution concept into a paper that is nominally about something else is considered poor form.

Economic theorists have become extremely efficient in communicating models to each other. This efficiency depends on having an effective language for defining primitives and a small set of handy solution concepts. Confronted with a new solution concept, theorists switch to a slower, more critical, and less efficient reception mode.

Our solution concept was new-ish. Conceptually, it was traditional. On the other hand, it wasn't bread-and-butter competitive equilibrium because there were no clearly articulated supply, demand, or endowments. Rather, our approach was inspired by Rothschild and Stiglitz's 1976 paper: they had invented a new solution concept in the *spirit* of competitive equilibrium, specialized for an insurance market model that departs from linear prices. Their concept was later applied to other settings, but it was initially introduced in that specific context of an insurance market. Likewise, Kfir and I wanted to define a solution concept in the spirit of competitive equilibrium, specialized for a "market for keywords" model. In the contemporary culture of economic theory, an exercise that introduces new primitives *and* a new solution concept is harder to get across.

From a broader perspective, which goes far beyond our little study of search engines, the competitive-equilibrium approach has a built-in limitation. Historically, the textbook definition was developed by Arrow, Debreu, and others in the context of rigidly structured market models. Agents in these models arrive with endowments or technologies, and prices must be linear. At the time, this seemed like the entire universe of economics, so economists didn't internalize its narrow scope. In this sense, game theory is much more flexible: its language can accommodate more diverse primitives. As a result, when theorists like Rothschild and Stiglitz wanted to carry the spirit of competitive equilibrium over to insurance markets with nonlinear pricing, they felt a need to invent a new solution concept, whereas a game theorist would need only write a new game form.

Recently, Michael Richter and Ariel Rubinstein developed an interesting research agenda that addresses this limitation. They argue that "competitive equilibrium" is a modeling attitude with much broader scope than what we have been conditioned to believe. Their approach (which they launched in Richter and Rubinstein 2015) was to present an abstraction of the competitive-equilibrium model that would go beyond the standard exchange/production economy and beyond prices as regulators of economic activity. This was more grandiose than our own exercise, but it had a similar underlying impulse.

Our audiences' distrust of our nonstandard solution concept was accompanied by the more general suspicion of models that involve hand-waving about invisible hands. If some competitive force is going to bring our sellers' profits to zero, then why won't we write down a game-theoretic model in which sellers have explicit moves that capture this force?

Ultimately, it wasn't clear to our audiences why we were so keen to abandon the mechanism-design approach. Under that approach, we would need to innovate only at the level of primitives: a new allocation problem that is concerned with assigning sellers to search pools. We wouldn't need to innovate at the level of the solution concept. Given the presentational advantages of this approach, our willful refusal to take it seemed annoying.

### Conversion

Faced with such a clear communication failure, Kfir and I didn't even bother to submit our paper for publication. Instead, we decided to soften our intransigence and describe our exercise entirely in mechanism-design terms.

We started with so-called (anonymous) direct mechanisms. In this telling, every seller reports whether she is of a Mozart or Stravinsky type. The mechanism responds to every report with a probabilistic assignment to search pools and a per-impression fee. Given the reporting strategies of other sellers, each seller can compute the number of impressions and transactions she will experience in each pool, and use it to evaluate her possible reports. The mechanism is incentive-compatible if no seller wants to misreport her type given that all other sellers are truth-telling.

And that's it! Of course, this description seems so much shorter than my earlier pitch in this chapter because I've already presented the primitives. So the proper comparison is between this conventional definition of incentive-compatible direct mechanisms and our earlier definition of market equilibrium. The familiarity of standard mechanism-design definitions contributes to the efficiency in communicating our idea.

The most interesting comparison between the two approaches concerns the *questions* that each of them generates. The mechanism-design description immediately suggests the following question: Are optimal search pools implementable by an incentive-compatible mechanism, even without imposing the restriction that sellers earn zero profits? The answer turns out to be an unqualified *yes*, using a basic result from the theory of mechanism design due to Rochet (1987). This question had no counterpart in the competitive-equilibrium version.

When we ask whether the search engine can implement the optimal search pools and at the same time extract the sellers' entire profits, we get a problem that is formally equivalent to the question we posed to our competitive-equilibrium model. And indeed, the answer is the same: the twin objectives of implementing optimal search and extracting sellers' profits are attainable if and only if the inequality (*) holds. But these twin objectives sound rather strange in a mechanism-design context. If the designer is the search engine, why should it regard search-time minimization as a primary motive? And if the designer is a benevolent social planner, why should it care about extracting advertisers' surplus? This is a neat demonstration of how the mechanism-design approach leads the analyst to identify with a specific designer and refrain from asking questions that do not correspond to the designer's natural motivations.

To maintain the interpretation of the designer as a search engine and to rationalize its interest in implementing optimal search, we can assume that it also collects access fees from the search engine's *users*. Their willingness to pay these fees will depend on the quality of their search experience. The lower the search time, the higher the access fee the search engine can charge them. This is what Kfir and I did. We rewrote our model of user behavior as a rational search model (instead of the mechanical sequential search process that we originally assumed) and introduced user access fees. In this manner, the search engine doesn't have twin objectives but a single, conventional one: maximizing profits. But that's exactly the kind of modeling strategy we had originally wanted to avoid. Not only does it carry the "unpaid Google employee" mindset further, but it also leads to something that we *don't* see in reality: user access fees. It is a feature that is demanded not by realism but by the mechanism-design modeling strategy.

Another problem that the mechanism-design pitch demands is finding "indirect," auction-like mechanisms, to complement the analytically convenient but unrealistic direct mechanisms. As we had expected, analyzing Nash equilibria in such auction games forces the analyst to consider all kinds of deviations from equilibrium play. Some of these deviations make sense, while others are excess baggage that one must accept if one is going to apply Nash equilibrium to the game. It's part of the deal, but it's a distraction that the competitive-equilibrium approach avoided.

Finally, once we learn that the search engine cannot always implement the "first-best" (maximizing and fully extracting social surplus), it is conventional in mechanism design to look for the "second-best": what is the maximal profit that the search engine can generate with an incentive-compatible mechanism? Once again, it is a question that doesn't arise in the competitive-equilibrium framework. This is a question we knowingly left open.

After we rewrote our paper as a strict mechanism-design exercise, without any reference to competitive equilibrium, it became a much easier expositional task. There were fewer misunderstandings, fewer lapses of communication. The stark assumptions we made exposed us to valid criticisms about the limited scope of our exercise—especially if one expected it to be a model of Google search, an expectation abetted by the mechanism-design style, unlike the more detached competitive-equilibrium approach. But it was easier to convey what we were doing.

## Recap: Why Did We Eschew Mechanism Design in the First Place?

The research directions that the switch to a mechanism-design approach forced us to consider demonstrate the reservations about the approach that had motivated us from the beginning. Let us recall these concerns.

First, the mechanism-design approach leads the analyst to identify with the designer and therefore ask questions that are of importance for the designer, possibly at the expense of questions that are more interesting for an outside observer. And indeed, we found ourselves reformulating the problem in terms of a profit-maximizing designer.

Second, according to this mechanism-design protocol, when the designer is unable to implement her "first-best," figuring out the "second-best" seems like an obvious next step. The pressure to pose such a question under a competitive-equilibrium approach is weaker.

Third, another question that arises naturally under the mechanism-design approach is the quest for realistic, auction-like indirect mechanisms. But Nash equilibrium analysis of such mechanisms forces the analyst to consider stability with respect to deviations that aren't always natural or interesting.

Fourth, the mechanism-design perspective impels the analyst to expand the set of instruments at the designer's disposal, even if these instruments aren't realistic. And indeed, to reformulate our original question as a profit maximization problem for the search engine, we were led to introduce unrealistic user access fees into our model.

As to the crowding out of interesting questions, the very notion of broad match may be a case in point. The large Econ-CS literature on sponsored search, with its mechanism-design orientation, almost never addressed broad match. The overwhelming majority of works on auction-theoretic aspects of keyword pricing focus on the case of a *single* query. Very few address the case of multiple queries and the notion of broad match that arises in them. Those that do typically view broad match as a means for thickening auction markets, or examine the computational complexity of bidding in a multi-keyword environment.[9] Broad match as a fundamental feature of search engines that enables them to fulfill the "vocabulary expansion" role—we found none of that in this sizeable literature. I believe that the mechanism-design perspective is responsible for this neglect. It creates this tunnel vision that pushes the researcher to go deep in certain directions at the expense of others.

## Epilogue

After the mechanism-design expositional overhaul, Kfir and I submitted our paper to the *American Economic Review* at the start of 2015, and our paper was rather quickly accepted for publication. In material terms, this was a successful outcome.

And yet, looking back, I think I still prefer the older, competitive-equilibrium version. The mechanism-design gambit led us to ask questions that appear "natural" through that particular prism. However, it may have muted other, more interesting problems that revolve around a question I still find fascinating: *Can market forces regulate effective organization of human knowledge?*

By accepting the mechanism-design mindset, Kfir and I were eventually, despite our initial intentions, acting like Google minions. The detached, bird's-eye view of competitive equilibrium seems to buy you a certain freedom and independence that the more practically minded "market design" culture doesn't. When the great transformation from competitive equilibrium to market design is complete and the dust settles, we should recognize this subtle cultural change as an important by-product.

# 9    A Placebo Trilogy

Academic researchers are specialists: they develop expertise in a particular area of study. Therefore, we expect their work to exhibit some amount of repetitiveness. Economic theorists who develop an expertise in a subfield are likely to revisit the same class of models or economic environments.

In this chapter I address a different kind of recurrence in theorists' work; a more personal and "artistic" recurrence of themes or mottos that are in principle independent of modeling choices or substantive economic questions.[1] I am thinking of the analogue of things like the Coen brothers' recurring theme of "evil meets stupidity"—or even smaller-scale mannerisms, like the image of a fat old man yelling at the protagonist from behind a large desk, which appears in many of their films. These are motifs, themes, or schticks that, for whatever reason, the artist keeps returning to, but placed in such different contexts that this ceases to be a simple matter of repeating oneself.

Within the world of economic theory, a rare example of a theorist's attempt to introspect about "recurring motifs" in his work is Avinash Dixit's semi-humorous piece "My System of Work (Not!)":[2]

As you can see, my approach to research is too opportunistic to have a constant direction. But taking stock of it for the purpose of writing this piece, I could see a recurrent if not dominant theme. Scale economies and sunk costs keep appearing in my papers with great regularity. Imperfect competition is the norm, and market equilibria are not socially optimal (but government interventions have more subtle effects than naive intuition would suggest, and may actually make matters worse).

If you think that the above quote holds no interest ("Who cares if you like to put sunk costs in your models? What are you, Fellini?"), Dixit offers the following broader interpretation of his professional mannerisms:

And therein lies an irony. The left-wing critics of the late 1960s and 1970s, who influenced many youngsters when I started out, reserved their strongest criticism for the perfectly competitive equilibrium of the neoclassical system. Of course they did little by the way of offering a viable alternative. It has been the unexciting incremental work, to which I have contributed a little, that has built into a major shift in our understanding of how the economic system operates when the assumptions of neoclassical economics fail.

Now this is an observation with interesting political connotations. The "personal tics" of sunk costs and economies of scale suddenly become Dixit's way of expressing a "third way": a moderately progressive approach to economics, against the background of radical left-wing progressivism that surrounded him during his formative student years.

This chapter is an attempt at a more systematic introspection, using my own work for raw material. I hope this won't come across as too self-indulgent. I am perfectly aware that few would take intrinsic interest in recurring mottos in an economic theorist's oeuvre. I am not Fellini. Nevertheless, I think that whoever takes an interest in the culture of economic theory may find something to learn from such an introspective exercise. And I hope the examples themselves have entertainment value.

I refer to my recurring motto as the *placebo theme*. It is the idea that certain actions or products may have zero intrinsic value but generate stable demand nonetheless, due to some error of reasoning committed by economic agents. I have been fascinated by this idea for many years and I keep returning to it. I'd like to share three of these examples, which are based on a trio of papers (Spiegler 2006, 2013, 2016). Though different from each other in terms of economic substance and modeling technique, they all share the placebo theme. I conclude by speculating about the political and psychological significance of this fixation.

## Consumers: The Dieter's Dilemma (2016)

We are all familiar with the motto "correlation doesn't imply causation." Economists use it to admonish or make fun of laypeople (or, even better, other scientists) for jumping into conclusions about causal effects from observed correlations. Yet, in the spirit of behavioral economics, shouldn't we also try to *model* how such people reason, and what the behavioral implications of confusing correlation with causation might be? Of course we should. So here's a story.

Imagine a population of identical consumers. Each consumer chooses whether to buy a food supplement, thinking this might have an effect on her long-term health. In reality, the food supplement has no such effect: the consumer has a 50% chance of being healthy, independently of whether she consumes the supplement. In the population of consumers, we will see two statistically independent variables: consumers' choices and their health outcome. However, if consumers realized their choice has no effect on their health, they would all refrain from buying the costly supplement, and so there would be no variation in the consumer-behavior variable.

Now add a third variable to our story, the blood level of some chemical—the like of cholesterol, vitamin D, or serotonin. In reality, the chemical blood level is determined by the other two variables: it is abnormal if and only if the consumer's underlying health is poor *and* she doesn't consume the supplement. Since the consumer doesn't care about the chemical blood level per se, and since it plays no role in the mapping from her action to the health outcome, the consumer should ignore this variable altogether.

However, suppose that our consumer believes that the three variables are causally related in a way that can be described by the following diagram:

$$s \rightarrow c \rightarrow h$$

In this diagram, $s$ stands for the supplement consumption quantity, $c$ stands for the chemical blood level and $h$ stands for the health outcome. In what follows, consumption quantity can take only the values 0 and 1. Likewise, good and bad health are denoted $h = 1$ and $h = 0$. Normal and abnormal chemical levels are denoted $c = N$ and $c = A$.

This diagram is an example of a *directed acyclic graph* representing a causal model: $s$ is perceived to be a direct cause of $c$, which is in turn perceived to be a direct cause of $h$, and there are no other causal transmissions. There is a wonderful literature at the intersection of artificial intelligence and statistics that applies directed acyclic graphs to probabilistic and causal inference. Judea Pearl's recent *The Book of Why* is a highly recommended entry point.[3] The model I am about to describe makes use of very basic concepts from this literature.

Our consumer forms a belief about the health implications of her consumption decision by *fitting her causal model* to objective observational data. This means measuring the empirical distribution of chemical blood levels conditional on supplement consumption, as well as the empirical distribution of health outcomes conditional on the chemical blood level, and putting them together in accordance with the consumer's causal model. Formally, the consumer's subjective probability of $h$ conditional on $s$ is

$$\Pr(c = N \mid s) \cdot \Pr(h = 1 \mid c = N) + \Pr(c = A \mid s) \cdot \Pr(h = 1 \mid c = A)$$

The consumer regards this conditional probability as a causal quantity, measuring the causal effect of her action on the probability of being in good health. As a result, her subjective estimate of the health effect of buying the supplement is

$$[\Pr(c = N \mid s = 1) - \Pr(c = N \mid s = 0)] \cdot [\Pr(h = 1 \mid c = N) - \Pr(h = 1 \mid c = A)]$$

All the terms in this formula can be measured from the objective empirical joint distribution over the variables $s$, $c$, and $h$. However, the formula delivers a *wrong* estimate of the causal effect of $s$ on $h$, because it is the result of imposing a wrong causal model on objective data, and therefore a wrong causal interpretation of observed correlations.

The correct causal model that underlies the objective joint distribution over the three variables is represented by the following graph:

$$s \rightarrow c \leftarrow h$$

The consumer's subjective model inverts the true causal relation between chemical levels and health. In reality, the chemical level is a consequence of the consumer's health condition, yet in his own mind the direction of causality is flipped. In other words, the consumer is committing a *reverse causality* fallacy.

Let us now compute the terms in the formula that describes the consumer's estimated health effect of buying the supplement. Denote $\Pr(s = 1) = q$. This is the fraction of consumers in the population who buy the supplement.

- $\Pr(c = N \mid s = 1) = 1$. Because by assumption, each consumer in the population ensures a normal chemical level if she consumes the supplement.
- $\Pr(c = N \mid s = 0) = 0.5$. Because by assumption, if a consumer doesn't buy the supplement, her chemical level is determined by her underlying health condition. Since half the consumers in the population are healthy, it follows that half the consumers who do not buy the supplement have a normal chemical level.
- $\Pr(h = 1 \mid c = A) = 0$. Because by assumption, the consumer must be unhealthy in order for her chemical to be abnormal.

- The fourth term, $\Pr(h=1\,|\,c=N)$, requires a more elaborate calculation. The fraction of consumers with normal chemical blood level is

$$\Pr(s=1)+\Pr(s=0)\cdot\Pr(h=1)=q+(1-q)\cdot 0.5$$

The fraction of consumers who are healthy and have a normal chemical level is 0.5. Therefore, by Bayes' rule,

$$\Pr(h=1|c=N)=\frac{0.5}{q+(1-q)\cdot 0.5}=\frac{1}{1+q}$$

Plugging these four terms in the formula, we obtain the consumer's estimated effect of buying the supplement on the probability of being in good health:

$$[1-0.5]\cdot\left[\frac{1}{1+q}-0\right]=\frac{1}{2+2q}$$

Two things about this formula are noteworthy. First, it is strictly above zero, which is the objective health effect of buying the supplement. In other words, the consumer's reverse causality error leads her to assign value to something with no intrinsic value.

Second, the consumer's subjective estimate of the health effect of her action depends on the action frequencies in the *consumer population*. This dependence would never arise if the consumer had a correct model: by definition, the conditional objective probability $\Pr(y\,|\,x)$ is invariant to the marginal probability $\Pr(x)$. This invariance does not extend to the *subjective* conditional distribution, which is based on a wrong causal model.

Moreover, the formula is *decreasing* in $q$. The larger the fraction of consumers who buy the supplement, the lower its subjective value. For example, suppose that the cost of buying the supplement is 0.4. Then, as long as $q<0.25$, consumers will conclude that the benefit from buying the supplement exceeds its cost. Conversely, when $q>0.25$, consumers will conclude that the cost exceeds the benefit. This suggests a natural *equilibrium* characterization of subjectively optimal behavior: when $q=0.25$, all consumers are indifferent between the two actions because the estimated benefit of buying the supplement is equal to its cost. Therefore, the pattern in which 25% of the consumer population purchase the supplement is stable.

We have thus learned two lessons from this example. First, reverse causality can lead consumers to assign value to intrinsically worthless products. Second, subjective optimization under reverse causality needs to be analyzed as an equilibrium phenomenon, even though we are dealing with *individual* decision-making.

I am proud of this little parable, which I called *the dieter's dilemma*. With it, I managed to produce a coherent description of a decision-maker who "mistakes correlation for causation." In Spiegler (2016), I developed a broader modeling framework out of this little example, which put the language of directed acyclic graphs to productive use and enabled me to study in greater generality behavioral implications of causal misperceptions. Yet it all started with this "placebo" story about the poor consumer who throws good money at a no-good remedy.

### Industries: The Market for Quacks (2006)

Our next story turns from the individual consumer, contemplating the purchase of an intrinsically worthless product, to an entire industry devoted to selling such products.[4]

Imagine a population of identical consumers having some underlying problem. Every consumer is willing to pay 1 for anything that will fix her problem. The consumers enter a market with $n$ revenue-maximizing firms that propose solutions to their problem. Firms incur an arbitrarily small cost when selling their products. Each consumer must choose one of the $n+1$ available alternatives: the firms' products and the outside option ("doing nothing"). The probability that a consumer's problem is fixed is $q$, independently for each consumer, and—most importantly—independently of the action she takes. In particular, firms' products have no advantage over the outside option! For this reason, I refer to the firms as "quacks" and to this industry as a "market for quacks." If consumers understood how this market works, they would have no business entering it: in order to turn a profit, firms would have to charge a strictly positive price, and yet the outside option is free of charge and offers consumers the same quality. Therefore, the market for quacks would be inactive if all market agents were individually rational.

Every reader will think of her own real-life analogue of this market for quacks. For some, many kinds of alternative medicine would qualify. This is actually trickier in practice because of placebo effects: a patient's mere belief in the healing power of a potential remedy may trigger physiological processes that effectively endow it with actual healing powers. My example assumes away such placebo effects. A more indirect parallel (and an obviously more important one) is with the market for active money management. A strong form of the *efficient market hypothesis* maintains that since market prices of financial assets reveal all underlying information, active money managers have no advantage over a passive index fund. From this perspective, active money managers are "quacks" relative to the outside option, which is a relevant index fund.

Back to the parable. Assume the firms play a simultaneous-move game: each firm independently chooses a product price between 0 and 1. This is the script of the textbook model of Bertrand competition. The difference is in how consumers make their choices. In the standard model, they correctly perceive that all firms sell the same product and · know how to evaluate this product. If the product had value relative to the outside option, they would choose to buy from the cheaper firm, as long as its price is below the product's value.

In contrast, in the current model, consumers rely on a *sampling procedure* to evaluate alternatives. Each consumer obtains an "anecdote" about each of the $n+1$ alternatives. An anecdote about an alternative is an independent random draw from the binary lottery that is associated with it: success in fixing a consumer's problem with probability $q$, and failure with probability $1-q$. Having gathered her $n+1$ anecdotes, the consumer chooses the best alternative in her sample. This means choosing the cheapest among all successful alternatives in the sample. If the sample contains no success story, the consumer opts out. Some tie-breaking rule is needed in case of ties in the sample. Although this is immaterial, for the present purposes it is simplest to assume that the consumer breaks ties between a firm and the outside option in favor of the firm.

The consumers' choice rule captures in a stylized manner two familiar psychological biases. First, the consumer behaves as if she believes that a small sample is representative of the underlying probability distribution. In particular, if the consumer hears a success story about one firm, she acts as if she believes that the firm will fix her problem with certainty. This type of exaggerated inference from small samples was studied by Tversky and Kahneman (1971) who gave it the ironic name "the law of small numbers." Second, anecdotes are by nature rich with contextual detail, and this makes them more memorable and affective than dry statistical data. This "vividness" of anecdotes makes them more likely to sway impressionable decision-makers, against their better judgment.

The consumers' choice model defines the payoff function in the firms' simultaneous-move game. For instance, when the firms' prices satisfy

$p_n > p_{n-1} > \ldots > p_1$, firm 1's market share is $q(1-q)$. The reason is that the firm's clientele consists of consumers who heard a success story about its own product and a bad anecdote about the outside option. Whether or not they heard a good anecdote about other products is irrelevant, because they are more expensive. The firm's revenue is $p_1 \cdot q(1-q)$. By the same logic, firm 2's revenue is $p_2 \cdot q(1-q)^2$. For any $k > 2$, firm $k$'s revenue is $p_k \cdot q(1-q)^k$. Since the firms are conventional revenue-maximizing players who play a simultaneous-move game, using Nash equilibrium to describe a stable outcome of their strategic interaction is also conventional.

Looking at the expression for firms' market share, we can develop an alternative interpretation for consumer demand, which is entirely consistent with conventional rationality. While we assumed that firms sell an objectively homogeneous product (which happens to be worthless), suppose instead that they sell *differentiated* products, for which consumers have idiosyncratic tastes. For each consumer and each alternative, the consumer values the alternative at 1 with independent probability $q$ and at 0 with probability $1-q$. In other words, $q$ is the probability that the consumer likes the alternative. From this point of view, $q$ is a parameter that determines the distribution of consumer valuations. These valuations reflect intrinsic, subjective tastes, rather than random estimates of commonly valued, objective quality.

This picture of consumer demand is formally equivalent to our sampling-based procedure. Therefore, Nash equilibrium analysis of firms' behavior will be the same as if they were facing rational consumers with differentiated demand parameterized by $q$. In this sense, there is nothing really "new" in the market-for-quacks model. What is unusual is the interpretation of consumer demand and the normative conclusions one draws from the market equilibrium analysis. Note that in many settings, the differentiated-taste reinterpretation will be patently absurd (can we imagine it being relevant when firms are money managers?) and therefore only useful as a purely formal analogy.

There is a unique Nash equilibrium in this game, which is therefore symmetric. Firms play a mixed strategy: a continuous probability distribution over the interval $[(1-q)^{n-1}, 1]$. The exact distribution does not matter. What *does* matter is two immediate conclusions we can draw from what we already know.

First, the market for quacks is active. Indeed, the industry profits it generates in equilibrium are equal to $nq(1-q)^n$. Why is that? Mixed-strategy Nash equilibrium requires that every price in the interval

$[(1-q)^{n-1}, 1]$ is optimal for a firm against the mixed strategies played by its rivals. In particular, the price $p=1$ must be optimal. It is easy to calculate the market share that this price generates. When a firm charges $p=1$, it is the most expensive alternative in the market. Therefore, only consumers who hear a good anecdote about this firm and a bad anecdote about each of the other $n$ alternatives will pick the firm. This implies a market share—and therefore a revenue—of $q(1-q)^n$. This is the payoff that an individual firm earns in equilibrium, and there are $n$ such firms in the market.

When we examine the expression for equilibrium industry profits, we see they are increasing in the number of firms $n$ as long as it is below some critical level (which can be awfully large if $q$ is small). How can greater competition lead to higher industry profits? Well, in the market for quacks, supply creates its own demand. The larger the number of firms, the higher the chances that a consumer will hear a good anecdote about one of them and decide to enter the market on the strength of this anecdote. This "aggregate demand" effect is countered by the standard competitive effect (the larger the number of firms, the lower the expected price they charge), but for low $n$, the former effect dominates.

The second interesting observation is that when $q$ is close to zero—that is, when the consumers' underlying problem is nearly hopeless—equilibrium prices in this market for quacks will be very high, close to the "monopoly price" of 1. The reason is simple. When a firm gauges the competitive forces it faces, it cares about the number of good anecdotes in the consumer's sample. When $q$ is small, this number will be small: with high probability, the firm will be effectively a monopolist if the consumer hears a good anecdote about it. Therefore, the firm faces very little effective competition, which drives its price upward. The differentiated-taste reinterpretation of the model helps clarifying this effect: a small $q$ corresponds to a market for highly differentiated products, such that a consumer who likes one product is unlikely to find a substitute.

The market equilibrium when $q$ is close to zero reminded me of the phenomenon of *guruism* (in the derogatory sense). Many consumers opt out entirely because they fail to hear a good story about any market alternative. But each firm attracts a small coterie of fans, who see value in the firm and no value in any other alternative. The firm can exploit this fan base and charge high prices from them, which the fans are happy to pay because they see no substitute.

To summarize the lessons from this parable, when consumers' value judgments are based on naïve extrapolation from anecdotes, equilibrium in the market for quacks turns firms into charlatans who command undeserved fees. When the consumers' problem is nearly hopeless, these charlatans become "gurus." Industry profits do not represent value added: they are a pure wealth transfer from consumers to firms. Moreover, this welfare loss for consumers can increase with the number of firms. Quite a market. Are some real-life industries essentially "markets for quacks"?

## Voters: Placebo Reforms (2013)

For our final story, let us turn from consumers evaluating market alternatives to voters evaluating policymakers. Although I use the term "voters," there will be no explicit model of the electoral process. Rather, "voters" are in the background, exerting an accountability pressure on policymakers.

The model is dynamic. At every time period $t = 1, 2, 3, \ldots$, a distinct policymaker chooses an action that may affect the evolution of a variable of public interest—say, GDP. Let's use $x(t)$ to denote the value of GDP at time $t$.

Two of the available actions are salient, and the public recognizes them as *interventions*. Let's call them $s$ and $r$. Taking such an action $a$ at time $t$ implies that at every subsequent period $t' > t$ until some future policymaker chooses an intervention,

$$x(t') = x(t'-1) + b_a + u_a(t') - u_a(t'-1)$$

We need to explain what $b_a$ and $u_a$ are. The term $b_a$ is a deterministic trend parameter associated with the action $a$. The term $u_a(t')$ represents the period-$t'$ realization of a random noise variable that takes two possible values, $-k_a$ and $+k_a$, with equal probability (independently across time periods). Prior to the first intervention, $x$ evolves as if one of the actions $s$ or $r$ was taken at period 0. The subtraction of $u_a(t'-1)$ means that the stochastic process exhibits *mean reversion*: shocks are transient and do not affect the future evolution of $x$.

Suppose the trend parameters are $b_s = \varepsilon$ and $b_r = 1$, where $\varepsilon > 0$ is arbitrarily small. The noise parameters satisfy $0 < k_s < 1$ and $k_r > 3$. This means that the intervention $s$ is a relatively *safe* action that induces nearly zero growth and carries small fluctuations around this trend, whereas the intervention $r$ is a *risky* action that induces a larger growth rate as well as wider noise fluctuations.

But there is also a *third*, non-salient action, referred to as a *default* and denoted $d$. This action cannot affect the course of $x$: when a policymaker chooses $d$, $x$ continues to evolve according to the most recent intervention. There is deliberate redundancy in this description: whether a policymaker chooses $d$ or a salient action that happens to coincide with the most recent intervention, the evolution of $x$ is the same. The only thing that can change the evolution of $x$ is an intervention that *differs* from the latest one. An intervention that replicates the most recent one is pure theatre, a *placebo reform*.

What motivates individual policymakers? Assume all a policymaker cares about is the *credit* that voters give her for affecting a change in GDP. This assumption is based on the everyday observation that real-life policymakers seem obsessed with claiming credit for good developments and dodging blame for bad ones. Of course, this motivation is largely the result of basic short-term goals such as winning elections. However, policymakers care about posterity even if they never plan to run for office again: It's why they always come out right in those boring autobiographies they write in their retirement. At any rate, we'll take this motivation as given, without trying to derive it from more basic assumptions.

And here comes the key piece in this model. Our voters attribute credit or blame according to a *simple rule*. If a policymaker chooses the default action $d$, she gets zero credit. If, however, she chooses an intervention, her credit is the change in $x$ from the moment she acts until the next time some policymaker chooses an intervention. (To close the model, we need to define what happens if no future policymaker ever intervenes. This need not bother us here.)

As with the consumers in the dieter's dilemma and the market for quacks, the voters' rule in this model captures an intuitive model of causal misattribution. I see it all around me. Daniel Kahneman's famous flight instructor story is one example.[5] Here's another one. Esther Duflo and Abhijit Banerjee (2011, chap. 3) argue that false inferences of this kind are partly responsible for major distortions in the demand for medical interventions, such as the overuse of antibiotics:

Because most diseases that prompt visits to the doctor are self-limiting (i.e., they will disappear no matter what), there is a good chance that patients will feel better after a single shot of antibiotics. This naturally encourages spurious causal associations: Even if the antibiotics did nothing to cure the ailment, it is normal to attribute any improvement to them. By contrast, it is not natural to attribute causal force to inaction: If a person with the flu goes to the doctor, and the doctor does nothing, and the patient then feels better, the patient will correctly infer that it was not the doctor who was responsible for the cure.

The voters in our story act like the patients in Duflo and Banerjee's example. The question is how their attribution rule affects our policymakers' behavior. The basic observation is that a policymaker has a stronger incentive to pick a salient action following a bad shock. The stochastic process exhibits mean reversion, as in the antibiotics example. Therefore, a negative shock artificially improves the credit that a policymaker gets if she intervenes when this shock hits. In contrast, a positive shock increases the policymaker's incentive to pick the default action, because a salient action is more likely to generate negative credit.

The strategic interaction between policymakers exacerbates this incentive. When a policymaker contemplates whether to intervene, she takes into account the *selective* subsequent interventions. Future policymakers' tendency to intervene after bad shocks pushes the expected credit that the present policymaker receives from an intervention *downward*. This strategic consideration gives a boost to the tendency to reserve interventions to bad shocks.

How does this play out? The policymakers are rational players in an infinite-horizon dynamic game, in which each player moves once. The conventional solution concept for such games is *subgame perfect equilibrium*: each policymaker's action is optimal (given the history at which she acts) against the strategies of all subsequent policymakers.

And this is what subgame perfect equilibrium looks like. Policymakers always intervene after a negative shock (whether it is $-k_r$ or $-k_s$) and opt for the default action after a positive shock (whether it is $k_r$ or $k_s$). Moreover, when they intervene, they choose the *safe* action $s$.

What this result means is that all the interventions voters witness along the equilibrium path, except possibly the first one, are pure theater. They are placebo reforms that do not change the evolution of $x$; their only role is to take advantage of voters' intuitive attribution rule in pursuit of credit. On average, interventions take place every two periods. But neither of these interventions, except maybe the first one, has any real effect. At the same time, since these placebo reforms maintain the safe action, the long-run growth rate is nearly zero. This entails a significant loss of societal welfare relative to the alternative of playing $r$, which is risky in the short run but brings much higher returns in the long run.

Let us see why this is an equilibrium. Consider a policymaker who moves at some time period $t$ following a shock $u(t)$. She takes it as given that whatever she does, the next policymakers will act only after negative shocks. Since positive and negative shocks are equally likely, the next negative shock will arrive after two periods in expectation. Therefore, if the policymaker chooses the safe intervention $s$, the expected credit she'll get is $2\varepsilon - k_s - u(t)$. Likewise, if she takes the risky action $r$, her expected credit will be $2 - k_r - u(t)$. Since $k_r - k_s > 2$, the policymaker will prefer $s$ to $r$. And since $\varepsilon$ is nearly zero, $2\varepsilon - k_s - u(t) > 0$ only when the shock $u(t)$ is negative. We have established that if the policymaker expects subsequent policymakers to intervene only after negative shocks, her optimal response is to do the same and adopt the safe action when that happens. This means that our guessed strategy is consistent with subgame perfect equilibrium. Showing no other equilibria exist is more intricate, and so I'll skip this part.

The assumption that policymakers are replaced every period is critical for this argument. Consider an alternative model in which policymakers move every $T$ periods, where $T$ is very large. Then, an individual policymaker faces much weaker competition for credit by subsequent policymakers. The difference between the two interventions' growth rates dwarfs the effect of adverse selection in future policymakers' timing of interventions. It is the long-run trend, not the short-term fluctuations, that dictates policymakers' choices, and they will always intervene and choose the risky action. Voters will still witness placebo reforms on the equilibrium path, but the selective intervention and risk aversion will disappear. This comparison resonates with the common intuition that short government terms inhibit major reforms. In the model, the reason is that short-term fights for credit lead to adversely selective interventions, which in turn lead policymakers to prefer low-risk, low-return measures.

In this last installment of the placebo trilogy, it is no longer consumers in a particular market but the general public that pays the price of using intuitive but ultimately wrong methods of causal attribution.

## What Does It Mean?

Perhaps the most basic tenet of modern economics is its theory of value. According to this theory, the value of products and services inheres in peoples' willingness to pay for it—that is, in their preferences. These preferences are primitive and should be respected by the economic analyst: *"de gustibus non est disputandum,"* as Stigler and Becker (1977) argued.

The placebo theme challenges this basic attitude. The economic value of objects or actions, as measured by how much people are willing to pay for them, can be a consequence of systematic attribution errors. If economic agents confuse correlation with causation, if they draw exaggerated inferences from anecdotal evidence, or if they fail to understand mean reversion, they may end up assigning value to intrinsically worthless things. And the broader implications? Transactions that are normally recorded as part of GDP are mere transfers. Sectors that seem to have great added value are nothing but a machine for transferring wealth from one group of people to another. Careers and reputations of business executives and policymakers live or die by stakeholders' poor methods for assigning credit and blame. The broad economic significance of the three placebo parables is that we need to take seriously the role of attribution errors in the formation of subjective value.

## Analyze This

More personally, what is it about the placebo theme that I find so irresistible as a researcher? I can only speculate.

Part of it has to do with aesthetic or pedagogic appeal: when studying the economic consequences of inference errors, it is convenient to consider a case with a very clear correct-beliefs benchmark. Actions with zero objective value offer such a neat benchmark. In this way, anything "interesting" will be due to the novel model of inference errors. There is a downside to this methodology. An "uninteresting" benchmark is extreme and usually unrealistic, which makes the exercise less plausible as a realistic description of the economic system in question. Once again, we have a clash between "pure" and "applied" attitudes, which has been a running theme in this book. The "pure theory" mentality will welcome the crisp benchmark, while the "applied theory" mentality will aim at a more realistic one, even at the cost of muddying the task of figuring out which effects are due to the novel behavioral element.

Part of it could be politics, an aspect of a "leftist" mentality that doubts the value system underlying our economic and political systems. I do seem to be obsessed with the broader idea that some economic agents receive unmerited rewards. My very first research paper, written when I was still a master's student at Tel Aviv University, proposed that intermediaries who contribute nothing to overall welfare can use exclusive-dealership contracts to extract the entire surplus that other agents generate.[6] This theoretical effect had nothing to do with inference errors, yet it foreshadowed the "why do the wicked prosper" mindset of the placebo trilogy.

Or it might have to do with *professional* politics and with a childish rebellious streak that my wife insists (against my mild protest) that I possess. During my formative years, the economics profession had a "center-right" flavor, and so mocking it from the left was the appropriately juvenile prank to pull. With the profession's leftward shift in recent years, I can imagine the same childish impulse producing pieces that would attack it from the right—for example, making fun of some of my "applied micro" peers' apparent belief that they can reconcile dispassionate scientific objectivity in their papers with vigorous activism on their Twitter account.

Looking inward more deeply, beyond the aesthetic and political layers, is it possible that the placebo theme springs from professional insecurity, a fear of being called out as an overpaid know-nothing? Under this interpretation, I am the charlatan who commands undeserved fees. Or is it envy of former schoolmates who pursued careers as executives and financiers? Do I get a kick from showing that they earn their money peddling worthless propositions, if only in the fantasy world of my models? In other words, is my obsession with the placebo theme an expression of something I share with every male primate, especially in a time of soaring inequalities: status anxiety?

If this kind of inward probing seems overly self-indulgent, note that it can be directed outwardly just as well. There is a flipside to the final question of the previous paragraph. Those countless studies that go out of their way to show how the alpha males of our economy rightfully earn their money and status; could they, too, spring from status anxieties of a similar nature?

Whatever the answers to these questions may be, the placebo theme illustrates how economic theory can serve as an "artistic" medium that channels raw psychological and political motives. Does this diminish the value of economic theory? Or does it make it more interesting?

# 10    Tiki-Taka (an Epilogue)

In 1996, the science writer John Horgan published a book called *The End of Science*.[1] The book offered a pessimistic assessment of various scientific fields, which in his opinion were fast approaching the limits of their ability to make great discoveries. Horgan coined the term *"ironic science"* to describe the kind of work that tends to flourish in such circumstances: a speculative kind of scientific activity that is hard to confront with credible empirical facts. The term "irony" means different things in different contexts, but a common feature that is especially relevant in this one is a heightened awareness of the gap between reality and its representation, coupled with a detached, bemused attitude to this gap.

Horgan was thinking of high-prestige scientific areas like elementary-particle physics or neuroscience. Yet, the scenario he describes has always been a reality for economic theorists. An economic model is a representation of reality, but the many layers of simplification and abstraction that separate the two imply that their correspondence is extremely subtle. This distance creates a sense of irony, and therefore has a humoristic potential. When economists say that our models are *caricatures* of reality, we may be reminded that in popular discourse, the term has humorous connotations.

Pieces of economic theory thus contain latent irony. Some, like the market-for-quacks paper I described in chapter 9, wear their irony on their sleeve. Some, like the e-mail game we saw in chapter 2, take a realistic aspect of economic behavior to an absurd extreme that turns the latent irony into a genuinely funny joke. Others, like the jury model we encountered in chapter 3, go through the motions of the "applied-theory style" and leave irony to the receptive reader. (Or was this actually masterful deadpan humor by the authors?)

As a child of the 1980s and 1990s, I grew up on a heavy irony diet. I savored the movies of David Lynch and the Coen brothers. (The opening titles of *Fargo* announce that the film is based on true events, a deliberate misdirection given that the story is entirely fictional. How much more ironic can you get?) Their work was widely admired, but a certain kind of critical acceptance eluded them for a long time because of a perceived deficit of seriousness. My greatest artistic hero, ever since I discovered him in my last year of high school, was the composer Igor Stravinsky—who, since the 1920s, wore the ironic stance as a badge of honor but for the rest of his life was detracted for offering (in the words of the musicologist Richard Taruskin) "trifles for snobs."[2]

Turning from the lofty world of art to the lowly world of economics, in my years as a graduate student in Tel Aviv in the 1990s I was exposed to some of the world's top theorists—especially during a marvelous series of long summer conferences known as Summer in Tel Aviv. The ironic style was everywhere, delivered with great sophistication and self-confidence: from musings about the foundations of incomplete contracts to speculations about the evolution of preferences. My PhD supervisor was Ariel Rubinstein, a practitioner of ironic science by my definition—"the economic model as a fable," as he called it. His repeated claim that economic theory is "useless" is not so different from Stravinsky's notorious meme about music being "powerless to express anything."[3]

The ironic style describes a big chunk of my own academic work. It is probably the professional communication mode I am most comfortable with. I cook up a model, enjoy the subtle ways in which it corresponds to an economic reality, and keep this correspondence at arm's length, leaving it to the reader to connect some of the dots. I tend to shy away from "taking the model seriously," in the customary sense of offering policy prescriptions or staking refutable (and typically refuted) scientific predictions.

The ironic style carries a certain risk. Its practitioners appear to be jesting, which of course they sometimes are. The bemusedly detached attitude may seem frivolous, unworthy of a handsomely paid social scientist. The seriousness of an ironic economic theorist is often in doubt. It's a professional hazard, not entirely unrelated to the critical ambiguities that surrounded the Coen brothers or Stravinsky. Even if I strongly believe that the ironic use of toy models is a profoundly serious mode of understanding economic phenomena, there is no easy way to impart this belief to skeptics who expect to see a more straightforwardly scientific pitch.

What I find remarkable is that, by and large, the economics community has been willing to sustain the irony-suffused culture of economic theory in its midst, through all these years. I am grateful for it. True, there has always been a current of resentment against this style of doing economic research. But it has been largely accepted as an ingredient that adds spice to the broader culture of economics, beyond theorists' supply of technical know-how for "real economists." Dani Rodrik, not exactly a hard-core theorist, recognized in his excellent book *Economics Rules* that economic theory enriches economic thought by expanding its "library of models" (although I can't rule out that Rodrik and I mean different things by "economic theory," and I won't be surprised if we don't share the same appreciation of its irony content).[4] Somehow, economic theory hasn't lost as much of its appeal and prestige as one might have expected from the common suspicion of its inherent irony.

With the generational change and what looks like an anti-irony zeitgeist, is this tolerance toward "bemusedly detached" economic theory going to persist? Or will theorists experience stronger pressure to adopt a less ambivalent stance toward the relation between their models and reality? In that scenario, some theorists will choose to insist on a tighter connection, and thus classify themselves as applied theorists who are expected to meet scientific criteria to validate the relevance of their work. Other theorists will be happy to define themselves as developers of techniques that applied economists can use. Still others will prefer to stay out of "applied" territory and relegate themselves into the small and increasingly "irrelevant" niche of purely abstract theory.

I am using the future tense, but I believe that this process is already in motion. For one thing, the rhetoric that surrounds theory papers has become increasingly "applied." As I remarked in chapter 3, one way to pass as an "applied" theorist is to pursue the technical development of established models that have already received the "applied" stamp of approval. This avenue doesn't require too much rhetorical warfare. Otherwise, theorists who present new classes of models need to work harder than before at establishing the models' relevance for their audience, which is increasingly intended to be the imaginary "general reader." The harder the work, the weaker the irony: ironists aren't supposed to sweat.

It's not just the rhetoric; the anti-ironic turn seems to affect the substance of economic theory. The increasing appeal of the "market design" field lies in its practitioners' ability to go through the regular motions of an economic-theory exercise while insisting on a straightforward, non-ironic connection to an economic reality. The "economist as engineer," as Al Roth (2002) called it; irony is not meant to be an engineer's thing. Market design methodology focuses on tightly regulated economic environments whose actors are expected to follow rigid rules. As a result, the gap between model and reality appears small enough to curb the irony impulse. In an auction, bidders really do follow the rules that the game-theoretic model describes. In a school-choice algorithm, parents and schools actually follow the mathematical model's script . . .

. . . Well, only if one narrows the scope of investigation and ignores the *unscripted* human activities that surround the scripted ones. I am thinking about parents exchanging opinions and forming preferences over schools. Or about how their preferences over schools are partly preferences over their child's peers—or, even better, the *parents* of the child's peers—and about the complex social forces that shape these preferences. Or about how winners and losers of a spectrum auction engage in free, unscripted market competition. In fact, Philippe Jehiel and Benny Moldovanu studied this aspect of auctions,[5] but then again, this work is probably not considered part of "market design."

Another direction that seems to be a good fit for an anti-irony age would be the development of complex, analytically intractable models that are amenable to numerical analysis and computer simulations. "Econophysics" researchers have been advocating this style of research for many years, but they have been neglected by mainstream economic theory (myself included, in my role as journal editor). Of course, numerical investigation of analytically inscrutable models has been the bread and butter of *macroeconomics* for several decades. But macroeconomists work with the same kind of models that microeconomic theorists have developed, only extended to the point where transparent analytic characterizations become impossible. What I have in mind is future *microeconomists* who will imagine new types of work that the broader research community will welcome as part of economic theory, independently of macroeconomic applications.

An economic theory that is more conducive to computerized numerical analysis, simulations, and visualization would enable practitioners to develop and showcase the kind of skills to which so much of today's quantitative IQ seems to be pouring. It would also give practitioners a sense they are doing actual science—not unlike climatology or epidemiology, both highly topical fields. It will therefore become a magnet for a new pool of talent. But it is hard to imagine a complex model with many moving parts delivered ironically. Whatever it is, a "fable" it is not. My prediction is that, in twenty or thirty years, much of what goes under the title of "economic theory" will look like this: more computer-based modeling, fewer fable-like toy models.

The influence of computer science is likely to flow in multiple channels. In the past, economists were said to suffer from "physics envy." These days, computer science has arguably supplanted physics as the high-prestige discipline that economists bow to. I may be susceptible to this trend myself: the directed-acyclic-graph formalism we encountered in chapter 9 was developed to a large degree by artificial-intelligence researchers like Judea Pearl. However, I (possibly echoing Pearl himself) saw this particular influence as a continuation of Herbert Simon's vision of artificial intelligence and human bounded rationality as two sides of the same coin.[6] By comparison, the broader computer-science impact on economic theory that I expect to see in the near future is of the kind that will strengthen economists' engineering orientation and solidify the applied math, operations-research strain of economic theory.

A related likely trend is a rise in the level of mathematical technique that the field will demand from its practitioners. This kind of craftsmanship has always been part of economic theorists' identity. However, it shouldn't be a controversial observation that economic theory is less sophisticated mathematically than physics or computer science. This reminds me of the comparison between pop and classical music. Pop music can be sophisticated, but there is a limit of technical intricacy that it will not exceed—or, if it exceeds it, then it will cease to pass as pop music. Consequently, we tend to be less interested in external manifestations of pop musicians' musical technique, compared with classical musicians. No one cares whether John Lennon had absolute pitch. To me, contemporary economic theory is like pop, rather than classical music. It can be subtle and deep, but an essential simplicity is a defining feature. This simplicity is a feature, not a bug. A future jump in the level of math that theorists are expected to display will signify a big change in the nature of economic theory.

Tastes change. A penchant for irony may reemerge. When it does, the curious culture of economic theory will still have much to offer. There are so many different angles from which it can gain insights into the social and economic world. Some angles will emphasize psychological factors, others sociological or anthropological factors. Some will emphasize individual decision-making, others collective behavior. Some will put emphasis on human agency, others on the growing role of algorithms in economic systems. Whatever the angle, the medium of abstract yet *simple* mathematical modeling will be rich, absorbing, and, at its best, a springboard for new economic thought. And it will be able to offer its services to researchers who have the stomach for the ironic baggage that inevitably comes with it.

In *Take the Ball, Pass the Ball*, a wonderful documentary film about Pep Guardiola's 2008–2012 Barcelona soccer team, Jordi Cruyff, son of legendary player Johan Cruyff, recounts how the two of them watched Guardiola's debut game as the team's manager. It was a La Liga match against an inferior team. Barcelona lost 0:1, and yet Cruyff senior told his son it was one of Barcelona's best games he had seen in years. Both father and son knew he was exaggerating, but what he meant was something that other veterans of that legendary team say in the documentary: that the enjoyment from Guardiola's Barcelona was from the *seemingly* inconsequential midfield passes as much as from the goals and wins they led to. I think about the relation between economic theory and the broader economics discipline in a similar way. We all want to score a goal or two, but many of us are here for the tiki-taka.

# Notes

## Chapter 1

1. Angrist and Pischke (2009).

2. Colander and Klamer (1987, 1990).

3. Piketty (2014, p. 32).

4. https://www.nytimes.com/2009/09/06/magazine/06Economic-t.html.

5. Colander (2007).

6. *Quarterly Journal of Economics, American Economic Review, Econometrica, Journal of Political Economy, Review of Economic Studies.*

7. Heckman and Moktan (2020).

8. Royal Swedish Academy of Sciences (2020)

9. https://marginalrevolution.com/marginalrevolution/2020/10/robert-wilson-nobel -laureate.html.

10. Lucas (2011).

11. Rubinstein (2006, 2012).

12. Wimsatt and Beardsley (1954).

## Chapter 2

1. See Halpern (1986).

2. Rubinstein (1989).

3. See Osborne and Rubinstein (1994, chap. 6.5).

4. Morris (2002) discusses experimental investigations of the e-mail game. As a "retrospective" on the e-mail game, Morris's piece is a recommended complement to this essay.

5. Wilson (1987).

6. Carlsson and van Damme (1993).

7. I have tampered with the exact payoff functions in Rubinstein's and Carlsson and van Damme's papers, in order to make the comparison easier. The payoff function of figure 2.2 has become conventional in pedagogical expositions (for example, Morris and Shin [2003]).

8. The term "essentially" means that at $t = \frac{1}{2}$, players' actions is undetermined.

9. Harsanyi and Selten (1988).

10. Young (1993), Kandori, Mailath, and Robb (1993).

11. A useful reference would be the scientific background for the 2016 Nobel Prize in Economics (Royal Swedish Academy of Sciences 2016).

12. Slonim and Roth (1998).

13. Camerer (2003, p. 43).

14. Hoffman, McCabe, and Smith (1996).

15. Allais (1953).

## Chapter 3

1. Austen-Smith and Banks (1996); Feddersen and Pesendorfer (1996, 1997, 1998).

2. E.g., Battaglini et al. (2010), Esponda and Vespa (2014).

3. Roemer (2010).

4. I thank Stephan Lauermann for alerting me to McLennan's paper.

5. Kamenica and Gentzkow (2011).

6. We were inspired by Caplin and Leahy's (2004) model of supply of information by a "concerned expert," where the sender is partly motivated by the wish to make the receiver "feel good."

7. Eliaz, Spiegler, and Thysen (2021 a, b).

8. Glazer and Rubinstein (2001, 2004, 2006).

## Chapter 4

1. Thaler (2015).

2. Rubinstein (1998).

3. Rubinstein, Tversky, and Heller (1997).

4. Gilboa and Schmeidler (1995).

5. Düppe and Weintraub (2014).

6. David Levine's (2012) *Is Behavioral Economics Doomed?* may be viewed as an example of this attitude by a major theorist.

7. This is more or less how Laibson and List (2015) define the area.

8. Spiegler (2019).

9. DellaVigna and Malmendier (2006).

10. DellaVigna and Malmendier (2004).

11. My textbook *"Bounded Rationality and Industrial Organization"* (Spiegler 2011) presents theoretical research that deals with these questions and others.

12. Gul and Pesendorfer (2008).

13. Caplin and Schotter (2008).

14. Kőszegi and Rabin (2008).

15. Rubinstein and Salant (2012).

16. Here are a few instances: Epstein (2006), Sarver (2008), Dillenberger and Sadowski (2012).

17. Two big favorites of mine are Eyster and Piccione (2013), which studied a model of competitive asset pricing when market traders have heterogeneous subjective models, and Heidhues and Kőszegi (2014), a model of monopoly pricing when consumers are loss averse.

18. The lecture was eventually published as Tirole (1999).

19. Maskin and Tirole (1999).

20. E.g., Abdulkadiroğlu and Sönmez (2003).

21. For a far superior substitute to this potted history of the field, I refer the reader to the "scientific background" of the 2012 Nobel Prize to Roth and Shapley (Royal Swedish Academy of Sciences 2012).

22. Kreps (1990), Mas-Colell, Whinston, and Green (1995).

23. Tirole (1988).

24. https://www.core-econ.org/the-economy.

# Chapter 5

1. https://twitter.com/SonjaStarr/status/1273020355129552896.

2. Recently, there has been interest in statistical discrimination models in which agents have systematically wrong beliefs—for instance, see Bohren, Imas, and Rosenberg (2019); Heidhues, Kőszegi, and Strack (2019); and Campos-Mercade and Mengel (2023).

3. Becker and Murphy (1988).

4. Rogers, Milkman, and Volpp (2014).

5. Elster (1999), Rogeberg (2004).

6. https://en.wikipedia.org/wiki/Winner%27s_curse.

7. For a simple textbook example, see Osborne (2004, pp. 297–299).

8. Sims (2003).

9. Caplin and Dean (2013) referred to this formula as a "posterior separable" representation.

10. Shannon (1948).

11. See Hari (2022) for a recent popular book devoted to this phenomenon.

12. Aridor, da Silveira and Woodford (2023) is an example of an economic model that involves an explicit model of constrained information processing, which shares the information-theoretic orientation of the rational inattention model but departs from its richness assumption.

13. Matějka and McKay (2015).

14. See Billingsley (1995).

15. The Morris-Strack exercise fits more comfortably into another general model of costly information acquisition due to Pomatto, Strack, and Tamuz (2020). This model does not follow the belief-dependent cost paradigm.

16. For example, Denti (2022).

17. For example, Caplin and Dean (2015) or De Oliveira, Denti, Mihm, and Ozbek (2017).

18. Other works in economics that trafficked with this idea include Akerlof and Dickens (1982) and Bénabou and Tirole (2016).

## Chapter 6

1. This is the only essay in the book that does not discuss individual pieces of economic theory. The motivation behind it was my experience as the chief editor of *Theoretical Economics* (*TE*) between 2017 and 2021. The journal's team of editors tried to cope with the appendicitis phenomenon, as a glance at the "editorial standards" and "submit a paper" pages on *TE*'s website (https://econtheory.org) will confirm. Nevertheless, I chose to keep these experiences out of this essay. Although *TE* is certainly not a negligible player in the world of economic theory, it is neither so dominant that a change in its policy can instantly overturn trends that reflect deeper cultural currents. Therefore, this chapter makes the simplifying assumption that *TE* is a "price taker" that can be safely ignored when analyzing this cultural phenomenon.

2. For instance, at the *American Economic Review*, when readers click on the link to the published paper, they land in a page with the paper's title and abstract and a prominent link to the print version. They have to scroll down in order to find a smaller link to the SOAP. The main file need not include a direct link to the SOAP.

3. I thank Nathan Hancart for preparing the graph. It focuses exclusively on regular articles—ignoring notes and comments, for which SOAPs are irrelevant by definition.

4. One explanation is that this was in response to rising competition from television. See https://www.businessinsider.com/are-movies-getting-longer-2016-6.

5. But see Gelman (2017) for a skeptical take on robustness checks in empirical papers.

6. Myerson (1981).

7. Hart and Reny (2015), Yildiz (2003).

8. This orientation is recent for *Econometrica.*

9. For instance, a 45-page limit currently practiced by *Econometrica.*

10. The lecture was based on Athey (2001) and Reny (2011).

11. Iyengar and Lepper (2000).

12. I thank Heidi Thysen for this point.

13. For example, Spiegler (2006) and Piccione and Spiegler (2012).

## Chapter 7

1. Spiegler (2011).

2. See Kőszegi and Rabin (2006) and Heidhues and Kőszegi (2008, 2014). At the time, some of these ideas appeared in a working paper (Heidhues and Kőszegi [2004]), which contained relevant material that was never published, to my knowledge.

3. Spiegler (2012).

4. Dyson (1979, p. 105).

5. This paper was titled "The Winner's Curse in Bilateral Negotiations." It was later published under the title "Negotiation under the Winner's Curse" (see Samuelson and Bazerman 1984, 1985).

6. I thank Yair Antler for this analogy.

## Chapter 8

1. For example, see Mirowski (1989).

2. Roth (2015).

3. Edelmen, Ostrovsky, and Schwarz (2007).

4. See the reprinted version of their paper: Brin and Page (2012, pp. 3831–3832).

5. https://www.jeffely.com/post/intermediate-micro-course.

6. Maskin solved the Nash implementation problem in 1977, in a piece that had a big role in his 2007 Nobel Prize. The paper was published much later, in the 1999 special issue of the *Review of Economic Studies* that I mentioned in chapter 4.

7. I was quite militant about this at the time. In 2009, I organized an "econ-CS" conference at University College London in order to learn more about search engines. As I was constructing the conference program, I asked the bewildered computer-science speakers whether they could refrain from presenting mechanism-design papers.

8. The nice properties of BC make it a useful measure of similarity between probability distributions. As such, it received applications that involve classification of distributions— for instance, in text mining.

9. See Qin, Chen and Liu (2015) for a review article.

## Chapter 9

1. This chapter originated from a special lecture I gave at the University of Helsinki in 2017 as a recipient of the Yrjö Jahnsson award.

2. Dixit (1994).

3. Pearl and Mackenzie (2018).

4. For a pedagogical exposition, see Spiegler (2011, chaps. 6, 13).

5. You can read all about it in Michael Lewis's (2016) story of the Tversky-Kahneman collaboration.

6. Spiegler (2000).

## Chapter 10

1. Horgan (2015)

2. Taruskin (1996, p. 1591).

3. Stravinsky (1935).

4. Rodrik (2015).

5. Jehiel and Moldovanu (2000).

6. Simon (1982).

# References

Abdulkadiroğlu, Atila, and Tayfun Sönmez. "School Choice: A Mechanism Design Approach." *American Economic Review* 93, no. 3 (May 1, 2003): 729–747. https://doi.org /10.1257/000282803322157061.

Akerlof, George A. "The Market for 'Lemons': Quality Uncertainty and the Market Mechanism." *Quarterly Journal of Economics* 84, no. 3 (1970): 488–500. https://doi.org/10.2307 /1879431.

Akerlof, George A., and William T. Dickens. "The Economic Consequences of Cognitive Dissonance." *American Economic Review* 72, no. 3 (1982): 307–319.

Akerlof, George A., and Robert J. Shiller. *Phishing for Phools: The Economics of Manipulation and Deception*. Princeton, NJ: Princeton University Press, 2015. https://doi.org/10.1515 /9781400873265.

Allais, M. "Le Comportement de l'Homme Rationnel Devant Le Risque: Critique Des Postulats et Axiomes de l'Ecole Americaine." *Econometrica* 21, no. 4 (1953): 503–546. https://doi.org/10.2307/1907921.

Angrist, Joshua David, and Jörn-Steffen Pischke. *Mostly Harmless Econometrics: An Empiricist's Companion*. Princeton, NJ: Princeton University Press, 2009.

Aridor, Guy, da Silveira, Rava Azeredo, and Michael Woodford. "Information-Constrained Coordination of Economic Behavior." Working Paper, 2023.

Arrow, Kenneth J. "The Theory of Discrimination." In Orley Ashenfelter and Albert Rees, eds., *Discrimination in Labor Markets*. Princeton, NJ: Princeton University Press, 1973: 3–33.

Athey, Susan. "Single Crossing Properties and the Existence of Pure Strategy Equilibria in Games of Incomplete Information." *Econometrica* 69, no. 4 (2001): 861–889.

Austen-Smith, David, and Jeffrey S. Banks. "Information Aggregation, Rationality, and the Condorcet Jury Theorem." *American Political Science Review* 90, no. 1 (March 1996): 34–45. https://doi.org/10.2307/2082796.

Battaglini, Marco, Rebecca B. Morton, and Thomas R. Palfrey. "The Swing Voter's Curse in the Laboratory." *Review of Economic Studies* 77, no. 1 (2010): 61–89.

Battigalli, Pierpaolo, and Giovanni Maggi. "Rigidity, Discretion, and the Costs of Writing Contracts." *American Economic Review* 92, no. 4 (August 1, 2002): 798–817. https://doi .org/10.1257/00028280260344470.

Becker, Gary S. *The Economics of Discrimination*. Chicago: University of Chicago Press, 1957. https://www.biblio.com/book/economics-discrimination-becker-gary/d/601525174.

Becker, Gary S., and Kevin M. Murphy. "A Theory of Rational Addiction." *Journal of Political Economy* 96, no. 4 (1988): 675–700.

Bénabou, Roland, and Jean Tirole. "Mindful Economics: The Production, Consumption, and Value of Beliefs." *Journal of Economic Perspectives* 30, no. 3 (August 1, 2016): 141–164. https://doi.org/10.1257/jep.30.3.141.

Bernheim, B. Douglas, and Antonio Rangel. "Addiction and Cue-Triggered Decision Processes." *American Economic Review* 94, no. 5 (November 1, 2004): 1558–1590. https://doi.org/10.1257/0002828043052222.

Bester, Helmut. "Screening vs. Rationing in Credit Markets with Imperfect Information." *American Economic Review* 75, no. 4 (1985): 850–855.

Bhattacharyya, Anil. "On a Measure of Divergence between Two Statistical Populations Defined by Their Probability Distributions." *Bulletin of the Calcutta Mathematical Society* 35 (1943): 99–109.

Billingsley, Patrick. *Probability and Measure*. 3rd ed. Wiley Series in Probability and Mathematical Statistics. New York: Wiley, 1995.

Binmore, Ken, Ariel Rubinstein, and Asher Wolinsky. "The Nash Bargaining Solution in Economic Modelling." *RAND Journal of Economics* 17, no. 2 (1986): 176–188.

Bohren, J. Aislinn, Alex Imas, and Michael Rosenberg. "The Dynamics of Discrimination: Theory and Evidence." *American Economic Review* 109, no. 10 (October 2019): 3395–3436. https://doi.org/10.1257/aer.20171829.

Brin, Sergey, and Lawrence Page. "Reprint of: The Anatomy of a Large-Scale Hypertextual Web Search Engine." *Computer Networks* 56, no. 18 (2012): 3825–3833.

Brunnermeier, Markus K., and Jonathan A. Parker. "Optimal Expectations." *American Economic Review* 95, no. 4 (September 2005): 1092–1118. https://doi.org/10.1257/0002828054825493.

Camerer, Colin F. *Behavioral Game Theory: Experiments in Strategic Interaction*. New York: Russell Sage Foundation, 2003.

Campos-Mercade, Pol, and Friederike Mengel. "Non Bayesian Statistical Discrimination." *Management Science*, forthcoming (2023). https://doi.org/10.1287/mnsc.2023.4824

Caplin, Andrew, and Mark Dean. "Behavioral Implications of Rational Inattention with Shannon Entropy." NBER Working Paper No. 19318, August 2013. https://doi.org/10.3386/w19318.

Caplin, Andrew, and Mark Dean. "Revealed Preference, Rational Inattention, and Costly Information Acquisition." *American Economic Review* 105, no. 7 (July 2015): 2183–2203. https://doi.org/10.1257/aer.20140117.

Caplin, Andrew, and John Leahy. "The Supply of Information by a Concerned Expert." *Economic Journal* 114, no. 497 (July 1, 2004): 487–505. https://doi.org/10.1111/j.0013-0133.2004.0228a.x.

Caplin, Andrew, and Andrew Schotter. *The Foundations of Positive and Normative Economics: A Handbook*. Oxford: Oxford University Press, 2008.

Carlsson, Hans, and Eric van Damme. "Global Games and Equilibrium Selection." *Econometrica* 61, no. 5 (1993): 989–1018. https://doi.org/10.2307/2951491.

Cho, In-Koo, and David M. Kreps. "Signaling Games and Stable Equilibria." *Quarterly Journal of Economics* 102, no. 2 (1987): 179–221. https://doi.org/10.2307/1885060.

Colander, David. *The Making of an Economist, Redux.* Princeton, NJ: Princeton University Press, 2007.

Colander, David, and Arjo Klamer. "The Making of an Economist." *Journal of Economic Perspectives* 1, no. 2 (December 1987): 95–111. https://doi.org/10.1257/jep.1.2.95.

Colander, David, and Arjo Klamer. *The Making of an Economist.* New York: Routledge, 1990.

Cowen, Tyler. "Robert B. Wilson, Nobel Laureate." *Marginal Revolution*, blog, October 12, 2020. https://marginalrevolution.com/marginalrevolution/2020/10/robert-wilson-nobel -laureate.html.

Crawford, Vincent P., and Joel Sobel. "Strategic Information Transmission." *Econometrica* 50, no. 6 (1982): 1431–1451. https://doi.org/10.2307/1913390.

Dekel, Eddie, Barton L. Lipman, and Aldo Rustichini. "Representing Preferences with a Unique Subjective State Space." *Econometrica* 69, no. 4 (2001): 891–934. https://doi.org /10.1111/1468-0262.00224.

DellaVigna, Stefano, and Ulrike Malmendier. "Contract Design and Self-Control: Theory and Evidence." *Quarterly Journal of Economics* 119, no. 2 (May 1, 2004): 353–402. https:// doi.org/10.1162/0033553041382111.

DellaVigna, Stefano, and Ulrike Malmendier. "Paying Not to Go to the Gym." *American Economic Review* 96, no. 3 (June 2006): 694–719. https://doi.org/10.1257/aer.96.3.694.

Denti, Tommaso, Massimo Marinacci, and Aldo Rustichini. "Experimental Cost of Information." *American Economic Review* 112, no. 9 (2022): 3106–3123. https://doi.org/10.1257 /aer.20210879.

Dillenberger, David, and Philipp Sadowski. "Ashamed to Be Selfish." *Theoretical Economics* 7, no. 1 (2012): 99–124. https://doi.org/10.3982/TE674.

Dixit, Avinash. "My System of Work (Not!)." *American Economist* 38, no. 1 (1994): 10–16.

Duflo, Esther, and Abhijit Banerjee. *Poor Economics.* Vol. 619. New York: PublicAffairs, 2011.

Düppe, Till, and E. Roy Weintraub. *Finding Equilibrium: Arrow, Debreu, McKenzie and the Problem of Scientific Credit.* Princeton, NJ: Princeton University Press, 2014. https://doi .org/10.1515/9781400850129.

Dyson, Freeman. *Disturbing the Universe.* New York: Basic Books, 1979.

Edelman, Benjamin, Michael Ostrovsky, and Michael Schwarz. "Internet Advertising and the Generalized Second-Price Auction: Selling Billions of Dollars Worth of Keywords." *American Economic Review* 97, no. 1 (2007): 242–259.

Eliaz, Kfir, and Ran Spiegler. "Search Design and Broad Matching." *American Economic Review* 106, no. 3 (March 2016): 563–586. https://doi.org/10.1257/aer.20150076.

Eliaz, Kfir, Ran Spiegler, and Heidi C. Thysen. "Strategic Interpretations." *Journal of Economic Theory* 192 (March 1, 2021a): 105192. https://doi.org/10.1016/j.jet.2021.105192.

Eliaz, Kfir, Ran Spiegler, and Heidi C. Thysen. "Persuasion with Endogenous Misspecified Beliefs." *European Economic Review* 134 (May 1, 2021b): 103712. https://doi.org/10.1016/j.euroecorev.2021.103712.

Ellison, Glenn. "Evolving Standards for Academic Publishing: A q-r Theory." *Journal of Political Economy* 110, no. 5 (October 2002): 994–1034. https://doi.org/10.1086/341871.

Elster, Jon. *Strong Feelings: Emotion, Addiction, and Human Behavior.* Jean Nicod Lectures 1997. Cambridge, MA: MIT Press, 1999.

Epstein, Larry. "An Axiomatic Model of Non-Bayesian Updating." *Review of Economic Studies* 73, no. 2 (2006): 413–436. https://doi.org/10.1111/j.1467-937X.2006.00381.x.

Esponda, Ignacio, and Emanuel Vespa. "Hypothetical Thinking and Information Extraction in the Laboratory." *American Economic Journal: Microeconomics* 6, no. 4 (2014): 180–202.

Eyster, Erik, and Michele Piccione. "An Approach to Asset Pricing under Incomplete and Diverse Perceptions." *Econometrica* 81, no. 4 (2013): 1483–1506. https://doi.org/10.3982/ECTA10499.

Eyster, Erik, and Matthew Rabin. "Extensive Imitation Is Irrational and Harmful." *Quarterly Journal of Economics* 129, no. 4 (November 1, 2014): 1861–1898. https://doi.org/10.1093/qje/qju021.

Feddersen, Timothy J., and Wolfgang Pesendorfer. "The Swing Voter's Curse." *American Economic Review* 86, no. 3 (1996): 408–424.

Feddersen, Timothy J., and Wolfgang Pesendorfer. "Voting Behavior and Information Aggregation in Elections with Private Information." *Econometrica* 65, no. 5 (1997): 1029–1058. https://doi.org/10.2307/2171878.

Feddersen, Timothy J., and Wolfgang Pesendorfer. "Convicting the Innocent: The Inferiority of Unanimous Jury Verdicts under Strategic Voting." *American Political Science Review* 92, no. 1 (March 1998): 23–35. https://doi.org/10.2307/2585926.

Geanakoplos, John, David Pearce, and Ennio Stacchetti. "Psychological Games and Sequential Rationality." *Games and Economic Behavior* 1, no. 1 (March 1, 1989): 60–79. https://doi.org/10.1016/0899-8256(89)90005-5.

Gelman, Andrew. "What's the Point of a Robustness Check?" *Statistical Modeling, Causal Inference, and Social Science*, November 29, 2017. https://statmodeling.stat.columbia.edu/2017/11/29/whats-point-robustness-check/.

Gilboa, Itzhak, and David Schmeidler. "Case-Based Decision Theory." *Quarterly Journal of Economics* 110, no. 3 (August 1, 1995): 605–639. https://doi.org/10.2307/2946694.

Glazer, Jacob, and Ariel Rubinstein. "Debates and Decisions: On a Rationale of Argumentation Rules." *Games and Economic Behavior* 36, no. 2 (August 1, 2001): 158–173. https://doi.org/10.1006/game.2000.0824.

Glazer, Jacob, and Ariel Rubinstein. "On Optimal Rules of Persuasion." *Econometrica* 72, no. 6 (2004): 1715–1736. https://doi.org/10.1111/j.1468-0262.2004.00551.x.

Glazer, Jacob, and Ariel Rubinstein. "A Game Theoretic Approach to the Pragmatics of Debate: An Expository Note." In *Game Theory and Pragmatics*, edited by Anton Benz, Gerhard Jäger, and Robert van Rooij, 248–262. Palgrave Studies in Pragmatics, Language and Cognition. London: Palgrave Macmillan UK, 2006. https://doi.org/10.1057/9780230285897_9.

Goldstein, Itay, and Ady Pauzner. "Demand-Deposit Contracts and the Probability of Bank Runs." *Journal of Finance* 60, no. 3 (2005): 1293–1327. https://doi.org/10.1111/j.1540-6261.2005.00762.x.

Grossman, Sanford J., and Oliver D. Hart. "The Costs and Benefits of Ownership: A Theory of Vertical and Lateral Integration." *Journal of Political Economy* 94, no. 4 (1986): 691–719.

Gruber, Jonathan, and Botond Kőszegi. "Is Addiction 'Rational'? Theory and Evidence." *Quarterly Journal of Economics* 116, no. 4 (November 1, 2001): 1261–1303. https://doi.org/10.1162/003355301753265570.

Gul, Faruk. "Bargaining Foundations of Shapley Value." *Econometrica* 57, no. 1 (1989): 81–95. https://doi.org/10.2307/1912573.

Gul, Faruk, and Wolfgang Pesendorfer. "Temptation and Self-Control." *Econometrica* 69, no. 6 (2001): 1403–1435. https://doi.org/10.1111/1468-0262.00252.

Gul, Faruk, and Wolfgang Pesendorfer. "Harmful Addiction." *Review of Economic Studies* 74, no. 1 (January 1, 2007): 147–172. https://doi.org/10.1111/j.1467-937X.2007.00417.x.

Gul, Faruk, and Wolfgang Pesendorfer. "The Case for Mindless Economics." In Andrew Caplin and Andrew Schotter, eds., *Foundations of Positive and Normative Economics: A Handbook.* New York: Oxford University Press, 2008: 3–42. https://doi.org/10.1093/acprof:oso/9780195328318.003.0001.

Güth, Werner, Rolf Schmittberger, and Bernd Schwarze. "An Experimental Analysis of Ultimatum Bargaining." *Journal of Economic Behavior and Organization* 3, no. 4 (December 1, 1982): 367–388. https://doi.org/10.1016/0167-2681(82)90011-7.

Halpern, Joseph Y. "Reasoning about Knowledge: An Overview." In *Theoretical Aspects of Reasoning about Knowledge*: Proceedings of the 1986 Conference, Los Altos, CA: Morgan Kaufmann, 1986: 1–17. https://doi.org/10.1016/B978-0-934613-04-0.50004-1.

Hari, Johann. *Stolen Focus: Why You Can't Pay Attention—And How to Think Deeply Again.* New York: Crown, 2022.

Harsanyi, John C., and Reinhard Selten. *A General Theory of Equilibrium Selection in Games.* MIT Press Books. Vol. 1. Cambridge, MA: MIT Press, 1988. https://ideas.repec.org/b/mtp/titles/0262582384.html.

Hart, Oliver, and John Moore. "Property Rights and the Nature of the Firm." *Journal of Political Economy* 98, no. 6 (1990): 1119–1158.

Hart, Sergiu, and Philip J. Reny. "Maximal Revenue with Multiple Goods: Nonmonotonicity and Other Observations." *Theoretical Economics* 10, no. 3 (2015): 893–922. https://doi.org/10.3982/TE1517.

Heckman, James J., and Sidharth Moktan. "Publishing and Promotion in Economics: The Tyranny of the Top Five." *Journal of Economic Literature* 58, no. 2 (June 2020): 419–470. https://doi.org/10.1257/jel.20191574.

Heidhues, Paul, and Botond Kőszegi. "The Impact of Consumer Loss Aversion on Pricing." WZB, Markets and Political Economy Working Paper No. SP II 17 (2004). https://doi.org/10.2139/ssrn.658002.

Heidhues, Paul, and Botond Kőszegi. "Competition and Price Variation when Consumers Are Loss Averse." *American Economic Review* 98, no. 4 (September 2008): 1245–1268. https://doi.org/10.1257/aer.98.4.1245.

Heidhues, Paul, and Botond Kőszegi. "Regular Prices and Sales." *Theoretical Economics* 9, no. 1 (2014): 217–251. https://doi.org/10.3982/TE1274.

Heidhues, Paul, Botond Kőszegi, and Philipp Strack. "Overconfidence and Prejudice." arXiv 2019 preprint, arXiv:1909.08497.

Heidhues, Paul, and Philipp Strack. "Identifying Present Bias from the Timing of Choices." *American Economic Review* 111, no. 8 (August 2021): 2594–2622. https://doi.org/10.1257/aer.20191258.

Hoffman, Elizabeth, Kevin McCabe, and Vernon L. Smith. "Social Distance and Other: Regarding Behavior in Dictator Games." *American Economic Review* 86, no. 3 (1996): 653–660.

Horgan, John. *The End of Science: Facing the Limits of Knowledge in the Twilight of the Scientific Age*. New York: Basic Books, 2015.

Iyengar, Sheena S, and Mark, R. Lepper. "When Choice Is Demotivating: Can One Desire Too Much of a Good Thing?" *Journal of Personality and Social Psychology* 79, no. 6 (2000): 995. https://doi.org/10.1037/0022-3514.79.6.995.

Jehiel, Philippe, and Benny Moldovanu. "Auctions with Downstream Interaction among Buyers." *RAND Journal of Economics* 31, no. 4 (2000): 768–791.

Kahneman, Daniel, and Amos Tversky. "Prospect Theory: An Analysis of Decision under Risk." *Econometrica* 47, no. 2 (1979): 263–292.

Kamenica, Emir, and Matthew Gentzkow. "Bayesian Persuasion." *American Economic Review* 101, no. 6 (October 1, 2011): 2590–2615. https://doi.org/10.1257/aer.101.6.2590.

Kandori, Michihiro, George J. Mailath, and Rafael Rob. "Learning, Mutation, and Long Run Equilibria in Games." *Econometrica* 61, no. 1 (1993): 29–56. https://doi.org/10.2307/2951777.

Kay, John. "The Map Is Not the Territory: Models, Scientists, and the State of Modern Macroeconomics." *Critical Review* 24, no. 1 (March 1, 2012): 87–99. https://doi.org/10.1080/08913811.2012.684476.

Kőszegi, Botond, and Matthew Rabin. "A Model of Reference-Dependent Preferences." *Quarterly Journal of Economics* 121, no. 4 (2006): 1133–1165.

Kőszegi, Botond, and Matthew Rabin. "Revealed Mistakes and Revealed Preferences." In Andrew Caplin and Andrew Schotter, eds., *Foundations of Positive and Normative Economics: A Handbook*. New York: Oxford University Press, 2008: 193–209. https://doi.org/10.1093/acprof:oso/9780195328318.003.0008.

Kreps, David M. "A Representation Theorem for 'Preference for Flexibility.'" *Econometrica* 47, no. 3 (1979): 565–577. https://doi.org/10.2307/1910406.

Kreps, David M. *A Course in Microeconomic Theory*. Princeton, NJ: Princeton University Press, 1990.

Kreps, David M., and Evan L. Porteus. "Temporal Resolution of Uncertainty and Dynamic Choice Theory." *Econometrica* 46, no. 1 (1978): 185–200. https://doi.org/10.2307/1913656.

Krugman, Paul. "How Did Economists Get It So Wrong?" *New York Times*, September 2, 2009, sec. Magazine. https://www.nytimes.com/2009/09/06/magazine/06Economic-t .html.

Kuhn, Harold William. "Extensive Games and the Problem of Information." In H. Kuhn and A. Tucker, eds., *Contributions to the Theory of Games*. Vol. 2. Princeton, NJ: Princeton University Press, 1953: 193–216.

Laibson, David. "Golden Eggs and Hyperbolic Discounting." *Quarterly Journal of Economics* 112, no. 2 (May 1, 1997): 443–478. https://doi.org/10.1162/003355397555253.

Laibson, David. "A Cue-Theory of Consumption." *Quarterly Journal of Economics* 116, no. 1 (February 1, 2001): 81–119. https://doi.org/10.1162/003355301556356.

Laibson, David, and John A. List. "Principles of (Behavioral) Economics." *American Economic Review* 105, no. 5 (May 2015): 385–390. https://doi.org/10.1257/aer.p20151047.

Lehrer, Ehud, and Ady Pauzner. "Repeated Games with Differential Time Preferences." *Econometrica* 67, no. 2 (1999): 393–412. https://doi.org/10.1111/1468-0262.00024.

Levine, David K. *Is Behavioral Economics Doomed?: The Ordinary versus the Extraordinary*. 1st ed. Cambridge, UK: Open Book Publishers, 2012. https://doi.org/10.2307/j.ctt5vjtfs.

Lewis, Michael. *The Undoing Project: A Friendship That Changed the World*. London: Penguin UK, 2016.

Lipman, Barton L. "Limited Rationality and Endogenously Incomplete Contracts." Working Paper. Economics Department, Queen's University, October 1992. https://ideas .repec.org/p/qed/wpaper/858.html.

Lucas, Robert, Jr. "What Economists Do." *Journal of Applied Economics* 14, no. 1 (May 2011): 1–4.

Maćkowiak, Bartosz, Filip Matějka, and Mirko Wiederholt. "Rational Inattention: A Review." *Journal of Economic Literature* 61, no. 1 (2023). https://doi.org/10.1257/jel.20211524.

Mas-Colell, Andreu, Michael D. Whinston, and Jerry R. Green. *Microeconomic Theory*. New York: Oxford University Press, 1995.

Maskin, Eric. "Nash Equilibrium and Welfare Optimality." *Review of Economic Studies* 66, no. 1 (January 1, 1999): 23–38. https://doi.org/10.1111/1467-937X.00076.

Maskin, Eric, and Jean Tirole. "Unforeseen Contingencies and Incomplete Contracts." *Review of Economic Studies* 66, no. 1 (January 1999): 83–114. https://doi.org/10.1111/1467 -937X.00079.

Matějka, Filip, and Alisdair McKay. "Rational Inattention to Discrete Choices: A New Foundation for the Multinomial Logit Model." *American Economic Review* 105, no. 1 (January 2015): 272–298. https://doi.org/10.1257/aer.20130047.

McCloskey, Deirdre N. *The Rhetoric of Economics*. Brighton, UK: Harvester Press, 1985.

McLennan, Andrew. "Consequences of the Condorcet Jury Theorem for Beneficial Information Aggregation by Rational Agents." *American Political Science Review* 92, no. 2 (June 1998): 413–418.

Mirowski, Philip. *More Heat than Light: Economics as Social Physics, Physics as Nature's Economics*. Cambridge, UK: Cambridge University Press, 1991.

Morris, Stephen. "Coordination, Communication, and Common Knowledge: A Retrospective on the Electronic-Mail Game." *Oxford Review of Economic Policy* 18, no. 4 (December 1, 2002): 433–445. https://doi.org/10.1093/oxrep/18.4.433.

Morris, Stephen, and Hyun Song Shin. "Unique Equilibrium in a Model of Self-Fulfilling Currency Attacks." *American Economic Review* 88, no. 3 (1998): 587–597.

Morris, Stephen, and Hyun Song Shin. "Global Games: Theory and Applications." In *Advances in Economics and Econometrics: Theory and Applications, Eighth World Congress*, edited by Lars Peter Hansen, Mathias Dewatripont, and Stephen J. Turnovsky, vol. 1. pp. 56–114. Econometric Society Monographs. Cambridge, UK: Cambridge University Press, 2003. https://doi.org/10.1017/CBO9780511610240.004.

Morris, Stephen, and Philipp Strack. "The Wald Problem and the Relation of Sequential Sampling and Ex-Ante Information Costs." SSRN Scholarly Paper. February 18, 2019. https://doi.org/10.2139/ssrn.2991567.

Myerson, Roger B. "Optimal Auction Design." *Mathematics of Operations Research* 6, no. 1 (1981): 58–73.

Myerson, Roger B., and Mark A. Satterthwaite. "Efficient Mechanisms for Bilateral Trading." *Journal of Economic Theory* 29, no. 2 (1983): 265–281.

Netzer, Nick, and Florian Scheuer. "A Game Theoretic Foundation of Competitive Equilibria with Adverse Selection." *International Economic Review* 55, no. 2 (2014): 399–422.

O'Donoghue, Ted, and Matthew Rabin. "Doing It Now or Later." *American Economic Review* 89, no. 1 (1999): 104.

Oliveira, Henrique de, Tommaso Denti, Maximilian Mihm, and Kemal Ozbek. "Rationally Inattentive Preferences and Hidden Information Costs." *Theoretical Economics* 12, no. 2 (2017): 621–654. https://doi.org/10.3982/TE2302.

Osborne, Martin J. *An Introduction to Game Theory*. New York: Oxford University Press, 2004.

Osborne, Martin J., and Ariel Rubinstein. *A Course in Game Theory*. Cambridge, MA: MIT Press, 1994.

Pearl, Judea, and Dana Mackenzie. *The Book of Why: The New Science of Cause and Effect*. New York: Basic Books, 2018.

Phelps, Edmund. "The Statistical Theory of Racism and Sexism." American economic review 62, no. 4 (1972): 659–661.

Phelps, Edmund and Robert Pollak. "On Second-Best National Saving and Game-Equilibrium Growth." *Review of Economic Studies* 35, no. 2 (1968): 185–199. https://doi.org/10.2307/2296547.

Piccione, Michele, and Ran Spiegler. "Price Competition under Limited Comparability." *Quarterly Journal of Economics* 127, no. 1 (February 1, 2012): 97–135. https://doi.org/10.1093/qje/qjr053.

Piketty, Thomas. *Capital in the Twenty-First Century*. Cambridge, MA: Harvard University Press.

Pirsig, Robert. *Zen and the Art of Motorcycle Maintenance*. New York: Morrow, 1974.

Pomatto, Luciano, Philipp Strack, and Omer Tamuz. "The Cost of Information." arXiv, December 11, 2020. https://doi.org/10.48550/arXiv.1812.04211.

Qin, Tao, Chen, Wei, and Tie-Yan Liu. "Sponsored Search Auctions: Recent Advances and Future Directions." *ACM Transactions on Intelligent Systems and Technology (TIST)* 5, no. 4 (2015): 1–34.

Rabin, Matthew. "Incorporating Fairness into Game Theory and Economics." *American Economic Review* 83, no. 5 (1993): 1281–1302.

Rabin, Matthew. "Risk Aversion and Expected-Utility Theory: A Calibration Theorem." *Econometrica* 68, no. 5 (2000): 1281–1292.

Rabin, Matthew. "An Approach to Incorporating Psychology into Economics." *American Economic Review* 103, no. 3 (May 2013): 617–622. https://doi.org/10.1257/aer.103.3.617.

Reny, Philip J. "On the Existence of Monotone Pure-Strategy Equilibria in Bayesian Games." *Econometrica* 79, no. 2 (2011): 499–553. https://doi.org/10.3982/ECTA8934.

Richter, Michael, and Ariel Rubinstein. "Back to Fundamentals: Equilibrium in Abstract Economies." *American Economic Review* 105, no. 8 (August 2015): 2570–2594. https://doi.org/10.1257/aer.20140270.

Rochet, Jean-Charles. "A Necessary and Sufficient Condition for Rationalizability in a Quasi-Linear Context." *Journal of Mathematical Economics* 16, no. 2 (1987): 191–200.

Rodrik, Dani. *Economics Rules: The Rights and Wrongs of the Dismal Science.* Oxford: Oxford University Press, 2015.

Roemer, John E. "Kantian Equilibrium." *Scandinavian Journal of Economics* 112, no. 1 (2010): 1–24. https://doi.org/10.1111/j.1467-9442.2009.01592.x.

Rogeberg, Ole. "Taking Absurd Theories Seriously: Economics and the Case of Rational Addiction Theories." *Philosophy of Science* 71 (July 1, 2004). https://doi.org/10.1086/421535.

Rogers, Todd, Katherine L. Milkman, and Kevin G. Volpp. "Commitment Devices: Using Initiatives to Change Behavior." *JAMA* 311, no. 20 (May 2014): 2065–2066. https://doi.org/10.1001/jama.2014.3485.

Roth, Alvin E. "The Evolution of the Labor Market for Medical Interns and Residents: A Case Study in Game Theory." *Journal of Political Economy* 92, no. 6 (December 1984): 991–1016. https://doi.org/10.1086/261272.

Roth, Alvin E. "The Economist as Engineer: Game Theory, Experimentation, and Computation as Tools for Design Economics." *Econometrica* 70, no. 4 (2002): 1341–1378. https://doi.org/10.1111/1468-0262.00335.

Roth, Alvin E. *Who Gets What—and Why: The New Economics of Matchmaking and Market Design.* London: William Collins, 2015.

Roth, Alvin E., and Marilda A. Oliveira Sotomayor. *Two-Sided Matching: A Study in Game-Theoretic Modeling and Analysis.* Econometric Society Monographs. Cambridge, UK: Cambridge University Press, 1990. https://doi.org/10.1017/CCOL052139015X.

Rothschild, Michael, and Joseph Stiglitz. "Equilibrium in Competitive Insurance Markets: An Essay on the Economics of Imperfect Information." *Quarterly Journal of Economics* 90, no. 4 (1976): 629–649. https://doi.org/10.2307/1885326.

Royal Swedish Academy of Sciences. a. "Stable Allocations and the Practice of Market Design." *Scientific Background on the Sveriges Riksbank Prize in Economic Sciences in Memory of Alfred Nobel.* October 15, 2012. https://www.nobelprize.org/uploads/2018/06/advanced-economicsciences2012.pdf.

Royal Swedish Academy of Sciences. b. "Oliver Hart and Bengt Holmström: Contract Theory." *Scientific Background on the Sveriges Riksbank Prize in Economic Sciences in Memory of Alfred Nobel.* October 15, 2016. https://www.nobelprize.org/uploads/2018/06/advanced-economicsciences2016.pdf.

Royal Swedish Academy of Sciences. "The Sveriges Riksbank Prize in Economic Sciences in Memory of Alfred Nobel 2020." NobelPrize.org. October 12, 2020.https://www.nobelprize.org/prizes/economic-sciences/2020/press-release/.

Rubinstein, Ariel. "Perfect Equilibrium in a Bargaining Model." *Econometrica* 50, no. 1 (1982): 97–109. https://doi.org/10.2307/1912531.

Rubinstein, Ariel. "The Electronic Mail Game: Strategic Behavior under 'Almost Common Knowledge.'" *American Economic Review* 79, no. 3 (1989): 385–391.

Rubinstein, Ariel. *Modeling Bounded Rationality.* Zeuthen Lecture Book Series. Cambridge, MA: MIT Press, 1998.

Rubinstein, Ariel. "Dilemmas of an Economic Theorist." *Econometrica* 74, no. 4 (2006): 865–883.

Rubinstein, Ariel. *Economic Fables.* Cambridge, UK: Open Book Publishers, 2012. https://doi.org/10.11647/OBP.0020.

Rubinstein, Ariel, and Yuval Salant. "Eliciting Welfare Preferences from Behavioural Data Sets." *Review of Economic Studies* 79, no. 1 (January 1, 2012): 375–387. https://doi.org/10.1093/restud/rdr024.

Rubinstein, Ariel, Amos Tversky, and Dana Heller. "Naive Strategies in Competitive Games." In *Understanding Strategic Interaction: Essays in Honor of Reinhard Selten,* edited by Wulf Albers, Werner Güth, Peter Hammerstein, Benny Moldovanu, and Eric van Damme, 394–402. Berlin: Springer, 1997. https://doi.org/10.1007/978-3-642-60495-9_30.

Samuelson, William F., and Max H. Bazerman. *The Winner's Curse in Bilateral Negotiations.* Cambridge, MA: Massachusetts Institute of Technology, 1984.

Samuelson, William F., and Max H. Bazerman. "Negotiation under the Winner's Curse." *Research in Experimental Economics* 3 (1985): 105–138.

Sarver, Todd. "Anticipating Regret: Why Fewer Options May Be Better." *Econometrica* 76, no. 2 (2008): 263–305. https://doi.org/10.1111/j.1468-0262.2008.00834.x.

Savage, Leonard J. *The Foundations of Statistics.* The Foundations of Statistics. Oxford: John Wiley & Sons, 1954.

Shannon, Claude. E. "A Mathematical Theory of Communication." *Bell System Technical Journal* 27, no. 3 (July 1948): 379–423. https://doi.org/10.1002/j.1538-7305.1948.tb01338.x.

Simon, Herbert. A. "Rational Choice and the Structure of the Environment." *Psychological Review* 63, no. 2 (1956): 129–138. https://doi.org/10.1037/h0042769.

Simon, Herbert. A. *Models of Bounded Rationality, Vols. 1 and 2.* Cambridge, MA: MIT Press, 1982.

Sims, Christopher A. "Implications of Rational Inattention." *Journal of Monetary Economics* 50, no. 3 (April 1, 2003): 665–690. https://doi.org/10.1016/S0304-3932(03)00029-1.

Slonim, Robert, and Alvin E. Roth. "Learning in High Stakes Ultimatum Games: An Experiment in the Slovak Republic." *Econometrica* 66, no. 3 (1998): 569–596. https://doi.org/10.2307/2998575.

Spence, Michael. "Job Market Signaling." *Quarterly Journal of Economics* 87, no. 3 (1973): 355–374. https://doi.org/10.2307/1882010.

Spiegler, Ran. "Extracting Interaction-Created Surplus." *Games and Economic Behavior* 30, no. 1 (January 1, 2000): 142–162. https://doi.org/10.1006/game.1999.0713.

Spiegler, Ran. "The Market for Quacks." *Review of Economic Studies* 73, no. 4 (2006): 1113–1131.

Spiegler, Ran. "On Two Points of View Regarding Revealed Preference and Behavioral Economics." In Andrew Caplin and Andrew Schotter, eds., *Foundations of Positive and Normative Economics: A Handbook*. New York: Oxford University Press, 2008: 95–115.

Spiegler, Ran. *Bounded Rationality and Industrial Organization*. New York: Oxford University Press, 2011.

Spiegler, Ran. "Monopoly Pricing When Consumers Are Antagonized by Unexpected Price Increases: A 'Cover Version' of the Heidhues–Kőszegi–Rabin Model." *Economic Theory* 51, no. 3 (November 1, 2012): 695–711. https://doi.org/10.1007/s00199-011-0619-5.

Spiegler, Ran. "Placebo Reforms." *American Economic Review* 103, no. 4 (2013): 1490–1506.

Spiegler, Ran. "Bayesian Networks and Boundedly Rational Expectations." *Quarterly Journal of Economics* 131, no. 3 (2016): 1243–1290.

Spiegler, Ran. "Behavioral Economics and the Atheoretical Style." *American Economic Journal: Microeconomics* 11, no. 2 (May 2019): 173–194. https://doi.org/10.1257/mic.20170007.

Spier, Kathryn E. "Incomplete Contracts and Signalling." *RAND Journal of Economics* 23, no. 3 (1992): 432.

Stigler, George J., and Gary S. Becker. "De Gustibus Non Est Disputandum." *American Economic Review* 67, no. 2 (1977): 76–90.

Stiglitz, Joseph E., and Andrew Weiss. "Credit Rationing in Markets with Imperfect Information." *American Economic Review* 71, no. 3 (1981): 393–410.

Stravinsky, Igor. *Chroniques de Ma Vie*. Vol. 2. Paris: Denoël et Steele, 1935.

Strotz, R. H. "Myopia and Inconsistency in Dynamic Utility Maximization." *Review of Economic Studies* 23, no. 3 (1955): 165–180. https://doi.org/10.2307/2295722.

Taruskin, Richard. *Stravinsky and the Russian Traditions: A Biography of the Works through Mavra*. 2 vols. Berkeley: University of California Press, 1996.

Thaler, Richard H. *Misbehaving: The Making of Behavioral Economics*. 1st ed. New York: W.W. Norton & Company, 2015.

Thaler, Richard H. "Behavioral Economics: Past, Present, and Future." *American Economic Review* 106, no. 7 (July 1, 2016): 1577–1600. https://doi.org/10.1257/aer.106.7.1577.

Tirole, Jean. *The Theory of Industrial Organization*. Cambridge, MA: MIT Press, 1988.

Tirole, Jean. "Incomplete Contracts: Where Do We Stand?" *Econometrica* 67, no. 4 (1999): 741–781.

Tversky, Amos, and Daniel Kahneman. "Belief in the Law of Small Numbers." *Psychological Bulletin* 76 (1971): 105–110. https://doi.org/10.1037/h0031322.

Wald, A. "Sequential Tests of Statistical Hypotheses." *Annals of Mathematical Statistics* 16, no. 2 (June 1945): 117–186. https://doi.org/10.1214/aoms/1177731118.

Wilson, Robert. "Game-Theoretic Analyses of Trading Processes." In *Advances in Economic Theory: Fifth World Congress,* edited by Truman Fassett Bewley, 33–70. Econometric Society Monographs. Cambridge, UK: Cambridge University Press, 1987. https://doi.org/10.1017/CCOL0521340446.002.

Wimsatt, William, and Monroe Beardsley. "The Intentional Fallacy." In *The Verbal Icon: Studies in the Meaning of Poetry* (1954): 3–18. Lexington, KY: University Press of Kentucky.

Woodford, Michael. "What's Wrong with Economic Models? A Response to John Kay" (2011). https://doi.org/10.7916/D8MS3QPB.

Yildiz, Muhamet. "Bargaining without a Common Prior—An Immediate Agreement Theorem." *Econometrica* 71, no. 3 (2003): 793–811. https://doi.org/10.1111/1468-0262.00426.

Young, H. Peyton. "The Evolution of Conventions." *Econometrica* 61, no. 1 (1993): 57–84. https://doi.org/10.2307/2951778.

# Index